A PLUME BOOK

TIGER, MEET MY SISTER . . .

RICK REILLY was a front-page columnist for ESPN.com, and now regularly appears on *Monday Night Countdown*, *SportsCenter*, and *Sunday NFL Countdown*. He is the author of ten previous books, including the *New York Times* bestsellers *Hate Mail from Cheerleaders*, *Missing Links*, *Shanks for Nothing*, and *Who's Your Caddy?*

Praise for Rick Reilly and His Works

"Rick Reilly is one of the funniest humans on the planet, an indescribable amalgam of Dave Barry, Jim Murray, and Lewis Grizzard, with the timing of Jay Leno and the wit of Johnny Carson."
—*Publishers Weekly* for *Tiger, Meet My Sister . . .*

"Reilly was the closest thing sportswriting ever had to a rock star."
—Chris Chase, USAToday.com

"Reilly made you think, made you cry, made you LOL, made you get to know a subject, made you love sports and hate sports and love him and hate him. Above all, he made you read him, every column."
—Jay Mariotti, *Sports Talk Florida*

"[Reilly] knows and delivers a good story when he sees it. . . . Readers can't help but be touched by the sheer ingenuity of many of these games and the sheer courage of many of the participants."
—*Booklist* for *Sports from Hell*

Praise for *Missing Links*

"Don't get started reading this book. It will take three burly men to pull you away from it."
　　　　　　　　　　　　　　　　　　　　　　　　—Bob Costas

"You don't need to know your bogeys from your birdies to find at least three laughs per page in this novel."
　　　　　　　　　　　　　　　　—*The New York Times Book Review*

"Snappy prose, believable characters, and the funniest take on blue-collar hacking and gambling since Dan Jenkins's *The Glory Game at Goat Hill* . . . it's social satire and pure irreverence that keep this story in the groove."
　　　　　　　　　　　　　　　　　　　　　　—*Los Angeles Times*

Praise for *Who's Your Caddy?*

"Reilly could write about lawn bowling and make it funny, informative, and entertaining. You never know what the next page is going to bring."
　　　　　　　　　　　　　　　　　　　　　　—*Los Angeles Times*

"You might not think the story of a man carrying Tommy Aaron's golf bag for eighteen holes could make you laugh out loud, but you'd be wrong. *Who's Your Caddy?* is funny enough to coax a chuckle out of Vijay Singh. A great way to read about the game—and its people, too."
　　　　　　　　　　　　　　　　　　　　—*The Charlotte Observer*

A PLUME BOOK

TIGER,

Meet My Sister . . .

. . . And Other Things
I Probably Shouldn't
Have Said

RICK REILLY

PLUME
Published by the Penguin Group
Penguin Group (USA) LLC
375 Hudson Street
New York, New York 10014

USA | Canada | UK | Ireland | Australia | New Zealand | India | South Africa | China
penguin.com
A Penguin Random House Company

First published in the United States of America by Blue Rider Press,
a member of Penguin Group (USA) LLC, 2014
First Plume Printing 2015

All articles were previously published, in slightly different form, on ESPN.com from 2011–2013.

P REGISTERED TRADEMARK—MARCA REGISTRADA

THE LIBRARY OF CONGRESS HAS CATALOGED THE BLUE RIDER PRESS EDITION AS FOLLOWS:

Reilly, Rick.
Tiger, meet my sister : and other things I probably shouldn't have said / Rick Reilly.
p.   cm.
ISBN 978-0-399-17125-3 (hc.)
ISBN 978-0-14-218190-4 (pbk.)
1. Sports—Anecdotes. 2. Sports—Miscellanea. 3. Sports—Humor. 4. Sportswriters—
Anecdotes. 5. Newspapers—Sections, columns, etc.—Sports. I. Title.
GV707.R47   2014   2014008467
796—dc23

Printed in the United States of America
10 9 8 7 6 5 4 3 2 1

Original hardcover design by Michelle McMillian

To my actual sisters,
PATTI and **SALLY**,
who also have really good legs

Contents

Foreword

Now that I'm dead, I'd like to discuss my funeral.

First off, I want chili cheeseburgers. And Guinness. And the Miami Dolphins cheerleaders.

I want the Cure playing, live. I hid some money under the rock out back. Should cover it. If there's any left, get the Phoenix Gorilla, too.

I'll need a mix of crying and laughing, 25 percent/70 percent, if we could. The other 5 percent is going to be those who will be there howling happily to see that I've boxed. That will be Bryant Gumbel, Steve Garvey, and Sammy Sosa, people like that. Let them holler lousy things out about me now and then. I don't mind. I was hard on them.

A lot of my final rankings will be hanging on big posters on the walls of whatever hall you rent. (The back room at an Olive Garden ought to do it.) They are as follows:

NICEST PEOPLE:

1. Steph Curry
2. Jim Nantz
3. That bald guy with the mushroom-cloud ear hair who always comes up to me and tells me how much he loved my last column even though Mitch Albom usually wrote it

BIGGEST JERKS:

1. Barry Bonds
2. Barry Bonds
3. Robert (*Arliss*) Wuhl
4. Barry Bonds
5. Jay Cutler

MOST FUN:

1. Charles Barkley
2. George Clooney
3. David Feherty

GREATEST WITNESSED THRILLS:

1. Nicklaus wins the 1986 Masters
2. North Carolina State wins the 1983 NCAA March Madness
3. My first *SI* Swimsuit shoot. Oh. My. God.

LARGEST REGRETS:

1. Believed Lance Armstrong
2. Didn't believe Jose Canseco
3. Sold all my Apple at 125

DUMBEST QUESTIONS PEOPLE ASKED ME:

1. Where do they store the hockey ice at the arena when they switch over to basketball? (A: They cut it up in little squares and the players take it home and keep it in their freezers.)
2. Why has Greg Norman never been selected to play in the Ryder Cup? (A: Because Norman has a deal with U-Haul.)
3. When was the last repeat winner of the Kentucky Derby? (A: Sigh.)

PEOPLE I WAS SURE WOULD BE DEAD BEFORE ME:

1. Mike Tyson
2. Dennis Rodman
3. John Daly

BEST INSULT:

1. "Thanks for sending me your book. I'll waste no time reading it." (From a reviewer.)

PRESIDENTS MET:

1. Ford (stepped on my foot)
2. Carter (wouldn't let go of my wife)
3. Bush 41 (very fast, very bad golfer)
4. Clinton (smart)
5. Obama (fantasy football partner)

ANNOYANCES:

1. The readjust, re-Velcro, triple loogie done between pitches every freaking time
2. The stupid rule that won't let you pull it out of a divot
3. Guns

THINGS I'LL MISS:

1. Wife and kids and buddies
2. Third-and-8 and Peyton Manning deciding who he's going to burn
3. Piano bars

THINGS I WON'T:

1. "Can you take a look at my nephew's book? It's a true story!"
2. Wide receivers who pump their chest and point to the name on their back after a six-yard gain.
3. The 43 million waiters and waitresses in this country who set the plate down and say, "Enjoy." Hey, lady, it's a cheesesteak. Where do you think I'm putting it?

WHAT I LEARNED:

1. The faster a sprinter is, the slower he walks
2. There is no point talking to a 5-iron

3. The Kenyan with the most impossible name to pronounce will win the race

4. All other Kenyans will finish 2-through-10

5. Media company lawyers do not get paid to get your joke. They get paid to kill it

6. Even if there are 1,000 people in front of you enjoying your after-dinner speech, you will focus on the lady who's asleep

7. The guy you need the most to finish your story will be last out of the shower

8. Every hate e-mail starts with "I've enjoyed everything you've written, until _____", and ends with "hope you die in a fiery ____ accident"

9. Ninety-seven percent of athletes are lovely people and really boring columns

10. If you're not adding some tiny good to the world, then you're wasting everybody's time

Up on stage, there will be a bottle of Macallan scotch from every year I've been alive. Each person will come up to the stage and take a shot from the year they met me, then smash the glass. If you don't drink, we probably never met.

For flowers, I'd like the purple kind. They're pretty.

MC Vin Scully (he'll outlive us all) will get up and open—cold—with Sentences That Have Never Been Uttered in the History of the English Language. I have a whole collection I've been saving and they'll be perfect coming out of Vin's velvet voice box. A few sentences nobody's ever uttered:

- "Tiger, meet my sister."
- "Shaq, you shoot the technical."
- "Tebow says go screw yourself."

Then Vin is going to open it up for speeches.

But be warned: Rip me, roast me, rave about me, but don't be boring. I'm going to have Nate (No Neck) Syzmanski standing there. If you're dull, he'll disconnect the mike and "encourage" you off the stage.

If Charles Barkley shows, I'd like him to get up and tell about the time we were driving along and the steering wheel came off in his hands. Or the time we were walking along in Barcelona in 1992 and looked back to see 200 people following us.

I'd like John Elway to tell about the time we were playing golf and he tripped on a tee marker at the top of a steep par 3 and tumbled 30 feet cleat-over-baseball-cap. One of the best up and downs of his life.

And it'd be great if one of my buddies got up and read some of the dumb quotes I've had to stand there and write in my notepad. Do you know how hard it is to write about people who make their livings with their bodies, not their brains? For instance:

- "Oh, man, you'll never get up this thing in the winter." —Wayne Gretzky's Canadian friend, surveying Gretzky's steep L.A. driveway
- "We got our backs to the driver's seat."—Otis Armstrong, RB, Denver Broncos
- "I've won championships at every level, except high school and college."—Shaquille O'Neal

Oh, and I want a bunch of Nerf footballs in the crowd. I want people to just stand up and go, "I'm open!" and then have somebody wing one at them. I want Elway to have his own basket of them.

Now, I've taken the liberty of writing my own obit. If you'll just send it to the papers and the websites and whatnot:

RICK REILLY, 56, sportswriter, died this week of one thing or the other. He probably had it coming.

Reilly published or posted over 2 million words in his 37-year career, most of them making fun of Barry Bonds and the size of his head.

At least Reilly tried to tell the truth in his stories and columns. He might not have always done it, but he tried. He also tried to make it all add up to something. He tried to make you laugh or cry or treat somebody better. Or worse. Once in awhile, he pulled it off.

Reilly was a very odd sportswriter in that he didn't really write about sports. He wrote more about people who played sports than the sports themselves. The high school stud quarterback who took the loneliest girl under his wing. The blind woman who travels by bus, train and sidewalk to every Yankees game. The sports-fan kid who was supposed to be 17 and looked 80.

Reilly covered every major sporting event except the Indy 500, and every minor one, including the world sauna championship, in which he placed 103rd. He saw over 100 countries, including some behind the Iron Curtain that no longer exist. He went to every state but North Dakota, although he's not really welcome in Nebraska, possibly because of this joke he told in Omaha:

Q: What do you call a hot tub full of Nebraska cheerleaders?

A: Gorillas in the mist.

He got decent at the piano for a while. Knew enough magic to annoy you. George Clooney made one of his movies. He had a TV series that lasted one episode. Had his own interview show that lasted 15. Helped raise over $50 million to fight malaria via Nothing But Nets, which he came up with because he was desperate for a column one week.

He saw the northern lights. He ran with the bulls. He saw the best people could be and the worst. He loved writing about big people acting small and small people acting big. He liked writing about the star of the team, but he preferred writing about the nobody at the end of the bench. He wrote short, medium and long, which was probably what he did best, but it's probably also why he's dead at 56. He always said every one of them takes a year off your life.

The son of an alcoholic, he made his own way. He could've done
better. He could've done worse. His main deal was trying to write
sentences nobody had ever read before, entertain people, and not
have to get a real job. Also, to his undying credit, he never was on
one of those everybody-yells sportswriter shows.

Oh, and he once took $5 off Arnold Palmer on the golf course.

When the speeches are done or the scotch is gone, whichever comes
first, we'll drive up to the graveyard in monster trucks. It's going to be
great. I've arranged for junker cars to be parked along the way—
marked with a giant orange X—and every truck gets to go over at
least one of them. You're welcome.

At the grave site, there'll be an L.A. taco truck—best eating
known to man—and it's *carta blanca*. Leaving the grave site and getting a quesadilla is not only OK, it's encouraged.

After my caddie says a few nice words, such as, "He had a loop in
his backswing you could drive a Mack truck through, but at least he
tipped OK," everybody can bring one item to throw down into the
grave, depending on whether you liked me or hated me. A few items
I'd like to see thrown in:

- My 7-Eleven smock. I worked there for a while before I got
  the writing gig. I have also been a grocery bagger, rental-
  shop clerk, lawn mower, book packer, parking hut attendant,
  flower deliverer, bank teller, gas jockey, and car washer. Got
  fired from most of them. I kept the smock to remind myself
  that writing is all I can do.
- My 100-plus photo collection of people choking me, including Michael Phelps underwater. Made for funny pictures,
  except for the time Eli Manning didn't realize it was supposed to be a joke.
- My laptop. I don't want anybody reading some of the columns I started and ditched. "Why Ryan Leaf Is About to

Turn This League on Its Ear." "At 30, Phil Mickelson Is Done." "25 Reasons I'll Never Tweet." Things like that. Plus, my wife has the kind of body that keeps whiplash specialists in business and I don't want anybody clicking on the "My Pictures" tab.

Speaking of my wife, it'd be nice if she lost it at some point and dove on top of the casket as it's being lowered. But by then I figure she'll be too busy fending off advances from my single buddies. Or not fending them off. I can't blame either of them.

Then I'd like to leave this note for my kids: "Sorry I spent your inheritance. Love you. Hope you have as much fun as I did."

Lastly, I want the tombstone to say:

Here lies Rick Reilly

1958–2014

Tried to write well

Anyway, that's it. Don't feel sorry for me. It wasn't long, but it was a blast. And look at it this way, I FINALLY made deadline.

(P.S. I bet my buddy Two Down O'Connor, The World's Most Avid Golf Gambler, $100 that I'd break par before I died and I never did. So he's going to come up and pretend to sob over my coffin, but he's really going to be taking the C-note out of the inside left breast pocket of my black blazer. The bill is in there, just make sure I'm wearing it.)

Flaws

(Big People Acting Small)

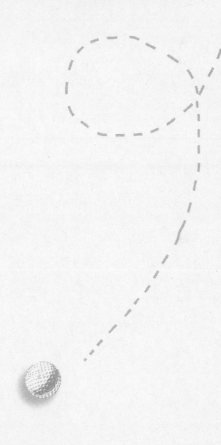

It's All About the Lies

January 27, 2013

Among my e-mails Wednesday morning, out of the blue, was one from Lance Armstrong.

> *Riles, I'm sorry.*
> *All I can say for now but also the most heartfelt thing too. Two very important words.*
> *L*

And my first thought was . . . "Two words? That's it?"

Two words? For fourteen years of defending a man? And in the end, being made to look like a chump?

Wrote it, said it, tweeted it: "He's clean." Put it in columns, said it on radio, said it on TV. Staked my reputation on it.

"Never failed a drug test," I'd always point out. "Most tested athlete in the world. Tested maybe 500 times. Never flunked one."

Why? Because Armstrong always *told* me he was clean.

On the record. Off the record. Every kind of record. In Colorado. In Texas. In France. On team buses. In cars. On cell phones.

I'd sit there with him, in some Tour de France hotel room while he was getting his daily post-race massage. And we'd talk through the hole in the table about how he stared down this guy or that guy, how he'd fooled Jan Ullrich on the torturous Alpe d'Huez into thinking he was gassed and then suddenly sprinted away to win. How he ordered chase packs from the center of the peloton and reeled in all the pretenders.

And then I'd bring up whatever latest charge was levied against him. "There's this former teammate who says he heard you tell doctors you doped." "There's this former assistant back in Austin who says you cheated." "There's this assistant they say they caught disposing of your drug paraphernalia."

And every time—every single time—he'd push himself up on his elbows and his face would be red and he'd stare at me like I'd just shot his dog and give me some very well-delivered explanation involving a few dozen F-words, a painting of the accuser as a wronged employee seeking revenge, and how lawsuits were forthcoming.

And when my own reporting would produce no proof, I'd be convinced. I'd go out there and continue polishing a legend that turned out to be plated in fool's gold.

Even after he retired, the hits just kept coming. A London *Times* report. A Daniel Coyle book. A U.S. federal investigation. All liars and thieves, he'd snarl.

I remember one time we talked on the phone for half an hour, all off the record, at his insistence, and I asked him three times, "Just tell me. Straight up. Did you do any of this stuff?"

"No! I didn't do s—!"

And the whole time, he was lying. Right in my earpiece. Knowing that I'd hang up and go back out there and spread the fertilizer around some more.

And now, just like that, it's all flipped. Thursday and Friday night we'll see him look right into the face of Oprah Winfrey and tell her just the opposite. He'll tell her, she says, that he doped to win.

I get it. He's ruined. He's lost every single sponsor. Nearly every close teammate has turned on him. All seven Tour de France titles have been stripped. He could owe millions. He might be in a hot kettle with the feds. Even the future he planned for himself—triathlons and mountain biking—have been snatched away. He's banned from those for life.

So I get it. The road to redemption goes through Oprah, where he'll finally say those two very important words, "I'm sorry," and hope the USADA will cut the ban from lifetime to the minimum eight years.

But here's the thing. When he says he's sorry now, how do we know he's not still lying? How do we know it's not just another great performance by the all-time leader in them?

And I guess I should let it go, but I keep thinking how hard he used me. Made me look like a sap. Made me carry his dirty water and I didn't even know it.

Look, I've been fooled before. I believed Mark McGwire was hitting those home runs all on his own natural gifts. I believed Joe Paterno couldn't possibly cover up something so grisly as child molestation. I bought Manti Te'o's girlfriend story. But those people never looked me square in the pupils and spit.

It's partially my fault. I let myself admire him. Let myself admire what he'd done with his life, admire the way he'd not only beaten his own cancer but was trying to help others beat it. When my sister was diagnosed, she read his book and got inspired. And I felt some pride in that. I let it get personal. And now I know he was living a lie and I was helping him live it.

I didn't realize that behind those blues was a bully, a coercer, a man who threatened people who once worked for and with him. The Andreus. Emma O'Reilly. Tyler Hamilton. Armstrong was strong-arming people in the morning, and filing lawsuits and op-ed pieces in the afternoon. We'd talk and his voice would get furious. And I'd believe him.

And all along, the whole time, he was acting, just like he had with Ullrich that day. So now the chase pack has reeled in Lance Armstrong, and he is busted and he's apologizing to those he conned.

I guess I should forgive him. I guess I should give him credit for putting himself through worldwide shame. I guess I should thank him for finally admitting his whole magnificent castle was built on sand and syringes and suckers like me. But I'm not quite ready. Give me fourteen years, maybe.

You're sorry, Lance? No, I'm the one who's sorry.

Postscript: *I figured that was the last e-mail I'd ever get from Armstrong, and good riddance. But about a month later, somebody was ripping me on Twitter for one thing or another and added, "Why should we believe you? You told us Lance was telling the truth." Out of the blue came a reply from Armstrong: "Don't blame Rick. I lied to him for 14 years." Hey, it's a start.*

Be Like Mike? No, Thanks

September 16, 2009

Michael Jordan's Hall of Fame talk was the *Exxon Valdez* of speeches. It was, by turns, rude, vindictive and flammable. And that was just when he was trying to be funny. It was tactless, egotistical and unbecoming. When it was done, nobody wanted to be like Mike.

And yet we couldn't stop watching. Because this was an inside look into the mind-set of an icon who'd never let anybody inside before. From what I saw, I'd never want to go back. Here is a man who's won just about everything there is to win—six NBA titles, five MVPs and two Olympic golds. And yet he sounded like a guy who's been screwed out of every trophy ever minted. He's the world's first sore winner.

In the entire twenty-three-minute cringe-athon, there were only six thank-yous, seven if you count his sarcastic rip at the very Hall that was inducting him. "Thank you, Hall of Fame, for raising ticket prices, I guess," he sneered. By comparison, David Robinson's classy and heartfelt seven-minute speech had seventeen. Joe Montana's even shorter speech in Canton had twenty-three. Who wrote your speech, Mike? Kanye West?

Not that Jordan's speech wasn't from the heart. It was. It's just that Jordan's heart on this night could give you frostbite. Nobody was spared, including his high school coach, his high school teammate, his college coach, two of his pro coaches, his college roommate, his pro owner, his pro general manager, the man who was presenting him that evening, even his kids!

"I wouldn't want to be you guys if I had to," he said as they squirmed in their seats.

He even mocked his own brothers, calling them maybe 5-foot-5 and 5-6. Actually, they're about 5-8 and 5-9. Michael was the one blessed with the height gene, not the tact one.

Jordan had decided that this was the perfect night to list all the ways everybody sitting in front of him had pissed him off over the past thirty years: Dean Smith, Doug Collins, Jerry Reinsdorf, Pat Riley, Isiah Thomas, Larry Bird, Magic Johnson, George Gervin and Jeff Van Gundy. It was the only one-man roast in Hall of Fame history. Only, very little of it was funny.

He was like that Japanese World War II soldier they found hiding in a cave in Guam twenty-seven years after the Japanese surrendered. The only difference is, Jordan won! What good is victory if you never realize the battle is over?

This is how Jordan really is, I just never thought he'd let the world see it. His old Bulls assistant coach, Johnny Bach, told me early on, "This guy is a killer. He's a cold-blooded assassin. It's not enough for him to beat you. He wants you dead."

I covered his entire career and saw examples of it throughout. Saw him break Rodney McCray in after-practice, $100 shooting games, humiliate him until McCray lost his stroke. Watched him race his car up the shoulder of Chicago interstates just because he didn't have the patience to wait in traffic. Heard how he'd kept his friends confined to his hotel room at the Barcelona Olympics so he could play cards—and keep playing until he won. For Jordan, it was never enough to win. He had to have scalps.

Now here he was, in Springfield without a filter or a PR guy to cut him off, while his staff must've been covering their eyes. And suddenly, it hit you: Michael Jordan is the guy who gets up at the rehearsal dinner, grabs the mike and ruins the night.

The thing Jordan doesn't understand is, it doesn't have to be this way. Terry Bradshaw won four Super Bowls and gave one of the greatest speeches in the history of the Hall of Fame. "Folks!" he hollered. "You don't get elected into the Hall of Fame by yourself! Thank you number 88, Lynn Swann! Thank you, Franco Harris! Thank you, Rocky Bleier! What I wouldn't give right now to put my hands under [center] Mike Webster's butt just one more time! Thank you, Mike!" He thanked linemen, tight ends, everybody but the ushers.

Had Jordan been in his shoes, he'd have said, "Hey, Steve Kerr! Remember when I kicked your ass in that fight?"

Jordan owes a roomful of apologies. But it'll never happen. I know firsthand.

Before his second comeback—with the Washington Wizards—I was the first out with the story by a month. Jordan and his agent, David Falk, denied it, said I was crazy, practically said I was smoking something. Then, after a month of lies, Jordan admitted it was all true. I saw him in the locker room before his first game back and said, "You wanna say something to me, maybe?"

And he said, "You know you don't get no apologies in this business."

So I wouldn't hold your breath.

They called it an "acceptance" speech, but the last thing Jordan seems to be able to do is accept it's over. In fact, Jordan hinted that he might make yet another comeback at 50.

I just hope Comeback No. 3 doesn't come with a speech.
Because then I'm really screwed.

Postscript: *Wright Thompson told this story about Jordan in* ESPN The
Magazine *not long ago: It seems Jordan brings his own chef to ad shoots
because she always makes his favorite cinnamon rolls. But when Jordan has
to leave his trailer to go shoot, he spits on each one, to make sure the security
guards don't take one while he's filming.*

Jay Cutler Is No Teddy Bear

January 13, 2011

For a man from Santa Claus, Indiana, Jay Cutler is one of the least jolly people you've ever met.

If he's not The Most Hated Man in the NFL, he's in the running. His expression is usually that of a man wearing sandpaper underwear. He looks everywhere but into your eyes. It's a tie as to which he enjoys more—smirking or shrugging.

It's hard to say what interests Cutler, but it's definitely not you.

Once, in his rookie year in Denver, forty-five minutes before a game, surefire Hall of Fame safety John Lynch was trying to explain something to Cutler about NFL pass coverage. Except Cutler wasn't looking at Lynch. He was texting.

"Man, I'm trying to talk to you!" Lynch protested.

Didn't help. Cutler was all thumbs, head down. Finally, Lynch slapped the phone out of Cutler's hands, smashing it to the floor.

He listened after that.

One time, Broncos coach Mike Shanahan thought it would be

helpful for Cutler and Broncos legend John Elway to have lunch. Let Cutler drink in some of Elway's experience.

The three of them sat down at a Denver steak joint. Elway, polite as ever, tried to impart some wisdom. Except Cutler wasn't looking at Elway. He wasn't looking at Shanahan, either. He was looking at the TV. The whole time. With his baseball cap on backward. All the way through dessert. Elway did not leave impressed.

So when Josh McDaniels, before he had even set his Samsonite down, started railroading Cutler out of town, almost nobody stood up for him.

Cutler was boxed up and shipped to Chicago, where, this Sunday, he will play his first playoff game of any kind since high school, this one at home against the Seattle Seahawks.

It's a huge moment for Cutler, if only because his disdain for making nice means everything rides on his wins and losses.

"In New York, they want to poke you in the eye," says former Bear and sports radio host Tom Waddle. "In L.A., they don't care about you. But in Chicago, they want to love you. They want to make a connection with you. Any kind of connection. But Jay doesn't really care."

Cutler could own Chicago if he wanted. In a city that has had as many good quarterbacks as Omaha has had good surfers, Cutler could have his name on half the billboards and all the jerseys. My God, the kid grew up a Bears fan! But he doesn't even try. He has zero endorsements and doesn't want any. If there is such a thing as a Jay Cutler Fan Club, Cutler is having a membership drive—to drive them out.

Example from Wednesday's fifteen-minute news conference, the only time he speaks publicly the entire workweek:

Reporter #1: So, did you enjoy the week off?
Cutler: Yeah, it's nice to kick back and watch the games.
Reporter #2: Wait. Last week, you said you never watch the games.

Cutler (disgusted): I said you could watch the games. I didn't say
   I watched the games. You've got to listen.

Cutler is the kind of guy you just want to pick up and throw into a
swimming pool, which is exactly what Peyton Manning and two
linemen did one year at the Pro Bowl.

"He's an arrogant little punk," former Broncos radio color man
Scott Hastings once said on a national show. "He's a little bitch."

Harsh? Yes. Heard before? Yes.

"I used to hear this kind of stuff a lot," says Marty Garafalo, a
freelance publicist who handled Cutler in Denver. "Elway was always
trying to give you the time of day, and Jay was always seeing which
door he could get out of quicker. It was a maturity thing."

Cutler's teammates will defend him when asked. "It's funny to me
how people form an opinion of a guy who've never even met him,"
says Bears tight end Greg Olsen, a close friend.

So what's the truth?

"He is what he is," Olsen says.

Not exactly something for your tombstone.

What he is is an RPG-armed, 27-year-old Vanderbilt product who
dates a reality TV star named Kristin Cavallari, battles type 1 diabe-
tes every day, and doesn't care who understands him and who doesn't.
He's a giving person who does things behind the scenes and hates it
when he gets found out. A few days before Christmas, he and Cavallari brought presents for an entire ward of sick hospital kids. A reporter for the *Sun-Times* got wind of it and asked him about it. Cutler
refused to discuss it.

He's a battler who's done amazingly well considering the swinging-
saloon-door offensive line he has to play behind. The man has been
sacked more times this season (52) than in his three seasons in Denver combined (51). Yet he never complains.

"He's as sharp an individual as I've ever been around," says Bears
offensive coordinator Mike Martz.

So why is Cutler as popular as gout?

Is it because he never makes eye contact?

Is it his seeming inability to answer a question without using "y'know"? (He once used it fifty-seven times in a five-minute interview with the NFL Network.)

Is it his penchant for making things difficult?

Reporter (after a game): What happened on that first interception, Jay?

Cutler: I threw the ball.

Reporter: Right, but what did you see developing there? Take us through it.

Cutler (archly): It seemed like a good place to throw the ball.

Then there was this:

Reporter: When you were a kid, which quarterback did you look up to?

Cutler: Nobody.

Reporter: Nobody? You didn't look up to anybody?

Cutler: No.

If he's lying, it makes him a miscreant. If he's telling the truth, it makes him a miscreant.

"Deep, deep down, I think he's a really good guy," Waddle says.

Maybe. But why do we have to look that deep?

Postscript: *Since this was written, Cutler married, immediately had a child and was, at last report, expecting a second. That figures. He always did get lousy protection.*

The Confounding World of Athlete Tattoos

November 11, 2009

This is the time of year when parents all over America take their children to the nation's sports facilities, sneak down to courtside and show the youngsters how dangerous it is to drink and ink.

How else do you explain Golden State Warrior Stephen Jackson's hands? Not the hands at the end of his arms. The tattooed hands on his chest and stomach, holding a handgun, praying. I am not kidding—two hands praying with a gun between them. Praise the Lord and pass the ammunition.

What is the message Jackson's stomach is trying to leave us? "God, please help me knock over this Kwik Stop?" "This is the Glock the Lord hath made?" Neither. Jackson says it represents him praying that he doesn't need to use a gun again.

Damn, Stephen. Where's your commute, Fallujah?

How else do you explain Kenyon Martin's lips? Not the lips on his face—the lips on his neck. They're fire-hydrant-red women's lips, smooching there for all time, a permahickey. They're a tracing of his girlfriend's lips, the rapper Trina. I hope they stay together. Because hell hath no fury like a woman who has to stare at another woman's lips every day and night. You're talking turtlenecks in July.

You need look only a foot farther to see something even more puzzling on K-Mart, whose skin is a kind of human bathroom stall—his ornate "I Shall Fear No Man But God" scrawled on his back. Uh, see Kenyon, the thing is: God isn't a man. Did you mean, "Fear No Man. Fear God?" That's the unfortunate thing about tattoo guns: no delete key.

Still, this is not as bad as the tattoo that Washington Wizards G/F DeShawn Stevenson added this past offseason—a Pittsburgh Pirates "P" on his cheek. The only problem is, it's backward. Did you do it yourself in a mirror, DeShawn? Because it looks like a 9. "If you're standing [farther away] it looks like a P," Stevenson told the *Washington Times* in what has to be the leader for Dumbest Quote of 2009.

Um, nope, still backward, DeShawn. From close up, from far away, from the Hubble telescope, still backward. Luckily, it's only on your face.

Many NBA tattoos seem to have all the foresight of a 4 a.m. Vegas wedding. Why else would Orlando Magic guard Jason Williams have "W-H-I-T" on the knuckles of his right hand and "E-B-O-Y" on the left? How often does a person arrange his fists side by side so that people can read them? Answer: Rarely. Which is why Williams must get these two comments quite a bit:

(1) "Nice to meet you, Whit."
(2) "E-boy? Is that a scouting website . . ."

Why would Celtic Marquis Daniels keep a tattoo of a guy blowing his brains out on his right arm? For the holidays? Why would LeBron James have "CHOSEN 1" scrawled across his back in a font usually reserved for "MAN WALKS ON MOON"? If a person really is The Chosen One, would we really need a tattoo parlor to spread the news? Why would Chicago Bull Brad Miller have the Saturday-morning cartoon character Scrappy-Doo—Scooby-Doo's nephew—tattooed on his arm? (Apart from the obvious intimidation factor, of course.)

Every tattoo parlor should come with a proofreader. This might have prevented Penn State tight end Andrew Quarless from tattooing "GODS" on one triceps and "GIFT" on the other. Quarless may be God's gift to football, but not to punctuation. It lacks an apostrophe, to say nothing of humility.

And why would Shawn Marion of the Dallas Mavericks get an ornate Chinese character tattooed down his leg without having a Chinese person in tow? See, Marion thought he was getting his nickname, "The Matrix," but instead got something that—crudely translated—comes out to "Demon Bird Mothballs." Still, it would be a very good intramural team name.

Boo-boo tattoos are everywhere. Why does Gilbert Arenas of the Wizards have the Barack Obama slogan "Change We Believe In" inscribed on the fingers of his left hand when (A) he forgot the word "can" and (B) he said on his blog he wouldn't even vote?

Why would New Orleans Saint Jeremy Shockey have a massive bald eagle and an American flag tattooed on his arm that—when half-covered by his jersey sleeve—looks like the Sam the Eagle Muppet? Why would Suns guard Jason Richardson have the And1 shoe logo tattooed on his arm when anyone with Junior Mints for brains could guess what would happen next? He signed with Reebok. And 1 more player who didn't think before he inked.

Of course, not all athlete tattoos are colorful proof that unbridled vanity will wind up slapping you and your ego around the school yard. For instance, Udonis Haslem of the Miami Heat has a giant map of Florida on his back. This is very useful for Haslem's friends.

Haslem friend No. 1: I think we're lost.
Haslem friend No. 2: Hey, Udonis, lean forward.
Haslem friend No. 1: See? When we got to his coccyx, we were
   supposed to go toward Coral Gables!

Nor do we guess every humiliating tattoo on athletes is Seagram's related. For instance, we think we know what happened to MMA fighter Melvin Costa. Written in elaborate scroll underneath his belly button, it says—and may God take my eyesight if I'm lying—"I Have a Small Penis."

Melvin, how many times have we told you? Never fall asleep at the tattoo parlor.

Postscript: *Readers sent in enough other bad tattoos to cover Shaq head to toe. Former NFL star LaDainian Tomlinson has "INSPERATION" on his torso. David Bey, a former heavyweight boxer, has his own name spelled incorrectly on his arm. And then a man named Henry Mullen sent in one about a guy who went in for "TEXAS" and came out with "TAXES," which is weird because people usually move to the former to avoid the latter.*

Woods Needs to Clean Up His Act

July 22, 2009

Tiger Woods has outgrown those Urkel glasses he had as a kid. Outgrown the crazy hair. Outgrown a body that was mostly neck.

When will he outgrow his temper?

The man is 33 years old, married, the father of two. He is paid nearly $100 million a year to be the representative for some monstrously huge companies, from Nike to Accenture. He is the world's most famous and beloved athlete.

And yet he spent most of his two days at Turnberry last week doing the Turn and Bury. He'd hit a bad shot, turn and bury his club into the ground in a fit. It was two days of Tiger Tantrums—slamming his club, throwing his club and cursing his club. In front of a worldwide audience.

A whole lot of that worldwide audience is kids. They do what Tiger does. They swing like Tiger, read putts like Tiger and do the celebration biceps pump like Tiger. Do you think for two seconds they don't think it's cool to throw their clubs like Tiger, too?

He's grown in every other way. He's committed, responsible, smart, funny and the most talented golfer in history. I just thought we'd be over the conniptions by now.

If there were no six-second delay, Tiger Woods would be the reason to invent it. Every network has been burned by having the on-course microphone open when he blocks one right into the cabbage and starts with the F-bombs. Once, at Doral, he unleashed a string of swearwords at a photographer that would've made Artie Lange blush, and then snarled, "The next time a photographer shoots a [expletive] picture, I'm going to break his [expletive] neck!"

It's disrespectful to the game, disrespectful to those he plays with and disrespectful to the great players who built the game before him. Ever remember Jack Nicklaus doing it? Arnold Palmer? When Tom Watson was getting guillotined in that playoff to Stewart Cink, did you see him so much as spit? Only one great player ever threw clubs as a pro—Bobby Jones—and he stopped in his 20s when he realized how spoiled he looked.

This isn't new. Woods has been this way for years: swearing like a Hooters bouncer, trying to bury the bottom of his driver into the tee box, flipping his club end over end the second he realizes his shot is way off line.

I can still remember the 1997 Masters—arguably the most important golf tournament ever played. Woods, then 21, was playing the fifteenth hole on Sunday. He had just hit a fairway wood out of the rough and was watching it. A young boy came up from behind just to touch him—just to pat the back of this amazing new superhero. That's when Tiger pulled the club way back over his head and slammed it down, nearly braining the kid he couldn't see behind him. And this was with a huge lead.

Look, in every other case, I think Tiger Woods has been an A-plus role model. Never shows up in the back of a squad car with a black eye. Never gets busted in a sleazy motel with three "freelance models." Never gets so much as a parking ticket. But this punk act on the golf course has got to stop. If it were my son, I'd tell him the same thing: "Either behave or get off the course."

Come to think of it, if I were the president of Nike, I'd tell him the same thing.

Put it this way: Will Tiger let his own two kids carry on in public like that?

I know what you're saying. We see more Tiger tantrums because TV shows every single shot he hits. And I'm telling you: You're wrong. He is one of the few on Tour who do it. And I keep wondering when PGA Tour commissioner Tim Finchem is going to have the cojones to publicly upbraid him for it.

Golf is a gentlemen's game. Stomping and swearing and carrying on like a Beverly Hills tennis brat might fly in the NBA or in baseball or in football, where less is expected, but golf demands manners. It's your honor. Is my mark in your way? No, I had 6, not 5. Golfers call penalties on themselves. We are our own police. Tiger, police yourself.

Tiger does a boatload of work for kids. He raises millions for his Tiger Woods Learning Center, which has helped teach thousands. But teaching goes the wrong way, too. Tiger is teaching them that if he can be a hissy hothead on the course, they can, too.

I remember Tiger's dad, Earl, telling a story. One day, when Tiger was just a kid, he was throwing his clubs around in a fuming fit when his dad said something like "Tiger, golf is supposed to be fun." And Tiger said, "Daddy, I want to win. That's how I have fun."

Well, it's not fun to watch.

Postscript: *This was written before Woods hit a fire hydrant and set himself on fire. After the sex scandal, he promised to be a better example. He* *even started wearing a Buddhist bracelet to remind him. None of it helped. His spoiled-brat attitude on the course hasn't changed. YouTube is full of him dropping F-bombs on the course. But uglier still are his manners when he's not on TV. Read Hank Haney's* The Big Miss. *Unforgettable talent. Inexcusable behavior.*

We Take Care of Our Own

April 2, 2012

In San Jose, California, this week, Kevin Woods will sit in his wheelchair a few feet from his television, watching his half brother play the Masters. He has to. He can't see otherwise.

Can't stand much lately, either. Can barely use his left arm at all. He can feel his hands and feet going a little more numb every day. Kevin was diagnosed with multiple sclerosis in 2009, and it's not getting better.

"I'd say 60 to 70 percent worse now," says Kevin's brother, Earl Woods Jr. "He's not going to be able to keep his house much longer."

All three men had the same father, Earl Woods, but Earl Jr. says they haven't heard from Tiger since they buried Earl's ashes in Kansas six years ago.

"I leave messages," Earl Jr. says. "I leave updates on Kevin, but for whatever reason I don't get a response. . . . Kevin loves Tiger. A call from Tiger would really pump Kevin up. When he doesn't call, it just makes him feel worse."

Earl Jr., Kevin and sister Royce are the children of Earl Woods and Barbara Gary, of Kansas. They're 20, 18 and 17 years older than Tiger, who is the offspring of Earl's second marriage, to Kultida Pun-sawad. Though they lived in different houses, the four kids visited often and say they remained close until Tiger turned "about 15 or 16," Earl Jr. says. "But the more universal Tiger got, the less we heard from him."

Royce, who also lives in San Jose, stayed close with Tiger during his two years in college, fixing him meals and doing his laundry. In thanks, Tiger bought her a house. But since the funeral, none of them have been able to contact him.

"I would live in a shack," Royce told author Tom Callahan for his 2010 book *His Father's Son*, "literally a shack, if I could have my relationship with my brother back."

When contacted regarding Kevin now, Royce would only say, "He has an illness and we're dealing with it the best we can."

The three have stayed almost entirely out of public view. None of the three have written a book, and they are rarely quoted.

"We haven't asked Tiger for a dime," says Earl Jr., who lives in Phoenix. "Not even tickets to a tournament. But Kevin's losing his home. He needs a caregiver and he can't have a caregiver and keep his home at the same time. And we can't do that, we don't have the means. He can't move into Royce's house because of the stairs. And he's got a dog.

"Nobody's asking for money here, but [a caregiver] really would be nice for Kevin. It would make Kevin comfortable. He wouldn't have to leave his house. . . . But we'd at least like to be able to find out how Tiger is, to find out if he's OK, and to let him know if we're OK."

A spokesman for Tiger said that he's preparing for the Masters and wouldn't be returning my call to talk about it.

Tiger is not without a heart. His Tiger Woods Foundation has reached millions of young people around the world. But there has clearly been a falling-out between Tiger and his half siblings, and nobody seems to know what caused it. Tiger is close with Earl Jr.'s daughter, Cheyenne Woods, who attends Wake Forest and won the 2011 ACC women's golf championship.

"Tiger had Cheyenne down to Florida for three days to spend Thanksgiving on his boat," Earl Jr. says. "I asked her [afterward], 'Did he ask about us?' She said, 'No.'"

Royce is Kevin's caretaker now, taking him to his appointments and seeing to him. She also tended to Earl Sr. in his last years as he fought pancreatic cancer, even moving into his house in December 2005.

Since his diagnosis, the 54-year-old Kevin hasn't been able to work. MS is a genetic disease that often comes on later in life. One of Kevin's cousins also got it, in his mid-40s.

"We see him suffering," says Barbara Gary Woods, 78, who lives in Modesto, California. "He can hardly walk. Can't hardly hold things. . . . I'm very disappointed in Tiger. Before he got all famous, they were in touch a lot."

The wall that's up between Tiger and Kevin burns Earl Jr.

"I'd like to [slap] Tiger, wake him up," he says. "I'd like to say, 'Don't come knocking on the door when you need a bone-marrow transplant.' To see this is the response we get? Maybe when you see the world like he does, you don't see what other people are going through. But, seriously? You've got problems with your knee? That's nothing compared to what Kevin is going through. Nothing."

I can't help wondering what things would be like if their dad were still alive.

"A lot different," insists Earl Jr., who looks a lot like his father. "My dad was a bonding agent. He encouraged us to keep in touch, protect each other, circle the wagons."

For Kevin's part, he tells his siblings that Tiger must be busy. He has not asked Tiger for anything and has not tried to contact him. He remains a Tiger fan and will have his face close to the TV as Tiger attempts to continue his comeback at Augusta.

Of course, some comebacks are harder than others.

Postscript: *As expected, nothing has changed in anybody's life but Woods's. He recently passed $1 billion earned in winnings and endorsements, according to* Forbes.

An Ad Doesn't Take Care of Everything

March 29, 2013

Sometimes you wonder where Tiger Woods gets his public-relations advice.

Gary Busey?

After a 2009 sex scandal that would make Magic Mike blush, it seemed as if Woods was finally coming around. Back to No. 1 in the world. Got himself a girlfriend he could bring home to Mom. People even were starting to feel a little sorry for him.

And then he allows Nike to release an ad that spits goo in the eye of anybody who was on the fence. It ran on social media after Woods won in Orlando last week. It was a picture of him with the caption: "Winning Takes Care of Everything."

The only problem is, it's a big whopping jelly-filled lie.

Winning doesn't take care of everything. There are some stains winning can't scrub clean. Like the worst sex scandal in pro sports history. Like talking about being sorry but never walking it. Like pretending you're going to curb your temper and your filthy mouth on the golf course and then doing nothing of the kind.

(Last week, Woods texted Rory McIlroy: "Get your finger out of your a— and win this week." Remind me: What charm school did he attend again?)

Life is life and lies are lies. Playing golf well doesn't buy you forgiveness or redemption or peace. The road to heaven isn't paved with giant novelty checks.

Ask Lance Armstrong if winning takes care of everything. Ask Pete Rose. Ask Joe Paterno's family. If winning took care of everything, why is the winning prison softball team still in prison?

I have one rule on Tiger Woods: Admire the game, not the man. The game is the greatest I've ever seen. But the man is rude and vulgar and has a screw-you-I'm-Tiger-Woods policy that's not the least bit becoming. The arrogance it takes to allow this ad to run is Reason No. 7,393.

If you're Elin Nordegren, his ex-wife, and you see that line "Winning Takes Care of Everything," don't you throw your laptop across the room? He cheated on her with a parade of porn stars, Vegas escorts and even a daughter of a neighbor. I'm thinking another win at Bay Hill isn't going to take care of much for her.

The problem isn't "winning takes care of everything." The problem is that Woods clearly believes it does.

This ad was easy for Tiger to approve. It spouts his guiding principle, after all. The fact that it also generates some heat and attention for Nike is just a bonus. And if you think he didn't OK it, you don't understand who Tiger Woods is. He's a detail demon down to the tips of his shoelaces. If he rents your house for a tournament, he allegedly has all of your furniture taken out and duplicates of his own brought in, so he feels at home. You think he's going to let a national ad go out without seeing it first?

Further, you don't think that Nike—which stuck by him when every other national corporation dumped him after the sex scandal broke—didn't have this cued up? You don't think they said: "OK, big guy. You're back to No. 1. Now it's payback."

And it worked. It's been a perfect storm of attention for Nike. People either hate it or they love it, but they're clicking on it like crazy. It's cocky. It's smug. And it's a solid 8-iron over the line.

Remember, Nike's done this before. They're the people who brought you Charles Barkley's "I Am Not a Role Model" and the 1996 Olympic anthem "You Don't Win Silver, You Lose Gold."

They are nothing if not provocateurs. The more you squirm, the better they like it. When Tiger was in the deepest end of the cesspool, Nike brought his father, Earl, back from the dead, using a sound bite that pretended to guide Tiger through the mess. You think they'd be afraid to trot out this saucy little number?

I love reading fiction, which is why I relished Nike spokesman Beth Gast's attempt to pretend this was all innocent: "When asked about his goals, such as getting back to No. 1, [Tiger] has said consistently winning is the way to get there. The statement references that sentiment and is a salute to his athletic performance."

Please.

My son writes for a big Chicago ad firm. He says every sentence, every word, every syllable is stared at, considered, rewritten, discussed and torn apart. For months. Every conceivable message that one phrase could send to the public is pored over, analyzed and tested. It has to be. If they put out an inadvertent message the client didn't intend, everybody's fired. Don't you watch *Mad Men*?

Oh, they knew what they were doing. And they meant every level you can read into it. Tiger and the creatives and the suits must've looked at all the options, ignored the pesky moral implications and said, "Just do it."

This is Tiger's "I'm back and I never changed and you have to like me anyway." This is his deodorant, and he's quite sure we'll all shrug and agree.

Can you imagine how little he thinks of us?

Postscript: *Maybe I'm the only one who cares about messages and morality. Despite the scandal, Woods has never left the perch as the No. 1 endorser of products in America.*

Please, No Signs Allowed That Might Make the Coach Feel Sad

September 3, 2008

Do you miss Beijing? Are you pining for some good ol'-fashioned totalitarianism? Enjoy seeing any small voice squashed like a ladybug under a Hummer?

Then come to the University of Virginia!

At Virginia a new rule bans signs of any kind at all sporting events, including football and basketball.

Not advertising signs, of course. Not "Beer: $8" signs. Not "Give to the Virginia Scholarship Endowment" signs. No, only signs about Virginia teams, such as the one then third-year biomedical engineering student David Becker held up at last year's Duke football game, which read "Fire Groh!" That's Al Groh, the Virginia football coach who always manages to beat the Davids, but rarely the Goliaths.

"No signs," the gendarme told Becker in taking away the sign. Becker asked why. Nobody knew. So he made another sign, this time smaller, thinking maybe it violated some kind of size-limit rule. They took that one, too. Becker asked why again. "Word from the Athletics Department," the guard said. So he wrote "Fire Groh!" on a sheet of notebook paper. The guard took that, too, saying signs of a negative nature weren't allowed and that if Becker wanted to go for one more, he'd gladly pitch him out under an Exit sign.

Now—no signs at all, pro or con. At Virginia! The nation's first secular university! Founded by Thomas Jefferson himself in 1819! Framer of the Constitution! Champion of "certain inalienable rights," like free speech! The man who once wrote: "A little rebellion now and then is a good thing"!

Who, exactly, is Virginia protecting here? Groh? The man can handle himself. After all, he was once the head coach of the New York Jets.

"Seems odd," says former Virginia star and current Bucs corner-back Ronde Barber. "You'd think if there was one university that would stand up for free speech, it'd be Virginia. When I was there, the signs were really clever."

I'll go further than that. I've covered plenty of games where the only clever part of the game was the signs. College football without signs is like pretzels without salt. Who can forget these signs from last season?

"WE WANT A NEW CARR WITH LES MILES!" —Michigan fan

"KANSAS FOOTBALL: A TRADITION SINCE SEPTEM-BER!"—Jayhawk fan

"IF YOU CAN READ THIS, YOU ARE NOT A CORN-HUSKER."—Colorado fan vs. Nebraska

Or, my favorite sign of all time in any sport, from a Bruins game in the '70s: "JESUS SAVES AND ESPOSITO SCORES ON THE REBOUND!"

Virginia's athletic department says it instituted the policy to promote a "positive game-day environment." Ugh. Sounds like some $150/hour therapist wrote that one. Someone with tissues in all their pockets and a "Ban Dodge Ball" bumper sticker on their car. Whoever wrote it doesn't get this: 99 percent of sports signs are positive.

Can you imagine what Jefferson himself would've thought of this new jackbooted policy? True, he grew to rue freedom of expression a little toward the end of his life, since the press was hammering him on his longtime affair with one of his slaves, Sally Hemings. (This might be why, to this day, Virginia still doesn't have a journalism school.) But I ask you: What's the point of founding a free university if that university is going to tell its students what they can say?

For instance, how are Virginia students supposed to express themselves about the Cavs' 52–7 home-opener loss to USC last Saturday? White T-shirts and Sharpies? Sign language? Hats worn at an angry angle?

"That's the thing," says Robert O'Neil, director of the Jefferson Center for the Protection of Free Expression, also in Charlottesville. "We don't quite know what constitutes a sign. Paint on someone's chest? A T-shirt? It's not quite clear."

One thing is clear. This is un-American. This isn't Havana. What's next? No yelling? No grumbling? No heavy sighing? How are students supposed to effect change at their school? Morse-code flashlights? And if they can censor students at the stadium, what's to keep them from doing it on The Lawn?

And if we're worried about a "positive game-day environment," shouldn't Groh be held to it, too? Remind me: What's so "positive" about 52–7?

This Saturday, the Cavs play Richmond and they'll be wearing special throwback jerseys. Seems superfluous. Virginia's already a throwback. To 1775.

Here's what Virginia students should do for every home game from now on: Bring signs that say nothing. Bring signs that say, "This

Is Not a Sign." Or bring 60,000 signs and let the Athletics Department goons try to sort them out.

Because sometimes rebellion isn't just a good thing. It's the only thing.

Postscript: *At least once a week somebody will ask why I switched from* Sports Illustrated *to ESPN. What happened to this column was one reason. After it ran, the students at Virginia rose up. They forwarded this column all around campus and came up with a plan. With two minutes left in each quarter, 7,000-plus Virginia students stood up, silently, wearing blank T-shirts and holding signs with nothing written on them. It worked. That Monday, the Virginia AD reversed his decision. It would've never happened at* SI, *whose readers are wonderful, but whose idea of forwarding an article involves stamps.*

Make $100 the Sleazy Way

June 6, 2010

Are you a male who'd like to make $100 the sleazy way? Then I have a deal for you, but you have to act by June 25.

Of course, you'll have to cash in your basic moral decency to do it and incur the wrath of every woman in your life—including your mom—and feel worse about yourself than Donald Trump's barber. But we're talking $100!

Here's how to do it, but I wouldn't let the wife read this:

It so happens that on May 8, 2004, the Oakland A's had a Mother's Day promotion. There was a fight-breast-cancer 5K run before the game, free mammograms, and the first 7,500 women through the gate got floppy plaid sun hats from Macy's. Nice day for the ladies.

Except that last part really hacked off a man named Alfred G. Rava. He was incensed that men weren't getting a floppy plaid sun hat for Mother's Day. He was so mad about it that he sued.

It gets worse. He has nearly won. A judge has given preliminary approval to a $510,000 settlement—roughly half to lawyers and the rest to the "victims"—the poor, downtrodden gender-disadvantaged waifs like Rava who didn't get their floppy Mother's Day hats. This is where you come in.

If you can prove you were one of the first 7,500 people there that day, you get $50 in cash, two-for-one A's tickets and a $25 Macy's coupon. It won't be hard. All you have to do is (A) state under oath that you are a male, (B) show some kind of receipt for your ticket and (C) swear you were there early. That's good enough. There's no video, and nobody's going to spend $5,000 deposing you about $100.

So how many guys have lined up to get their rightful floppy-hat-equivalent payment that was stolen from them by those selfish Mother's Day–manipulating women? "Well, I haven't taken a single call so far," said the 1-888 operator at the firm handling claims. "And I'm here just about every day."

A's fans are not just ignoring Rava in droves; they're pissed. "The entire settlement should be donated to the Breast Care Center at UCSF," says A's fan Ben Huber. "No good deed goes unpunished."

Isn't it good to know that most American males still have a spine? Save for (cough, cough) one.

Turns out Rava is a lawyer. In fact, this is not his first men-inism lawsuit. He's been part of more than forty male antidiscrimination lawsuits, sometimes as the plaintiff, like in Oakland, and sometimes as the plaintiff's attorney. He has sued Club Med for a ladies-only promotion. He's sued the Angels for giving away a $1.45 tote bag to women in 2005. He has sued restaurants and nightclubs and theater companies. Mr. Rava gets incensed a lot.

Oh, and he doesn't even work in Oakland. He works in San Diego. Gee, I wonder what a sue-happy lawyer from San Diego would be doing at an A's-Twins game the very day that they were holding a women-only giveaway? I called and asked.

But Rava wouldn't say.

"Season-ticket holder?" I asked.

Rava wouldn't say.

"You went to a game on Mother's Day, to a game that was promoting breast cancer awareness, and you felt victimized by not getting a floppy plaid sun hat?"

Rava insisted it was a fishing hat.

And he thinks the fact he didn't get one is offensive. Not just to him, he says, but to the state of California, "which has a very strong policy against discriminating on the basis of sex."

"Dude!"

"Look," Rava says, "if ESPN were giving away free autographed Nolan Ryan baseballs to men only on Father's Day, would that be fair?"

"These weren't autographed baseballs. They were women's sun hats. Plaid, floppy sun hats."

Rava: "Fishing hats."

I'm surprised he didn't want his free mammogram, too.

Personally, I find Mr. Rava as odorous as a bag of dyspeptic hamsters. He's a greasy manipulator who has found a small leak in American law and stuck an open wallet under it. When they wrote California's Unruh Civil Rights Act in 1959—the act Rava cites in his suits—they never thought soulless creatures like him would someday slink about the earth.

We are not a collection of legal briefs, appellate rulings and city ordinances. We are people. We are grandfathers and sisters and uncles and girlfriends, all woven into the fabric of this wonderful thing called sports. And if once in a while we want to do something nice for each other—and not want anything for ourselves—is that so wrong?

What are you going to do, sue?

Yes, Al Rava is going to sue and keep suing. What's next, Mr. Rava? Kids' Helmet Night? (Age discrimination!) Wheelchairs along the rail with a view? (Health discrimination!) Mullets Get In Free Day? (Clean-hair statutes!) Lawyers like Rava suck the fun out of everything.

What's amazing is that Rava's own mother died of breast cancer at age 53. How would she feel about his crass-action lawsuit?

"I am sure my mom would be proud of my lawsuit against this major league baseball franchise that denied male and female consumers under 18 years of age free fishing hats based on sex and age," he says.

Sun hats, tool.

Postscript: *The latest brave victory for Mr. Rava's organization—the NCFM (National Coalition for Men)—was over a Los Angeles–area Four Seasons' "Ladies' Night" promotion, which caused "discontent, animosity, harm, resentment, or envy among the sexes." And you just thought it was half-off drinks.*

Don't Hate Donovan. He's Not the Only Player Drawing a Blank

December 3, 2008

Donovan McNabb is getting $6.3 million this year to play in the NFL, and yet was clueless that a regular-season game can end in a tie after one overtime. Then he added, "I'd hate to see what happens in the Super Bowl. You'd have to settle with a tie."

(Sound of America slapping its forehead.)

Oy. It'd be like a pro golfer going, "You mean I have to get it all the way into the stupid hole?" So I devised a little unscientific quiz to see if it's just Duhnovan who's brain-dead about his line of work, or if other players are rules-challenged, too. Cover your eyes. It's not pretty.

Q: *What does happen in the playoffs if the game is tied after the first overtime?*

- Sam Madison, CB, Giants: "Are they gonna do a coin toss? The rule needs to be changed."
- Shaun O'Hara, C, Giants: "Yeah, we don't want the Super Bowl decided by a coin flip."

CORRECT ANSWER: Play continues until one team scores.

Q: *How many points do you get for returning a blocked PAT all the way?*

- Calvin Pace, LB, Jets: "Two? Isn't that the rule in college?"
- Kerry Rhodes, S, Jets: "Wait, you're trying to trick me. It's either two or none. I say none."
- Nick Mangold, C, Jets: "Seven? I have no idea."
- Dustin Keller, TE, Jets: "I think it's two."
- Madison: "Two."

CORRECT ANSWER: Zero.

Q: *If a punt is in the air while the game clock expires and the receiver signals and makes a fair catch, is the game over?*

- Danny Clark, LB, Giants: "Yes."
- Madison: "Yes."
- Damon Huard, QB, Chiefs: "If the punter touched it, then the game is over."
- Ray Rice, RB, Ravens: "Yes."
- Pace: "Yes. It's an untimed play, isn't it?"

CORRECT ANSWER: No, the receiving team can try a fair-catch kick.

Q: *What is a fair-catch kick?*

- Brendon Ayanbadejo, LB, Ravens: "The ball is put on the tee, or maybe there's a holder holding it, but there's nobody covering."
- Jarret Johnson, LB, Ravens: "You kick from the 50, off the tee. You can cover it. We've gone over it in meetings, but you don't practice it because it's the kicker kicking off a tee."

CORRECT ANSWER: A fair-catch kick is a field goal attempt following a fair catch. It can be a placekick or dropkick, but no tee may be used. It cannot be defensed.

Q: *What is the penalty for running into the kicker on a quick kick?*

- Clark: "Personal foul."
- Jonathan Goff, LB, Giants: "Same as on a normal punt."
- O'Hara: "Personal foul."

- Ayanbadejo: "Roughing the kicker? Automatic first down? No, wait! If he's showing that he's running the ball, then you can hit him just like anybody else."
- Johnson: "Fifteen yards and a first down."
- Chester Pitts, G, Texans: "It's a fifteen-yard penalty. If you annihilate him, I guarantee someone will throw a flag."
- Eric Barton, LB, Jets: "No idea."
- Pace: "There isn't a penalty. I just took a wild guess on that one."

CORRECT ANSWER: No penalty.

Q: *What's the maximum number of challenges a coach can make in a game if he's always right?*
- Clark: "As many as he wants."
- Goff: "Two per half."
- O'Hara: "Four."
- Barton: "If he's right, why stop him?"
- Pace: "Six."
- Mangold: "I don't know. There goes my coaching gig."
- Rhodes: "Three. You're not going to get me."

CORRECT ANSWER: Three.

Q: *When can the first-string QB reenter the game if the third-string quarterback is inserted before the fourth quarter?*
- Huard: "After the fourth quarter, the first-string quarterback can come in."
- Johnson: "You have to declare who your first- and second-string quarterbacks are?"
- Pitts: "They're interchangeable. If someone wanted to wake up and start the third quarterback and then put in the first quarterback on the next series, they could."

CORRECT ANSWER: Never. If the third quarterback is inserted before the fourth quarter, a team's first two quarterbacks cannot be used in the game at any position.

Q: *Can the kicking team recover its own blocked punt and advance?*
• Johnson: "No, it's dead."
• Barton: "I don't think you can advance a blocked punt."
• Mangold: "Don't know. Great question."
CORRECT ANSWER: Yes, if the kick is caught or received behind the line of scrimmage.

Q: *Are most of these players very much hoping their coaches don't read this?*
CORRECT ANSWER: Yes.

Postscript: *And here's a question nobody on earth can answer: What is a defenseless receiver?*

It's Hard Being a Cowboys Cheerleader

September 21, 2009

If you're going to make it in the Cowboys organization, you better cram like a sardine, because you'll take written tests on everything from Cowboys history to Texas culture to world affairs.

Not to make the football team. To make the cheerleading team.

The players don't have to take any quizzes. If you're 290 and can turn a running back into an oil stain, you could read at the equivalent of a mealworm and make it.

It's the cheerleaders who get grilled like it's Final Jeopardy. They take a nearly 100-question test during tryouts and are asked to name everything from the governor of Texas to a country that borders Iraq.

Remind me: What's this got to do with pom-poms?

Tryout coordinator: "Amber, that was a terrific triple-twisting salchow, and landing in a split was a surprise, but I'm afraid you gagged on the cold-fusion question. Get out."

"We want our cheerleaders to be knowledgeable and well-spoken in interviews," says Cowboys cheerleading boss Kelli Finglass. "If they're not, it's a deal breaker."

Cowboys players get interviewed every day. Shouldn't they have to take it? "Well, their job description is winning football games," Finglass says.

Riiiiight.

Besides, if Cowboys players had to pass the same quiz before they could make the team, many of them would be bouncers at Showgirls today.

Which is exactly why we gave it to them.

Why not? Why should the cheerleaders have to know more than the players? It's not like anybody from Fox is going up to a cheerleader after the game, asking, "Incredible game! Where do you think it ranks in Cowboys history?"

We coerced twelve players into taking it. To their credit, they did it with good humor and open minds, just not always clever ones. All these questions are from the cheerleader test:

Q: *Name the Six Flags of Texas.*

A very tough question. Only backup QB Jon Kitna nailed it. "Oh, my kids have been schooling me on this. Mexico, Spain, France, United States, Republic of Texas and the Confederacy. Thanks to my kids, I just learned that!" Nearly all eleven others thought it was an amusement park question. Need to get some kids.

Q: *Name the two ex–Cowboys quarterbacks in the Pro Football Hall of Fame.*

Everybody got it right except G Travis Bright, who answered Troy Aikman but forgot Roger Staubach, and S Pat Watkins, who answered, "Joe Namath and Troy Aikman." Yep, who can forget ol' Beltway Joe?

Q: *Name a country that borders Iraq.*

Ten of twelve got it right (Iran, Kuwait, Jordan, Syria, Saudi Arabia and Turkey), although WR Miles Austin and CB Orlando Scandrick said Afghanistan, which is about 750 miles away. Gotta at least pause at CNN once in a while, boys.

Q: *Who is the governor of Texas?*

This one was hopeless. Only TE Jason Witten and DE Marcus Spears got it right: Rick Perry. Interesting fact about the governor of Texas: He doesn't have to take a quiz, either.

Q: *List three lean proteins.*

"Like, foods?" asked LB Keith Brooking.

Uh, yes, foods.

"Tuna fish," he tried. "I don't know, man."

Watkins replied, "Fish, chicken, duck."

WR Sam Hurd listed, "Steak, chicken and pasta."

Pasta? No. Some correct answers: fish, skinless poultry, lentils, beans, soy products and lean meats. Definitely not duck.

Q: *In how many Super Bowls have the Dallas Cowboys appeared?*

Pretty simple question, right? One that might come up in interviews, appearances, book signings? But only one player in twelve—Bright—answered correctly, with eight. Not to be harsh, but 70 percent of Texas schoolkids will get that one right.

Overall, some of the Cowboys would've flunked before they got to show off their herkies, except DE Marcus Spears. He nailed nearly every question. That figures. Spears, who went to LSU, says friends made fun of him back when he was a kid for getting good grades and being smart.

Me, if I were a Cowboy and things got crazy on the sideline

this season and I had no idea what the coach just meant, I'd find Spears.

Or, better yet, a cheerleader.

Postscript: *Did you know that the original Cowboys cheerleaders in the early 1960s were half men? No, I mean, they were full men, it's just that in those first three years, they were allowed to be with the women. No, see, what I mean is . . . oh, forget it.*

Bad Lies at U.S. Open Qualifying

June 8, 2012

For every hug-happy U.S. Open qualifying love story—like Oregon's Casey Martin making it this year on one leg—there are 100 more left-your-fly-open stories. Guys who were supposed to shoot 69 and shot 99 instead.

When that happens, the USGA wants to know why. They dispatch a letter asking why you said you were a 1.4 handicap or better and then shot yourself a radio station—a ZOO-103 or a KOZY-105.

You better have a good excuse, or you'll be banned from any USGA event for the next three years. Let the stammering begin . . .

One guy wrote, "The reason I played poorly was the night before my wife took my clubs, so I had to go to the neighbor and borrow some. That [expletive] really knew how to hurt me."

Another man explained, "The color of the greens bothered me. I just never played on that color of green before."

One golfer said that he'd recently uncovered "incriminating" evidence that Richard Nixon, Ronald Reagan and Stephen King had plotted to assassinate John Lennon and that FBI agents were "hiding behind every bush and tree" as he played.

The USGA called the Secret Service on that one.

"One fella came down to our offices, mad as a hive of bees," says Larry Adamson, who was the director of USGA championship administration for twenty-five years. "He was yelling, 'Get your clubs, Mr. Adamson! Any local course you wanna go to! Right now! I'll show YOU I can play this game!'"

When security got him settled down and off the property, he still had to answer the letter.

If you try to qualify for a U.S. Open (this year it's at Olympic Club in San Francisco, June 14–17), as over 9,000 golfers did this year, try not to play like a drunken yeti. You'll get a letter requiring proof your handicap isn't phonier than a ski slope in Dubai.

"Just show us some scores from some reputable tournament," says Betsy Swain, who has Adamson's job now. "We're not even going to check them."

One guy, who'd shot in the high 80s both rounds, answered that with: "But I only hone my game for the U.S. Open every year."

To which Adamson replied, "Hone it somewhere else."

"We have to," says USGA Director Mike Davis. "It's not fair to the guy who's trying to shoot 68-68 to be paired with somebody shooting 90-90 and looking for balls all day. There's no way for him to get any kind of rhythm."

But golfers are prideful animals, if not always honest ones. They'll pull two hamstrings trying to explain why they're better than their score. You know, the old: "I can play better, I just never have."

One guy wrote to say that while looking for his ball in a pond, his glasses fell off his face and he couldn't see for the rest of the day.

Another said that the night before qualifying, his girlfriend had a baby and "I found out it wasn't mine. Kinda hard to get that off your mind."

And one golfer, who showed up to a Florida qualifier with his clubs in a plastic bag, admitted he just wanted to play with "famous golfers."

Reverse sandbagging has become an epidemic at Open qualifying, because golfers realize that for just the $150 entry fee, they can play a practice round and a tournament round at a sweet course they could never get on otherwise.

For instance, for local qualifying this year, you could've teed it up at Trump National in Westchester, New York, or Newport Beach Country Club in California. It's a good deal if you can live with the lying.

Some golfers have legit excuses. One guy no-showed because he was taken off to prison. Others were called into active duty. Some were doctors dealing with emergencies mid-round. All of those are accepted. Many are not.

"A lot of guys say they played bad because their wife was about to have a baby," Swain says. "And we're thinking, 'You haven't known the due date for nine months?'"

Adamson tried to use empathy with the particularly stubborn cases. "I'd ask them, 'Think about this: How would you like to play with you?' I remember one guy saying, 'Hell, I'd have quit.'"

And then there was this handwritten letter, which Adamson saved. It was from a 20-year-old in Ohio:

Dear Mr. Adamson,

This was the first USGA championship I'd ever entered.

But my Uncle Art died and my mom and dad said I had to go to the funeral.

I heard you can't get your money back, so I sent a friend of mine. His name was Curtis and he played under my name.

After he got home that night, he told me he shot 75–79. You tell me he shot 99–102. Now, somebody's lying and Curtis says it's not him.

I hope this is good enough.

Sincerely,

Name Withheld

(P.S. I sure am mad at Curtis.)

Postscript: *The highest score anybody ever shot in an actual U.S. Open round is 157, by J. D. Tucker, at the Myopia Hunt Club in Massachusetts in 1896. Which might be why qualifying was invented in the first place.*

Fortitude

(Small People Acting Big)

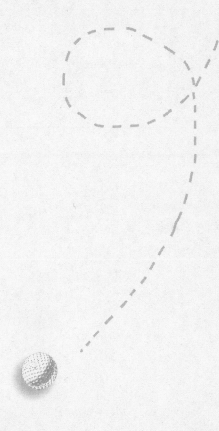

Special Team

November 11, 2012

How about a little good news?

In the scrub-brush desert town of Queen Creek, Arizona, high school bullies were throwing trash at sophomore Chy Johnson. Calling her "stupid." Pushing her in the halls.

Chy's brain works at only a third-grade level because of a genetic birth defect, but she knew enough to feel hate.

"She'd come home every night at the start of the school year crying and upset," says her mom, Liz Johnson. "That permanent smile she had, that gleam in her eye, that was all gone."

Her mom says she tried to talk to teachers and administrators and got nowhere. So she tried a whole new path—the starting quarterback of the undefeated football team. After all, senior Carson Jones had once escorted Chy to the Special Olympics.

"Just keep your ear to the ground," Liz wrote to Carson on his Facebook page. "Maybe get me some names?"

But Carson Jones did something better than that. Instead of ratting other kids out, he decided to take one in—Chy.

He started asking her to eat at the cool kids' lunch table with him and his teammates. "I just thought that if they saw her with us every day, maybe they'd start treating her better," Carson says. "Telling on kids would've just caused more problems."

It got better. Starting running back Tucker Workman made sure somebody was walking between classes with Chy. In classes, corner-back Colton Moore made sure she sat in the row right behind the team.

Just step back a second. In some schools, it's the football players doing the bullying. At Queen Creek, they're stopping it. And not with fists—with straight-up love for a kid most teenage football players wouldn't even notice, much less hang out with.

"I think about how sweet these boys are to her," says volleyball player Shelly Larson, "and I want to cry. I can't even talk about it."

It's working.

"I was parking my car yesterday, and I saw a couple of the guys talking to her and being nice," says offensive lineman Bryce Oakes. "I think it's making a difference around here."

And the best thing is? The football players didn't tell anybody.

"I didn't know about any of this until three weeks ago," says Carson's mom, Rondalee, who's raising four boys and a daughter by herself. "He finally showed me an article they wrote here locally. I said, 'Are you kidding me? Why didn't you tell me this?'"

All of a sudden, Chy started coming home as her bubbly self again. When her mom asked why she was so happy, she said, "I'm eating lunch with my boys!"

The boys take care of Chy, and she takes care of the boys. Carson, carrying a GPA of 4.4, got in a car accident last week; since then, Chy is always trying to carry his backpack. "I know his neck hurts," she says.

I get e-mailed stories like this a lot, but most of the time they don't pan out. They turn out to be half true, or true for the first week but not the second. But when I walked into the Queen Creek High

School cafeteria Tuesday, unannounced, there was 4-foot-high Chy with eleven senior football players, eating her lunch around the most packed lunch table you've ever seen, grinning like it was Christmas morning. It was Carson's birthday, and she'd made him a four-page card. On one page she wrote, in big crayon letters, "LUCKY GIRL."

I asked Chy to show me where she used to eat lunch. She pointed to a room in the back, away from the rest of the kids, the special-ed lunchroom. Much more fun out here, she said.

"I thank Carson every chance I see him," says Chy's mom. "He's an amazing young man. He's going to go far in life."

Nobody knows how far Chy Johnson will go in life. The life expectancy of those afflicted with her disease, microcephaly, is only 25 to 30 years. But her sophomore year, so far, has been unforgettable.

She'll be in the first row Friday night, cheering 10-0 QC as it plays its first playoff game, against Agua Fria. Some people think it will be QC's sixth shutout of the season. Sometime during the game, Carson probably will ask Chy to do their huddle-up "Bulldogs on Three" cheer, with everybody's helmet up in the air. You won't be able to see Chy, but she'll be in there.

"Why do I do these interviews?" Chy asked her mom the other night.

"Because you're so dang cute," her mom answered.

I've seen this before with athletes. Josh Hamilton used to look out every day for a Down syndrome classmate at his Raleigh, North Carolina, high school. Joe Mauer ate lunch every day with a special-needs kid at his St. Paul, Minnesota, high school. In a great society, our most gifted take care of our least.

But what about next year, when Carson probably will be on his Mormon mission and all of Chy's boys will have graduated?

Not to worry. Carson has a little brother on the team, Curtis, who's in Chy's class.

"Mom," he announced at the dinner table the other night, "I got this."

Lucky girl.

Postscript: *This column has more legs than a centipede. It was shared almost 150,000 times on Facebook. Hall of Fame quarterback Steve Young called Carson after it came out to congratulate him. Disney is talking about a movie. Carson and his team went on to win the state championship that year. Then Carson and Tucker went on their Mormon missions. While Carson is gone, Curtis keeps a close eye on Chy, as promised.*

When Cheering for the Other Side Feels Better than Winning

December 23, 2008

They played the oddest game in high school football history last month down in Grapevine, Texas.

It was Grapevine Faith vs. Gainesville State School and everything about it was upside down. For instance, when Gainesville came out to take the field, the Faith fans made a forty-yard spirit line for them to run through.

Did you hear that? The other team's fans?

They even made a banner for players to crash through at the end. It said "Go Tornadoes!" Which is also weird, because Faith is the Lions.

It was rivers running uphill and cats petting dogs. More than 200 Faith fans sat on the Gainesville side and kept cheering the Gainesville players on—by name.

"I never in my life thought I'd hear people cheering for us to hit their kids," recalls Gainesville's QB and middle linebacker, Isaiah. "I wouldn't expect another parent to tell somebody to hit their kids. But they wanted us to!"

And even though Faith walloped them 33–14, the Gainesville kids were so happy that after the game they gave head coach Mark Williams a sideline squirt-bottle shower like he'd just won state. Gotta be the first Gatorade bath in history for an 0-9 coach.

But then you saw the twelve uniformed officers escorting the fourteen Gainesville players off the field and two and two started to make four. They lined the players up in groups of five—handcuffs ready in their back pockets—and marched them to the team bus. That's because Gainesville is a maximum-security correctional facility seventy-five miles north of Dallas. Every game it plays is on the road.

This all started when Faith's head coach, Kris Hogan, wanted to do something kind for the Gainesville team. Faith had never played Gainesville, but he already knew the score. After all, Faith was 7-2 going into the game, Gainesville 0-8 with 2 TDs all year. Faith has seventy kids, eleven coaches, the latest equipment and involved parents. Gainesville has a lot of kids with convictions for drugs, assault and robbery—many of whose families had disowned them—wearing seven-year-old shoulder pads and ancient helmets.

So Hogan had this idea. What if half of our fans—for one night only—cheered for the other team? He sent out an e-mail asking the Faithful to do just that. "Here's the message I want you to send," Hogan wrote: "You are just as valuable as any other person on planet Earth."

Some people were naturally confused. One Faith player walked into Hogan's office and asked, "Coach, why are we doing this?"

And Hogan said, "Imagine if you didn't have a home life. Imagine if everybody had pretty much given up on you. Now imagine what it would mean for hundreds of people to suddenly believe in you."

Next thing you know, the Gainesville Tornadoes were turning around on their bench to see something they never had before. Hundreds of fans. And actual cheerleaders!

"I thought maybe they were confused," said Alex, a Gainesville lineman (only first names are released by the prison). "They started yelling 'DEE-fense!' when their team had the ball. I said, 'What? Why they cheerin' for us?'"

It was a strange experience for boys whom most people cross the street to avoid. "We can tell people are a little afraid of us when we come to the games," says Gerald, a lineman who will wind up doing more than three years. "You can see it in their eyes. They're lookin' at us like we're criminals. But these people, they were yellin' for us! By our names!"

Maybe it figures that Gainesville played better than it had all season, scoring the game's last two touchdowns. Of course, this might be because Hogan put his third-string nose guard at safety and his third-string cornerback at defensive end. Still.

After the game, both teams gathered in the middle of the field to pray, and that's when Isaiah surprised everybody by asking to lead. "We had no idea what the kid was going to say," remembers Coach Hogan. But Isaiah said this: "Lord, I don't know how this happened, so I don't know how to say thank you, but I never would've known there was so many people in the world that cared about us."

And it was a good thing everybody's heads were bowed, because they might've seen Hogan wiping away tears.

As the Tornadoes walked back to their bus under guard, they each were handed a bag for the ride home—a burger, some fries, a soda, some candy, a Bible and an encouraging letter from a Faith player.

The Gainesville coach saw Hogan, grabbed him hard by the shoulders and said, "You'll never know what your people did for these kids tonight. You'll never, ever know."

And as the bus pulled away, all the Gainesville players crammed to one side and pressed their hands to the window, staring at these people they'd never met before, watching their waves and smiles disappearing into the night.

Anyway, with the economy six feet under and Christmas running on about three and a half reindeer, it's nice to know that one of the best presents you can give is still absolutely free.

Hope.

Postscript: *They're making a movie out of this one—*One Heart*—with cameo appearances by Dallas Cowboys receivers Jason Witten and Miles Austin. And it's not just a movie. It's a movement. The One Heart people mentor prison youth and send them goodie bags in prison full of hygienic products, snacks and books. How cool is that?*

Camp Sundown Shines
in the Bronx

August 12, 2009

The team facing Yankees ace A. J. Burnett a few weeks back at Yankee Stadium has to go down as the oddest in baseball history.

For one thing, it plays only at night. The players have no choice. Even one minute of sunshine can kill them.

They're from Camp Sundown, in Craryville, New York, and they live life on the other side of the sun. All of them have the rare disease known as XP—xeroderma pigmentosum. If kids with XP catch the slightest UV ray, they can and do develop cancerous tumors. Even fluorescent lights fry their skin like boiling oil. Most of them don't live to be 20.

So how could they take the field at Yankee Stadium? Because this was 3 a.m. Superstar right-handers should be tucked into bed by then, yet there was Burnett, throwing Wiffle-ball splitters and chasing down line drives.

There is no cure for XP. If you're born with it, you're one in a million. There are only 250 known cases in the United States. Until Camp Sundown was founded fourteen years ago by Caren and Dan

Mahar, whose daughter Katie has the disease, few of these kids had met anyone else with XP. For most of them, Yankee Stadium was the first MLB ballpark they'd ever seen—and probably it will be the last.

Getting here wasn't easy.

To make the seven-foot trip from the front door of Camp Sundown to the curtained bus with double tinted windows that took them to Yankee Stadium, all the XPers had to wear hats, tinted eye shields, vats of sunblock, turtlenecks, long-sleeve shirts, long pants and gloves. Even with all that, they ran.

Because they couldn't leave until the sun was almost down, and because it was a three-hour drive, they knew they'd be able to see only the last couple of innings of the game. But then it rained, causing a more-than-two-hour rain delay. While the rest of the crowd cursed, the campers rejoiced. How lucky can you get? The bus arrived just before the first pitch. "It was almost like the game was waiting for them to show up," Yankees GM Brian Cashman said. "That kind of gave us goose bumps."

To get the kids out of the bus and into their VIP suite for the game, Yankees media-relations director Jason Zillo—the man who dreamed up the whole night—had to take them on a rat's route of back staircases and tunnels to avoid any fluorescent lights. After the Yankees beat the A's 6–3, the stadium lights had to be dimmed to 30 percent. Once they were, all the kids came running onto the field with smiles that could've lit up the Bronx.

"It's cool to be part of this," said Burnett, whom Zillo forced to leave at 3:15. "And it's kind of mind-boggling. I can't imagine if I couldn't take my children outside."

Eleven ghostly-pale XP campers took the field, including Yuxnier Beguebara, who is coming up on 71 operations, and Kevin Swinney, who has had over 200, and the rest of them, grinning through faces operated on so many times they seem to be covered in plastic. Feel sorry for them if you want, but they have one thing most kids will never have: For one night, the Yankees' field was theirs.

They high-fived Derek Jeter, ran madly around the bases and wallowed in the instant carnival the Yankees had set up—from the magician to the bouncy castle to reliever Alfredo Aceves strolling the yard, strumming his guitar while Cashman sang the Police's "Message in a Bottle." For one night, at least, these kids found out they are not alone in being alone.

Not that they don't play baseball at Camp Sundown. They do—at midnight, to the accompaniment of owls and bullfrogs—against the local fire department. "We're pathetic," says Caren Mahar. "But we always play."

By 3:30, it was time to go, and there was no time to waste. They had to make it back to Camp Sundown before sunup. Welcome to life lived like a vampire.

On board the bus, Katie Mahar, 17, was whipped. Her hearing is down to 50 percent, and her vision is going fast, and her words are starting to lack vowels. But anybody could understand her as she kept saying, "That was a blast! What a blast!"

And I keep thinking of my friend Jason Zillo and the fourteen years it took him to make this night happen.

"I saw one little girl," he said afterward, exhausted. "When the center-field wall opened and the whole carnival started coming out— she just started jumping up and down, over and over. She wouldn't stop, she was so excited. People wanted to thank me. But that's all I needed."

And you thought the warmest light came only from above.

Postscript: *Sadly, Kevin Swinney died six months later.*

The Ravens' (Very) Secret Weapon

January 14, 2010

Hey, Baltimore fans, this might make you spit out your crab cakes.

You realize who's been calling the first play of Ravens games lately? Like the one that went for an 83-yard touchdown against the Patriots?

If you said head coach John Harbaugh, you'd be wrong.

Offensive coordinator Cam Cameron? Wrong again.

QB Joe Flacco? Strike three.

The guy who's been calling the first play lately isn't a guy at all. It's a 14-year-old Baltimore kid. His name is Matthew Costello, he's got an inoperable brain tumor and he's on a lucky streak.

"You gotta meet this kid," says Cameron.

This all started when Matt, a third baseman and pitcher for Loyola Blakefield middle school, was hit in the eye with a pitch that tipped off his bat. He ended up with double vision. A few dozen doctors later, they found a malignant tumor. Now his days are mostly going to chemo sessions and wondering if he's ever going to get back to playing any of the three sports he loves.

Cameron's son, Danny—Matthew's classmate—told his dad about him, how he lives for the Ravens. Next thing you know, Cam Cameron was driving through the biggest snowstorm to hit Baltimore in years—getting stuck three times—with a Flacco-signed football, a signed hat and glad tidings for Matthew.

Why? Maybe because Cameron survived serious melanoma cancer at age 28.

Matthew's dad is a morning news anchor at WMAR in Baltimore, and he was on the air, live, when his phone spit out this befuddling text from his wife, Donna: Cam Cameron is on his way.

"I'm like, 'What?'" Jamie Costello recalls. "'In a driving snowstorm?'"

Yep. Cameron talked with Matt for twenty minutes, and then, as he was leaving, turned and said, "Hey, Matthew, whaddya wanna call for our first play Sunday?"

Mouth open. Eyes not blinking.

"Seriously," Cameron said.

Since Matt played QB for the school team, he knew when it was time to be audible. "Play-action pass," he said. "Be cool if you could get it to Todd Heap."

Sure enough, first snap against the Chicago Bears in Week 15—with the Ravens trying to make the playoffs—Flacco fakes the handoff and drops back to pass. Only, he bounces the ball off the turf for an incomplete pass. But later in that series Cameron looks at his play sheet. Scrawled on the side, he's written "Matthew Costello." So he calls Matt's play again and it goes for a 14-yard touchdown to Heap, the tight end. Ravens win, 31–7.

End of story, right? Except, three weeks later, the night before the Ravens' playoff game with New England, Cameron calls again.

"OK, Matt, whaddya wanna do Sunday?"

"Run the ball," pronounced Matt. "Ray Rice. He's hot."

So, first play against the Patriots, Flacco hands to Rice. There's a hole and Rice is through it like he's being chased by a bear.

"And I'm thinking to myself, 'Don't tell me this is going to go all the way,'" Cameron remembers. It does—83 yards, untouched, for a touchdown. "The whole way, I'm thinking of Matthew," Cameron says.

Nobody knows any of this except Cameron's and Matt's families. Jamie Costello is in the press box, screaming like his underwear is on fire. He hadn't told anybody that his teenage son was the new brains behind the Ravens' offense, so every single person gives him the stink eye. There's no cheering in the press box, dude. Unless you're cheering for a kid who's trying to survive.

Ravens win, 33–14.

Says Cameron: "I just looked to the sky and said, 'Maybe there's something to this kid!'"

Oh, there's definitely something to this kid. Since the chemo took his brown hair (the family calls him "Barkley" now) and a whole mess of his white blood cells, he only leaves the house to go to the hospital. Instead, he listens to comedy on his MP3 player. It's a crazy thing to see a kid, fighting for his life, constantly laughing.

This month sometime, Matthew will gulp hard and find out if his tumor has shrunk enough to begin radiation. If not, it's back to the chemo, Frank Caliendo going through his brain, prayers going through everybody else's.

Cameron knows a little how the kid feels. Earlier this fall, he had another cancer scare—this one prostate—but a battery of tests turned up nothing.

"My three boys and I talk about Matthew all the time," he says. "Anytime we're going through something a little tough, we say, 'How do you think Matthew's doing?'"

As for Matthew's dad, he can't find the words. "I used to worship Brooks Robinson," Jamie says. "But Cam Cameron is higher than that now for me."

The Ravens play Super Bowl–favorite Indianapolis on Saturday, on the road. Cam is planning the Matthew call for Friday night.

So, Matthew, whaddya wanna do?

"I haven't decided yet," he says. Smart. The Colts could be reading.

Not that he doesn't have a game plan.

"When I get better, I wanna do what Coach Cam did for me. I wanna make some kid feel the way Coach made me feel."

Funny, right? How a kid with double vision can see so clearly?

Postscript: *Saw Matt at a Ravens game not long ago and he was big and healthy and happy. He was never allowed to play contact sports again, but he still loves football. That's why he was off to work as a student coaching assistant under Cam Cameron, who's now the offensive coordinator at LSU.*

Drive Me Out to the Ballgame

July 13, 2013

There's only one baseball beat writer in this country who has a chauffeur pick him up in a new Lexus and take him up to the game every day: Hal McCoy of the *Dayton Daily News*.

He has to. He's legally blind.

McCoy has been that way for ten years now and yet continues to report, opine, blog, chat and broadcast about the Reds with humor and panache, his forty-second year on the beat.

"Hey, Hal!" Aaron Boone once yelled out in the Reds' clubhouse. "Do you realize you've been talking to a Coke machine for the last twenty minutes?"

It wasn't that funny that day in 2003, when the vision in McCoy's left eye went all dark and blurry, matching the fog in his right one from the year before. Optical strokes had hit them both—an event as rare as the unassisted triple play—and they left McCoy sure his Hall of Fame baseball writing career was done.

He walked into the office of his sports editor and told him that he was going to have to quit. They both had a good cry. Then the editor asked him to try one day of spring training.

A decade later, McCoy's eyesight is only worse, but he's still covering the Reds like a summer shower, thanks to his own bottomless knowledge of baseball, a very big flat screen in front of his seat in the press box, and his personal driver/Sancho Panza, Ray Snedegar, who got the job by answering this question in McCoy's blog:

". . . anybody out there with nothing much to do on their hands who would like to see most of the Reds home games this season . . . for free?"

McCoy got more than 400 applications from all over the country, but he only interviewed one man, Snedegar, whose wife, Barbara, had died two years before. He drives a hearse, but only part-time, and he's ex-military, so he's used to the twelve-hour days of a beat writer. Plus, they were both in their early 70s and loved the same things: Yuengling beer, old rock 'n' roll and the Reds.

Two hundred miles a day, fifty-five cents a mile, and no complaining about extra innings?

"Sold," Snedegar said.

How does a legally blind sportswriter cover a baseball team?

Really well.

McCoy writes for FoxSportsOhio.com, appears on Fox TV, writes stories for the *Daily News*, writes his blog, "The Real McCoy," and even covers road games from his garage. He's as popular as many of the players.

But he couldn't do it without Snedegar. "The last time I drove a car, I wrecked it," McCoy says. Snedegar survived a wreck himself—a plane leaving Saigon in 1975 that killed 138 people as part of Operation Babylift. A doubleheader in August wasn't going to scare him.

Snedegar answers occasional questions from McCoy like: "What just happened?" and "Who's that talking?" He takes his elbow when McCoy gets in heavy foot traffic.

"The worst part is people think I'm ignoring them," McCoy says. "I have to get up on a guy to two feet before I know who it is. So people will say hello to me and I won't say anything. They probably think I'm an arrogant jerk."

One day, he was interviewing Reds pitcher Mat Latos in the clubhouse. Latos, barefoot, finally stopped the interview and barked, "Dude, how many times are you going to step on my toes?"

Latos didn't know, and neither did McCoy.

Today, McCoy is interviewing Reds superstar first baseman Joey Votto. Afterward, I ask Votto if he knew.

"I've known for a few years now," Votto says. "Hal's got a very nice air about him, classy. So I'm glad to talk to him. But can I ask you a question? Is it true he can't see a fastball or a line drive?"

Sort of. Between the big screen and the cloud forest in his eyes he can just make out the ball—until it's hit hard or leaves the outfield. But then he just watches which way the batter's head turns. That's how he knows where it was hit.

"Cool," says Votto.

McCoy can tell where a home run lands by watching the fuzzy scramble of people in the bleachers. Or when a pitcher drops his head in shame. He knows where a line drive went by watching the relay line. In the clubhouse, he's memorized each player's walk and voice. And with his glasses and 20-point bold font, he can read his laptop.

"If the third baseman stays where he is, this guy is going to bunt," McCoy says to nobody in particular as the Reds are playing the Colorado Rockies.

Sure enough, Reds outfielder Derrick Robinson bunts.

"How'd you know that?" I ask.

"I know these guys," he says.

"It's flat-out amazing to me," says Reds reliever Bronson Arroyo. "Your eyes are your No. 1 asset. And he's covering the team. I'll bet half the guys on the team don't know."

———

It's two hours before the first pitch, and Reds manager Dusty Baker has saved the chair in front of his desk—and the first question—for McCoy, as always.

McCoy has already interviewed three players and the GM. After Baker, he'll go up, bang out a pregame story for Fox and then finally get something to eat.

There were years, even when he was sighted, when he didn't get to do that. When bombastic Marge Schott owned the Reds from 1984 to 1999, she'd often punish McCoy for breaking stories she didn't want broken by banning him from the press dining room.

No problem. McCoy was so respected that Eric Davis sent him a pizza. Another time, Tim Belcher. One night, for a laugh, the rest of the writers collected canned goods and piled them up in front of his space in the press box.

As McCoy is telling the story, the guy eating next to him makes a comment. McCoy turns and asks, "How long have you been sitting there?"

"About ten minutes," the guy says.

"See? I never even knew you were there. My peripheral vision is zero."

There's a bit of an awkward pause in the conversation . . . until McCoy adds: "Hey, it's not all bad. I'm now perfectly qualified to be an umpire."

The lovely part of McCoy's story is that it was a player who gave him a way to see his path forward.

The first day of that spring training in 2003, without a good eye, was a disaster. He had to outwait everybody at the luggage carousel because he couldn't tell which bag was his. He was lost in the Sarasota airport. When he stumbled into the clubhouse for the first time, "I suddenly couldn't recognize the faces of guys I'd known for years.

And I'm thinking, 'How can I cover a baseball team when I can't see?'"

McCoy was looking like a wrinkled pile of laundry with a person in it. Naturally, Boone figured it was a perfect time to give him crap.

"What happened to you?" Boone asked with a grin.

McCoy shuffled in the direction of the voice.

"Aaron, I think this is the last time you'll see me for a long time," McCoy said. "Both my eyes are gone. I have to quit."

Boone took him by the shoulders and sat him down in his chair.

"I don't want to hear you say 'quit' again," Boone said sternly. "That's not a good enough reason to quit. You're too good at your job to quit. You're still too young. We'll help you. We'll get it figured out."

McCoy was flabbergasted. A millionaire player caring about a lowly writer?

With at least one person believing he could do it, McCoy decided to stick around for two more days. Then somebody wrote a piece about him. Immediately, McCoy's e-mail box filled up with encouragement.

"People were telling me not to quit," McCoy remembers. "A soldier in Iraq telling me I was his hero. A guy with leukemia. And that day it hit me. I had it a lot better off than a lot of people. . . . But I would've quit that day if it weren't for Aaron."

In fact, when McCoy threw out the first pitch one night in 2009 at Cincinnati's Great American Ball Park, he asked Boone, then with the visiting Houston Astros, to catch it.

"That was so memorable," says Boone, now with ESPN. "Just to be able to come back to the mound and hug him and say, 'Love you, man.' I'm so proud of him. I'm proud to be linked to him."

On this night, the Rockies beat the Reds on Troy Tulowitzki's late two-run home run. McCoy won't be done until 11:30 p.m., and he and Snedegar and the Lexus will still have the ninety-minute ride home ahead of them.

"Are you going to be able to stay awake all the way back?" I ask Snedegar.

"Don't have to," he says. "Hal always drives home."

Postscript: *Hal is still driven. His autobiography is due out in late 2014.*

Mom, I Can Do This!

September 15, 2011

The marching band you see in front of you is like a lot of them in Ohio. They play the *1812 Overture*. They form tricky patterns. They even dot the "i" in Ohio.

The only difference is, the "i" they form is in Braille, because this marching band is blind.

They're the Ohio State School for the Blind Marching Panthers and—as far as I can tell—they're the only blind marching band in the world.

Brian Rowan is one of the bass drummers. He's 12. He has a tumor behind his eyes that has already taken the sight in his right eye and will soon take his left. Doesn't keep him off the field.

"I don't know why you guys cry so much," he told his parents—Karl and Shelly—when he was diagnosed. "I'm still going to do all the things I wanted to do. You watch."

They did. Last Saturday. Standing right next to me at a high school football game in Columbus, Ohio. Didn't help. Mom was still crying.

Which is the exact reaction that OSSB's Carol Agler, the woman who thought of this whole idea six years ago, doesn't want.

"We don't want any 'Awwwwww's when people see us play," she says. "We want 'Ohhhhhh!'s. We want people to be entertained. What we're trying to do is show the amazing abilities of the disabled."

They were pretty Ohhhhhhh! Saturday, sighted or nonsighted. (Some are visually impaired, not blind.) Twenty-three members strong, they whirled through four songs in nearly perfect pitch (a third of them have it) and nearly perfect order. Nobody tripped. Nobody smashed into anybody else. Nobody wound up in the parking lot.

How do they keep from running straight into the goalposts, you ask?

They're guided by nineteen volunteer "marching assistants." Of course, a lot of the time, the assistant is guided more by the band member than vice versa.

"I had no idea where I was going," said marching assistant Daniel Cook, 17, who plays trumpet in his own Franklin Heights (Ohio) High School marching band. "Brian did most of the work."

OK, so at one point, half of them were swinging left on "Sweet Georgia Brown" and the other half were swinging right. Nearly lost a few teeth there. But, overall . . .

"Pretty good!" pronounced the band director, Dan Kelley, who's been blind since birth. "We screwed up a couple little things. One group went out too far, but the rest of the band sort of came to them."

I blinked at him for a second or two.

How could you know that?

"Oh, I can hear them," Kelley says. "When they mess up with their feet, it messes up their playing."

Kelley is about as disabled as a road paver. He loves his chain saw. Sometimes, when all the cars are gone from the school parking lot, he likes to drive his buddy's car. With his buddy in it, of course.

He once made it onto the famed Ohio State marching band, sans assistant. "I was fine," says the trumpet-playing Kelley. "Just as long as I stayed right between my two piccolo players."

What was weird Saturday was that Kelley's heroes didn't get much applause from the 200 or so people in the stands. This might be because they played at a game involving two deaf football teams—the Ohio School for the Deaf vs. the Georgia School for the Deaf. Many of those in attendance were probably deaf themselves.

If you've never seen football played by deaf players, you should. The football is exactly the same (a deaf team invented the huddle) except that every now and then some tailback will go 80 yards because he never heard the whistle. That happened twice Saturday. Also, it is eerily quiet, like you're watching a game on mute. And being in a deaf football team's locker room at halftime is louder than standing next to a 727. They bang on the lockers with their helmets. They shriek. They usually have a big kettledrum that they pound on. They get psyched up for the third quarter by feeling all those vibrations.

It was a very odd afternoon when you thought about it. Here were two deaf football teams playing for a band that couldn't see them. Followed by a band playing instruments for football teams that couldn't hear them.

But the blind kids thrilled at the sounds of the crushing tackles. And the deaf kids could see the snappy blue-and-red OSSB uniforms with the bright red plumes in the hats. They could see the shiny sousaphones and tubas. And of course, they could feel the vibrations of the big bass drums. In the stands, the deaf fans wiggled jazz hands in glee.

If they'd been at the Rose Parade last year in Pasadena, they could've seen them marching in that, too. Six miles' worth. A very cool week for these kids, who range from 12 to 20. The day before, they got to touch all the floats. Float builders kept bringing them seeds and sticks and flowers to hold and feel and smell. Who gets to do that?

Hang around this school long enough—they have track (sprinters hold on to guide wires) and wrestling (grapplers start out touching) and goal ball (a kind of football)—and you'll be blown away at what they can do.

"I remember when he was born," says Jennifer Brandon, mother of band member Billy, 15. "I thought, 'How will he ever be able to do anything?' Well, this summer, we were both climbing an 8,000-foot mountain in New Mexico. We got about halfway up, and I said, 'Billy, maybe we should stop.' And he said, 'Mom, I can do this!' And I said, 'I know you can do this. I can't do this!' I had to stop there, but he made it all the way."

What do you give a kid who can dance 100 yards while playing a tuba and climb mountains?

Jazz hands.

Postscript: *After this ran, two band members—Brian and Boniface—had the honor of dotting the "i" during halftime at sold-out Ohio Stadium with the world-famous Buckeyes marching band. It came off without a hitch, despite all of Boniface's worries. "I didn't want my mouthpiece to fall out," she said afterward, "because that right there would be straight up embarrassing to see on national TV."*

Not Exactly on the Bubble

March 1, 2011

Coach K is good, they say. Roy Williams isn't bad. Rick Pitino can coach, I suppose.

But I'd like to see how those guys would've done with a roster of three valedictorians, six National Merit Scholarship finalists, seven mechanical engineers, three computer scientists, one debate team captain and one chess club president.

That's what peoples Caltech's men's basketball roster. Try taking that job. You'd be working at Home Depot inside three years.

How are you going to sneak a center with size 17 feet and an IQ to match into a school that ranks on many lists as the hardest to get into in America?

How are you going to coach at a school where your players can major in inorganic chemistry but not PE?

How are you going to win at a place where the students get a minimum of three hours of homework every night?

You couldn't beat an egg with that collection of nerdballs. That's why what Caltech's coach just did is so mind-melting.

Dr. Oliver Eslinger's Beavers, who hadn't won a Southern California Intercollegiate Athletic Conference game in twenty-six years, finally did last week, beating Occidental, 46–45, in the last game of the season. It wasn't a scoreboard hoax. After going 0-for-310, the rocket scientists finally figured it out.

Alumni were so proud that night their pocket protectors nearly burst.

Have you ever seen mathematicians storm the court? They looked like bankers at a rave. They were fanning on high fives and gently patting people on the back. It was such unfamiliar territory that some of the Caltech players doused the coach in water. (Sorry, wrong sport.)

At one point, Nobel laureate Dr. Robert Grubbs was hugging the school president at center court. If that's not a hoops first, I'll eat my calculator.

Nobody goes to Caltech to storm the court. You go there to storm space. You go there to work on the Mars rover, invent a car that runs on oxygen and get a corner office at Microsoft.

Only two guys on the team have girlfriends. The starting forward has *Star Wars* posters on his wall. The star of the team got a perfect ACT score. The coach starts each week asking, "OK, how many guys will have to pull all-nighters this week?"

This is a team that can figure out its shooting percentage as it's falling back on defense. It's not pretty. This season it was 37 percent. And the school's futility is not just in basketball. The baseball team has lost 415 straight conference games, and the women's volleyball team has never won one.

"My whole career," said Caltech's leading scorer, Ryan Elmquist (a computer science major), "people would say to me, 'You guys are never going to win a conference game. What's the point?'"

Elmquist won one game in his freshman season, one his sophomore and none his junior, going 0-25 last season. But Eslinger managed to recruit a bunch of freshmen who didn't have just beautiful minds but beautiful bounce passes, too.

Suddenly, Caltech basketball wasn't the equivalent of Auburn astrophysics. The Beavers had won a colossal four nonconference games.

This was their chance. Braun Gym was packed to the ceiling—387 people. Senior night. It was now or never for Elmquist. Losing by eight points with four minutes to play, never was looking like a very good bet.

"I felt like we could get this done," Eslinger said. "I just didn't know how."

Math is how.

"It was simple statistical probability," said freshman Todd Cramer (computer science) of Philadelphia. "After 310 games and getting so close so many times, you're bound to win one game, right?"

Elmquist went out and proved the theory. He scored the game's last seven points, including the winning free throw. What do you know? Spheres do fit in cylinders.

Caltech went absolutely irrational. Suddenly, the Beavers were no longer a null set. You'd have thought that somebody on campus had just solved the Hodge conjecture.

"I won two league championships in high school," Cramer said. "And it was nothing like this."

In a 900-student school that has had 31 Nobel winners—five of them still on the faculty—basketball was suddenly making national news. No wonder. None of these guys were even born the last time Caltech had won a conference game.

Elmquist went on the *CBS Evening News* with Katie Couric. Cramer got an e-mail from one of his professors, who celebrated the historic win with an unprecedented gift—a twenty-four-hour extension on his homework.

What's next? Well, Elmquist will program software for Google. A lot of the guys will end up launching rockets for the Jet Propulsion Laboratory next door to the school. One, guard Mason Freedman, plans to be an astronaut.

As for basketball, Caltech hasn't had a winning season since 1954, a record for heartache eclipsed only by the Detroit Lions. They're probably not ready for that any time soon, but that's their goal.

"When I tell people our goal is to win the conference, they go, 'Oh, that's cute!'" Cramer said. "But, honestly, we're not that far away."

These are space nerds. They know far away.

In the meantime, Caltech is living the dream. The other day, Eslinger got to coach the Washington Generals against the Harlem Globetrotters.

Must've been a comfort to him. The Generals once lost 2,495 games in a row.

Postscript: *Coach Eslinger is still at Caltech, while most of his players are off being Google programmers and NASA mathematicians. But one player has something he can brag on no matter where he works. Guard Mason Freedman not only helped break the basketball team's schneid, but, as a pitcher, he helped the baseball team break a 228-game losing streak that same year. Maybe the Cubs should sign him?*

Doing the Right Thing

September 4, 2013

WARNING: This college football column does not include illicit autograph sessions, under-the-table house payments or bloody-nose bar brawls. It will not require a thirty-minute suspension. It may even make you feel fuzzy all over about college football players. Proceed at your own risk.

As the operations manager for Buddy's Small Lots, a catchall chain store in New Jersey, Marci Lederman sees the worst from people daily on the fifty closed-circuit cameras in her stores.

"I see people stuffing two items into one box and then only paying for that one," she says. "I see people eating food in the store and hiding the wrapper. I see employees sitting around doing nothing because they think nobody's watching."

But she's never seen what she saw from four Division III football players last week.

It began when she got a call from the police that there had been an after-hours break-in at her Wayne, New Jersey, store. She expected the worst. Sure enough, on the video, she saw four large young men come in the front door, which was accidentally left unlocked after closing.

"My VP was looking at the video with me," Lederman remembers. "He saw those four boys and goes, 'Uh-oh, that's it. We've been robbed.'" But as the video played, they saw the oddest thing: integrity.

The four young men, who play football at nearby William Paterson University, picked up the items they wanted and then looked around for—get this—somebody to pay.

"We were down there for ten minutes looking for someone," wide receiver Anthony Biondi e-mailed me. "We thought everybody was in the back on break."

It was easy to see why they thought it was open. Buddy's always keeps some lights on after hours. Plus, the new motion-sensor Halloween monsters kept going off every time one of them got within five feet of them. "It was creepy," wrote defensive back Kell'E Gallimore.

Time was running out. They had to get to practice. So wide receiver Thomas James pulled out the $5 to cover the batteries and a video cord they needed, waved it at the surveillance camera above the cash register and laid it on the counter.

That's about the time on the tape when the VP slapped his forehead and said, "Uh-oh. I have to eat my words."

It gets better. One of them took eighty cents out of his pocket and laid it on the counter, too. Tax.

It was a first: surveillance cameras catching somebody in the act of honesty.

As if all that wasn't enough, the players went next door to Rite Aid to warn them that Buddy's was open but nobody was home. Eventually, Rite Aid called the police, who called Lederman to report a break-in. But it wasn't a break-in. It was a breakout. Of honor.

Nobody was watching and they still did the right thing.

When the closed-circuit video went viral on News 12 New Jersey and the players were identified, the coaches told them Buddy's manager wanted to speak to them.

Uh-oh.

"We thought we were definitely in trouble," remembered wide receiver Jelani Bruce.

"People are usually only on the news looking for people in a bad way," wrote Gallimore.

"I didn't know if it was a crime or not," wrote James.

Crime? This was a reward! Lederman just wanted to give them a $50 spending spree each to thank them for their honesty.

And why not? She expected shoplifting and got spirit-lifting instead.

"They were just so sweet and grateful," Lederman remembers. "They all bought pillows."

If there's one thing I've learned about parenting it's that the best gift you can give your kid is someone they'd hate to disappoint.

These four young men had that someone when it mattered most. For Biondi, it was his mother. For Gallimore, it was his whole family, who now call him "Honest Abe." For James, it was his father. "He sacrificed a lot for me," James wrote. "I want to make him proud of me. I don't want him to look at me like I was a waste of time."

I love this story. It makes me want to go hug somebody. I cover young, urban athletes nearly every week and 99 percent of them are fine and honest and good. Dreads and hoodies and baggy pants are not moral statements, they're fashion statements, nothing more. These four just made that a whole lot easier for me to explain.

I asked the four if there's one lesson they hope people will take from all this. Two of them gave the exact same answer: "You can't judge a book by its cover."

Somewhere, I hope George Zimmerman is listening.

Postscript: *An Internet snark called me "racist" for writing this, saying it was only me who expected young, urban athletes to steal and only me who was congratulating them for not doing so. If that's true, then by the end of it more than 750 media outlets, including the* Today *show, were racist. The truth is, in today's twenty-four-minute news cycle, a story about anyone doing the exact opposite of our fears was a refreshing pie in the face.*

Guei Made Sure That Everybody Won

February 28, 2013

The assist leader in college basketball this season doesn't play for Indiana or Kentucky or Duke. CBS hardly knows he exists. He won't show up on any national stat sheet.

His name is Allan Guei (pronounced: Gway) and he's the 5-foot-9, sixth-man point guard for Cal State Northridge. He's averaging only two dishes a game, but his sweet touch has helped seven people completely change their lives.

Two years ago, Guei walked into the gym at inner-city Compton High School (near Los Angeles) and sunk a single free throw to win a $40,000 college scholarship. But what he did a month later was even more breathtaking.

He gave the money away.

The whole story is told in a just-released, award-winning documentary called *Free Throw* by Court Crandall, an ad exec who wrote the Will Ferrell hit comedy *Old School*. But where *Old School* was about never wanting college to end, *Free Throw* is about eight kids hoping it begins.

Crandall's son, Chase, is a star high school hooper in ritzy Manhattan Beach, California, and Court had gotten to know a lot of Compton kids. He's also gotten to know how far out of reach college is for many of them.

A lightbulb went off.

Crandall got the cameras, bugged friends for $47,000 in donations—$40,000 to the winner, $1,000 each to the losers—and began the contest, open only to Compton High School students with a 3.0 GPA or higher. Eight names were drawn randomly out of sixty-five.

And whose name came up first? The captain of the basketball team—Allan Guei.

"Fix," people grumbled.

"Unfair," parents whispered.

"Oops," thought Crandall.

Even Guei himself wasn't sure he wanted to do it. "I knew they were all going to be mad about me being in it," he remembers.

Fast-forward to March 25, 2011. The Compton gym was crammed. The dance team was there. The cheerleaders. The marching band. Seven nervous kids (an eighth withdrew when she got pregnant). Their parents, fingers crossed.

The first round, best out of ten, cut the field to four: Guei (who made five free throws); Arturo Mendez (five), who spends most of his day caring for his grandmother; Donald Dotson (four), who'd given away his best basketball shoes to a kid whose toes were popping through his; and Diana Ramirez (four), who didn't know a free throw from a throw rug until the contest. Her arms were so weak she couldn't even get her practice shots to the rim. "So my dad told me to try it underhanded, so I did," she says. "And it worked."

The final round was one free throw each, winner take nearly all.

"I wasn't nervous until I got up to the line," says Diana, "and then everything crashed down on me. I was thinking, 'This one shot is going to determine how easy your future is.'"

Crandall was secretly hoping she'd sink it. Nobody wants to watch a documentary in which Bill Gates wins the lottery. "Diana was the David. I needed to beat the Goliath."

But Diana's Rick Barry granny shot rimmed out. Donald's wasn't close. Neither was Arturo's.

Which left Guei's. It hit the front of the rim, the backboard, the front rim again and then decided to drop through.

End contest. End a lot of dreams. End hopes for a dramatic documentary.

But then a funny thing happened. The predictable ending had a piano fall on it.

Guei was suddenly on the phone telling Crandall he'd been offered a full ride to play basketball at CSUN and asking him, "What would you think if I let the other kids have the money instead?"

Crandall pulled the phone away from his ear and stared at it.

"That would be amazing," Crandall spit out. "Let me make sure we have some film in the camera."

And so it was, on Graduation Day, Guei gathered the six around him—seven if you count the pregnant classmate—and told them they were all getting $5,714 toward college, to be parceled out over four years. They were all on their Guei to college.

"We were just speechless," Diana said. "All we could do is crowd around and hug him."

Today, Guei is a proud 20-year-old father of seven. "I'm so happy they're all still in school," he beams.

Mostly, they are. The only one not enrolled is Diana, but she'll be going back to Eugene Lang College in New York City in the fall when Allan's money kicks in again, when she'll work as an office assistant and pizza driver, and a very grateful student.

As for Guei, his life hasn't gone exactly as he thought, either. He's coming off the bench instead of starting, as he often did as a freshman. And, seems like about every day, his teammates poke at his psyche.

"They're always talking about, 'Man, you coulda did this or that. You coulda bought a car!'"

Actually, the $40,000 had to be used for college, but it would've been a very nice safety net for him in case he was thrown off the team or had a change of heart about basketball.

"Anything could've happened to him," says Diana. "What if he couldn't play anymore?"

But Guei has never looked back. "I'd do it again," he says. "I mean, if I already ate and somebody's starving next to me, I'm not going to eat again, right? People I've never met in my life find me and go, 'I'm so proud of you. I'm so proud of what you did. Friend me. Call me.' I've never had that kind of thing in my life."

And so it was Allan Guei became known as The Kid from Compton Who Gave Away $40,000.

"You know, when they first pulled Allan's name out, I thought, 'That's the absolute worst name that could've been drawn,'" says Efren Arellano, who is now at Long Beach City College. "And now I think it was the best."

Postscript: *Turns out Guei could've used that money. His mom got sick and his dad lost his job. Then Cal State Northridge decided to cut him. He's now at Humboldt State and trying to hang on. Anybody got a good job for a giving kid?*

Family

(Mine and Other People's)

Dad Played Golf and Drank—a Lot. But He Taught Me a Lot, Too

June 3, 2013

Since this is my first column for *ESPN The Magazine,* I figure I should introduce myself. And maybe the best way to tell you who I am is to tell you about my dad, Jack. He was an Irish tenor, a yarn spinner, a songwriter, a father of four, a crack golfer and a first-class drunk.

As kids, we blamed golf. We thought the game made him meaner than a dyspeptic rattler. We were sure it was more important than we were, or why was he never around? More than once he asked me, "What grade are you in again?"

He'd always come home drunk after playing golf, except for the times he'd come home dripping drunk. Then he'd be looking to bust something, maybe a lamp, maybe somebody's nose; my mom's, once. To this day, the sound of spikes on cement sends a shot of ice through me. That was him coming up the sidewalk.

In alcoholic families, the youngest kid becomes the mascot. That was me. I became the funny one, comic relief, third-grade vaudeville— anything to keep the furniture where it was. When he'd eventually stagger into bed, the rat in my stomach would finally stop gnawing.

When I was about 10 or 11, I started working through the thing backward. If I could play golf with him, maybe I could keep him from drinking. I'd be the hero! So I started asking him to take me. He did once, but my fear of him was so paralyzing that any instruction he gave sounded like a shotgun blast in my ear. After about three holes, I stormed off the course in tears and waited in the car.

I didn't play again until high school. I did it partly to understand what was so wonderful about a game that would keep a man from coming to his kids' games and piano recitals and birthday parties.

And I was happy to find out it wasn't the Titleist clubs that made him so mean, it was the Canadian Clubs. It was the whiskey. Golf was this green-and-blue launching pad for little white rockets. Golf taught me the lessons my dad never did, including the best one: You play life where it lies. You hit it there. You play it from there. Nobody threw you a nasty curve or forgot to block the defensive end. I learned that my mistakes were mine alone, not my boss's, not the cop's and, as much as I hated to admit it, not my dad's.

And then one day, out of the blue, maybe twenty-five years ago, my dad went to one AA meeting and quit drinking. Never had a drop after that.

It was five more years before I finally believed it. Then I invited him to the Masters. He was 70, I was 30. And it was on that two-and-a-half-hour ride from Atlanta to Augusta that we finally met.

He told me his life story, how he drank and fought to get the attention of his distant father, how he'd kept from us that he'd been married before, and how sorry he was to have let his family grow up while he was holding down the 19th Hole with his elbows.

He apologized and cried. I forgave him and cried. I never dreamed I-20 could be that emotional.

Suddenly he understood. He went home to Boulder, Colorado, and apologized to my mom and my brother and two sisters. They finally got to tell him how much he hurt them. He wrote us a poem about his love for us and his shame and why nobody would cry the day he died.

It took a lot of guts and a lot of courage, and the only lousy part was that it came so late. By the time I saw him for who he was—a strong man who took most of a lifetime to understand his crushing weakness—I was ears deep into my own family and career. So we didn't play much golf together before the warranty on his heart started to expire. I never got to really see the swing that won all those trophies. By then, the only time he used his putter was as a cane.

Two months ago, on the final night of his life, I sat alone in a chair next to his hospice bed, holding his hand and a box of Kleenex and proving how wrong poems can be sometimes.

As I looked at him, I realized that for better and worse, he'd shaped me. I think I'm a good father born of his rotten example. I'm a storyteller out of surviving him. I'm a man with more flaws than a 1986 Yugo, but I try to own up to them, because a very good Irish tenor showed me how.

And that's what I call a very good save.

Postscript: *Funny story, if that's possible, about the day my dad died: We were all circled around his bed, singing to him. He had a lovely tenor voice and his favorite song was "When Irish Eyes Are Smiling," so I went into the little nurse's office to find the lyrics on Google. Just as I hit "print," I heard somebody say, "This is it." I ran into his room, but he was gone. Five minutes later, we were still crying and hugging when the lyrics started printing in the little office, much to the shock of the nurse who was now sitting in there. She came in, wide-eyed, holding the piece of paper, trembling. She thought she'd witnessed a miracle. Turned out to just be a slow printer driver.*

Hey, Pro, Don't Want to Be a Role Model? It's Not Your Choice

February 25, 2009

This is a story I want to tell ALL athletes who think that what they do, how they act, the little kindnesses they give or withhold from fans, don't matter.

It'll take only a minute.

My wife, Cynthia, is adopted. At 36, she found half her biological family on the Blackfeet Indian Reservation in Montana. Turns out she had four half brothers, one named Lil' Bob, who was as big as a tree.

Lil' Bob, a bar owner, could pick a man up with one hand and throw him out the front door. He was gregarious and funny and always seemed to have his son, Jake, hanging on to one of his huge legs. Unfortunately, he was also a full-blown alcoholic. Many were the days that started and ended with a quart of Jack Daniel's, although you could never tell.

In size and in heart, Lil' Bob was one of Montana's biggest Broncos fans. His hero was John Elway. He joked that he wanted to be buried in an Elway jersey, with pallbearers in Elway jerseys, and an Elway football in his huge hand. His one regret was dropping out of school in eighth grade, ending his football career. His one dream was to take Jake to a Broncos game. Sometimes on the reservation, the dreams come small.

Last March, Lil' Bob's liver failed. One awful hospital day, Jake, now 13, walked up to the bed, took his dad's head in his hands, put his mouth on his forehead and told him he couldn't go yet. Told him he needed him to stay and take him to a Broncos game. Stay and watch him grow up and play for the Broncos.

Lil' Bob's death, a few days later, seemed to send Jake into that shapeless, black sinkhole where boys go when their best friend is gone for reasons they can't understand. "I tried to talk to him, but he was closed to it," says Jake's mom, Lona Burns. "He started doing bad in school. Kids picked on him. Every day I fought him just to go. His grades dropped. He didn't even care about going to football practice, didn't want to play."

Worse yet, since the day Lil' Bob died, Jake hadn't cried.

And then, this past October, one of Lil' Bob's best friends—a restaurant owner named Christopher Hamlet—decided to make good on an unfulfilled dream: He bought two plane tickets, packed up Jake and flew to Denver. Jake was finally going to a Broncos game.

As locals, Cynthia and I took them to lunch at one of Elway's restaurants so Jake could see all the jerseys and photos. The kid was so excited he hardly ate. And that was before a certain Hall of Fame QB walked in, all keg-chested and pigeon-toed. Immediately, Jake turned into an ice sculpture.

We introduced them, and it took a few seconds before Jake could even stick out his hand. Apparently, 13-year-olds are not used to meeting gods.

Elway took the time to sign Jake's football and pose for a picture. He even made us all go outside, where the light was better. Then, as we said good-bye—Jake's feet floating a foot off the ground—Elway turned and said, out of nowhere, "Hey, why don't you guys come by the box today?"

And the next thing Jake knew, he was in John Elway's box, asking him any question he wanted, all with a grin that threatened to split his happy head in half.

Then Elway said, "Comin' to dinner?"

And suddenly Jake was having his lettuce wedge cut for him by the legend, who tousled the kid's cowlick. Like a dad might.

Halfway through the night, a guy came out of the bathroom and said, "Are you guys with that kid? Because he's in there talking to his mom on the phone, crying. Is he OK?"

Yes, Jake would be OK.

"Jake came back a changed boy," his mom says. He started climbing out of that hole. He started making A's again. Started loving football again. He told his mom, "When I make it to the NFL, I'm going to buy you a big house in Denver so you can come to my games."

And I ask myself: Why did Elway do all that? Maybe because his late father, Jack, was his best friend, too? Maybe because his own son, Jack, went away to college last fall? Or maybe because that's how he is. In my twenty-six years of knowing him, I've never seen him turn down an autograph request, a picture request, a Can-I-just-tell-you-something? request.

A lot of athletes don't want the burden that comes with being a role model. But what I want to tell them is: You don't get to choose. You don't get to tell 13-year-old boys with holes in their hearts who can help them heal.

I know it's a hassle, but it matters. Because you never know when you might just lead a kid out to where the light is better.

Postscript: *Elway still asks, "How's Jake?" now and then when I see him. Answer: Well, he's huge now, for one thing—6-foot-7. He made the honor roll, still lives on the reservation, and misses his dad every day. One thing he's glad of, though: He says he's happy his dad didn't have to witness the Tebow era.*

Thanksgiving Comes Early

November 25, 2009

Really, what would you say?

You're a 52-year-old trucker, and you blew your chance with the Cincinnati Reds, blew your full-ride football scholarship at VMI, blew it all because you were just stubborn and rebellious and dumb.

And then one day, your 8-year-old granddaughter tells you that you ought to get on a thing called Facebook, and two weeks later, somebody on this Facebook thing is telling you that you have a son.

And not just a son, but Nick Jones, the strapping, two-time NCAA Division II discus champ and starting defensive end for Abilene Christian University.

Oh, and by the way? Abilene Christian is in the playoffs not ninety minutes from your house this Saturday, and hey, would you like to meet Nick before the game?

"I couldn't sleep," says Perry Hogsten, of Independence, Missouri. "I didn't know what to say. What do you say? 'I'm so sorry? I didn't know you were out there? Forgive me?'"

Some dads abandon their kids. Some get jailed. Some die. Perry

Hogsten missed out on the first twenty years of his son's life out of rotten luck.

Hogsten and his girlfriend, Stephanie Jones—Nick's mom—were planning on getting married when the Air Force sergeant was suddenly shipped off to Panama. This was 1988. Stephanie was supposed to stay in Abilene, Texas, and wait for him. Then she found out she was pregnant. The pregnancy turned high risk, so her mother brought her home to an Amarillo hospital, six hours from Abilene.

"I tried so many times to find him," Stephanie says, "but it happened all so fast. I had no idea how. We didn't have cell phones then, and international calls were too expensive."

When Hogsten came back six years later, he figured he'd been jilted.

Stephanie tried to explain it to her young son. "Your father would be here if he knew about you," she told him. "He's a good man. We never broke up. We just got lost."

She raised Nick and two other kids mostly by herself. There were weeks with no water, lights or heat, despite Stephanie working three jobs. By 11, Nick was the man of the house: up at 5 a.m. to do chores, work out for football, go to school, work out again, come back and make dinner, then homework. At games, there was no point in looking up into the stands like his teammates. Nobody was there for him.

"I'd always wonder at games," says Jones, a sophomore, "whether maybe he was secretly watching me. In high school, I'd wonder if he was one of my coaches."

Still, something inside him didn't want to search. Hogsten, meanwhile, had two other sons and divorced twice. Then, three weeks ago, he read a Facebook message from a Miriam Jones, Nick's wife.

Are you the Perry Hogsten who was in Abilene in 1988?

Next thing you know, he was driving toward the Ramada in St. Joseph, Missouri, butterflies in his stomach the size of Cessnas. In the parking lot, Nick "started coming at me pretty fast, and I just thought, 'My son's a big man!'" Hogsten remembers. "He's gotta be 6-foot-2, 245!"

Nick jogged toward him with his hand out, but Hogsten wouldn't have any of it. He put a helmet-to-helmet hug on him.

Suddenly, his life was on *Extreme Makeover*. He not only got a son, but he also got his girl, Stephanie, back, plus a grandson he didn't know he had—Little Nick, 15 months—and a daughter-in-law with very good detective skills.

As for him and Nick, it was like two strangers who'd never been apart. At Cracker Barrel, they ordered the same breakfast without knowing it. Same with lunch at Fazoli's. They looked the same, walked the same, laughed the same.

In Nick, Hogsten sees the life he lost. The college student. The young father. The track and football star who actually stuck with it. "My father told me, 'If you do this [give up his chance at college football or pro baseball], you'll regret it the rest of your life.' But I had to be the rebel. I joined the Air Force instead. And his words ring true every day to me."

Which is why he admires young Mr. Jones. "Just the way he carries himself, the way he talks. He's on scholarship, has a young child, has a wife, does his football, does his studies. I think he's the finest man I've ever met."

And now Stephanie and Hogsten are going to try to see whether love can start up again at the place Panama tore apart. He's trying to find a trucking job in Amarillo, where she still lives. Until then, there are actual cell phones this time.

As for Nick, all of a sudden, he's living life in reverse.

"I guess I just feel so much younger," he says. "I feel like a regular kid again, a kid with two parents. It's kind of a burden lifted off me. It's a relief."

This past Saturday, Abilene Christian got swamped by Northwest

Missouri State, 35–10, but it was the best loss of Nick's life. He did something he'd never done in a game before.

He kept looking up into the stands.

Postscript: *Sometimes these postscripts can wreck a happy ending. Stephanie and Perry tried to pick up where they left off, but it didn't take. Nick and his dad tried to become close, but that didn't take either. "It turns out," Nick says, "we're the same kind of person—neither of us likes to pick up the phone." Jones never played another football game after the one that weekend, but he did become the first discus thrower in history to win the NCAA title four straight years. He hopes to be in the 2016 Rio Olympics.*

Talking Football with Archie, Peyton, Eli

April 26, 2011

It's no good talking about the NFL draft unless you've talked to the first family of the NFL draft—the Mannings of New Orleans. Dad Archie went second overall (1971) and the two sons (Peyton and Eli) went first overall (1998 and 2004). That's a bigger draft family than the Busches of St. Louis.

I corralled all three of them in one room in Vail, Colorado, not long ago. It was a chance for the two brothers to give each other mountainous piles of crap while poor Archie, as usual, officiated.

They talked about growing up Manning, Super Bowl wins, the one rule the NFL needs to change, wedgies, how to cheat on concussion tests and, of course, their infamous ESPN commercial.

Q: *You guys were both overall No. 1s. Are you embarrassed to be sitting here with a guy who only went second?*
Peyton: Yeah, a little. Plus, Mom went fourth one year in the CFL draft.

Eli: When I was at Ole Miss, I called my dad up one time and said, "Hey, Dad, have you ever looked at your stats here? They're not very good."

Q: *They must've been pretty good. They changed all the speed limits on campus to eighteen to honor him.*

Archie: Yeah, but after Eli made that play to beat the Patriots in the Super Bowl [in 2008], I got about thirty texts from people saying, "They're going to change the speed limit to ten [Eli's jersey number] now."

Q: *Peyton, what do you remember about the Colts taking you?*

Peyton: I remember talking to Mr. Irsay [Colts owner Jim] at the combine, and saying, "Tell me what you're going to do." And he said they'd tell me in March. They were making it so dramatic, not making up their mind [between him and QB Ryan Leaf of Washington State]. And finally I was in his office one day and I said, "I would like to play for you, but if you don't pick me, I will kick your ass for the next fifteen years."

[Archie slaps his forehead.]

Peyton: That whole first-round draft choice thing isn't very long lasting. That's what I tell these guys—just get drafted and then be great.

Q: *Who's the best athlete of the three?*

Archie: Me. [laughing] I could outrun some guys in my day.

Eli: Me . . . I don't know. We're always trying to prove that. I remember one time, I was 17 and Peyton was 23 maybe. He was in college. He was home and we were playing one-on-one [hoops]. And it was just basically tackle basketball. Nobody got an open layup. And whoever lost didn't talk the rest of the day. So he had to go back to college and we promised to have a rematch. So the next time he came home, we went out there for the rematch and the goal was gone. Just gone. Dad took it off the wall. Mom made him.

Q: *Who's fastest?*

[Archie and Eli laugh knowingly.]

Eli: Peyton has never been timed in the 40.

Peyton: Well, I always had a little hammy problem when it came to run the 40 times. But my 40 time is not going to make or break it.

Eli: It may break it.

Q: *Peyton is five years older. Did Eli ever get to kick his ass?*

Peyton: Absolutely not. But he gave me a killer wedgie once. Got me up against a wall on a golf trip. He had all the leverage. But it wasn't an atomic wedgie.

Q: *What about in that ESPN commercial you're all in? [Peyton and Eli roughhouse at the back of a tour of ESPN, much to Archie's disapproval.] Looked like the two of them beat each other up pretty good in that.*

Archie: The director says to me, "OK, what would you do if your boys were screwing around like that?" And the boys both said, "We'd get The Look!" So he called action and I got it in one take! People come up to me all the time now and go, "That's the exact same look my dad used to give me!"

Peyton: It was so not fair. People go, "You got to kick Eli and it looked like it hurt him." But I only got one take. I had to get ten wet willies from Eli. And an ear infection.

Eli: I just didn't feel like I was getting it right. Not quite getting in there deep enough. So I asked for a few retakes.

Peyton: A few?

Eli: He got about five punches on my shoulder. I said, "Hey, Peyton, don't punch me so hard in the shoulder. That's my throwing shoulder." And, of course, the next take he just hauls back and really slugs me. After that it was serious. We just started going at it. Pictures were being knocked down along those walls. The director had to cut.

Q: *Sounds like that* Saturday Night Live *you did [in 2007], Peyton, when you were strafing little kids with footballs [as part of a United Way spoof].*

Peyton: We got out there and I told the director, "I don't know if I can throw the ball at those kids." It was just a Nerf ball that they'd scraped the "Nerf" word off it, but still. And he talked me into doing it. I felt better when I heard a parent of one of the actor kids saying to the director, "Hey, how come he's not throwing the ball at MY kid's face? I want him to throw the ball at my kid's face!"

Q: *Eli, you can relate, right?*

Archie: Oh, yeah he can. When Eli was 12 and Peyton was 17, Peyton needed somebody to throw to. Cooper had gone off to college [where he was a standout receiver at Ole Miss until a degenerative spine problem ended his career] and Peyton needed to work on his throws. It was kind of comical.

Peyton: It was so sad. I'd be throwing to a person who can't catch.

Eli: I was 12! They'd stuff me in a large T-shirt filled with padding, then stuff a bunch of pillows in there, too. And Peyton's arm had gotten too strong for the backyard, so we had to go out in the street. Our house is in an area of New Orleans where tours go by. And I'd be out there getting slammed by these rocket throws. And people would drive by and think, "What is wrong with this kid who keeps getting hit with balls on purpose?"

Q: *Eli was real quiet, right?*

Peyton: OK, driving him to school. His school was right on a direct line with my school, so I had to drive him. But I'd have a lot on my mind, right? I'm in high school. I've got a game that night. Test.

Whatever. So about ten times during the year, I'd pull into the school parking lot and realize Eli was still in the backseat. Just sitting there! And I'm like, "Eli, you let me drive right by your school! Why didn't you say anything?"

Eli: Well, I was in fifth grade. I had a lot on my mind, too. Girl troubles.

Peyton: Sheesh.

Eli: And the worst part was, you wouldn't even drive me back. One time, you called a cab!

Peyton: I'd call Mom.

Archie: Eli's gotten everybody back. He's a prankster. He can turn cell phones into any other language in about seven seconds. He'll do it to complete strangers, too. Chinese, Japanese.

Peyton: Yeah, he'll borrow some perfect stranger's phone. "Hey, can I borrow your phone?" And he'll change it to German. All the settings are gone. Everything.

Archie: And if you're on a golf trip with him, don't go to bed first. You will wake up with Sharpie marks all over you.

Peyton: Oh, yeah, he'll write across your forehead, color in your ears.

Eli: The best is to draw on the back of their calves, because they won't know it until they're on the golf course. They're wearing shorts and people are going, "What's that?" And it's always some kind of inappropriate drawing.

Q: *And yet you'll help him during the season with info on other teams, right?*

Peyton: Yeah, except if we're playing each other. But we'll share tidbits about who the other one is playing. Especially if they're playing somebody in the AFC South [Indianapolis's division]. I'll give him all he wants.

Eli: Yeah, like we played Jacksonville and he gave me a few things and we beat them. But then they played the [Philadelphia] Eagles and they lose!

Q: *And yet Peyton said one of the proudest moments of his life was watching your Super Bowl.*

Peyton: Yeah, Eli's big play in the Super Bowl. I watch it and I'm like, "How did he get that pass off?"

Eli: I remember after that catch, they went to replay. And I said to David [Tyree, the receiver], "Did you catch the ball?" And he goes, "Yes, yes I did." And I said, "Don't lie to me. You're a Christian man, don't lie to me." Because I need to know what the situation is going to be as soon as possible. Are we going to have a third down? Are we going to have a first down? What? Because I've asked receivers, "Did you catch it?" And they'll say, "Yes, absolutely I caught it." And then I'll look up at the replay on the scoreboard and the thing bounces three times before it even gets to him.

Peyton: But you have to watch that [Tyree] play closely, because when he thought there was no way to get out of it, he was about to shovel it to his left guard!

Eli: Well, you get desperate. You're looking for any white jersey. But when I saw the replay, I'm like, "Why is [guard Chris] Snee blocking no one five yards ahead of me?"

Peyton [sarcastically]: You should've passed it to him. Ya'll still would have won.

Q: *Archie, do you remember much about Peyton's Super Bowl win [in 2007 against the Chicago Bears]?*

Archie: I just remember how hard it was raining. The replay doesn't do justice to rain. I thought Prince would get electrocuted.

Q: *The game is so fast and violent. As a dad, do you worry about them?*

Archie: When I played, the collisions weren't as bad because the guys weren't in such great shape [like they are] now. Now, they're bigger and stronger than ever. I have two grandsons [He now has three

with Peyton's twins arriving March 31]. And I ask myself sometimes: Do I really want them to play?

Q: *What did you think last season in the game with the Jets, when blood
was just gushing from Eli's head?*
Peyton: That was overacting.
Eli: Those twelve stitches weren't overacting.

Q: *What do defensive ends say to you after they sack you?*
Eli: Sometimes they say, "Hey, I'm gonna see you here again in a few
minutes."
Peyton: [Baltimore Ravens linebacker] Ray Lewis is such a nice
guy, but he has this habit of using your body to help himself
up after a sack. You know, he really leans into you in order to
get up. . . .
Eli: Late hits bug me.
Peyton: Yeah, guys get called for late hits and they get fined—
Eli: Fifteen hundred dollars! These guys have millions! Fifteen hundred dollars? That's nothing!
Peyton: And they can write it off on their taxes! It's like, "I'm so glad
that you can write off my broken rib, buddy."

Q: *How do you feel about all the new research about concussions that's
coming out?*
Peyton: They have these new [brain] tests we have to take. Before the
season, you have to look at twenty pictures and turn the paper over
and then try to draw those twenty pictures. And they do it with
words, too. Twenty words, you flip it over, and try to write those
twenty words. Then, after a concussion, you take the same test and
if you do worse than you did on the first test, you can't play. So I
just try to do badly on the first test.
[Archie slaps his forehead again.]

Q: *Are we going to have a season this year?*

Peyton: I hope so. All I want to do is play football, and I'm running out of time. I can't afford to miss a year. [He's 35.] Eli could make it up, but not me.

Q: *So what are you doing during the lockout?*

Eli: Peyton and I went in before the lockout started and got everything we need. We're training every day.

Q: *Archie, let's finish with you. You had this terrific college and pro career. And then you have three star sons, two of whom grow up to be Super Bowl MVPs. Does it ever just stop you in your tracks?*

Archie: You know, I said to [Olivia] one night—I was in bed, reading something about the boys in a magazine—and I said, "Honey, we've been married thirty-five years now. Did you ever, in your wildest dreams, think you and I would have children that would do these amazing things?"

And she said, "Archie, very seldom are you in my wildest dreams."

Postscript: *Turns out Peyton got in some trouble with his crack about tanking the preseason brain tests. A lot of NFL beat guys got worked up. There have been rumors of players tanking, but nobody had ever admitted it before. But the man was joking! (I think.)*

Eli Manning Up

December 15, 2011

Here's to the little brother. Here's to the squirt. Here's to Beaver and Linus and Jim-Bob Walton.

Here's to the one who never gets the top bunk, never gets shotgun, never gets the last chicken leg.

Here's to Eli Manning, the ultimate little brother. Eli the Lesser, Eli the Forgotten, Eli the Oh Your Youngest Son Plays, Too?

Oh, he plays. The little brother with the perma-cowlick is one game away from his second Super Bowl in five seasons as the star QB of the New York Giants. If he can beat the San Francisco 49ers on Sunday in Candlestick Park, it would give him just as many Big Bowls as big brother Peyton, and in five fewer seasons.

Noogie!

Wouldn't that be a tiny, little, private smirk across the dinner table for Eli? For the sixth-grader who had to stand in the front yard catching howitzer passes from his five-years-older brother Peyton while wearing a pillow, gloves and a helmet. Had to stand there while Peyton hollered, "Hold still, Michelin Man!" Had to catch those things.

"Sometimes it just wasn't right," remembers their dad, Archie Manning, with a laugh. "He looked like some big fat kid out there. Cooper and Peyton just always messed with poor Eli. And you know Eli. He was always quiet, so he just kinda took it."

He's not taking it anymore.

And what about this—after all those years of Eli being the Boying to Peyton's Manning, is it possible that Eli is actually going to end up as the greatest Manning of all?

Settle down. It's possible. Consider:

- Eli's playoff record is better than his brother's. Eli is 6-3 to Peyton's -10.
- The scalps on Eli's belt are better. He got one off Tom Brady and the 18–0 New England Patriots of 2007 in Super Bowl 42. A week ago, he snagged one almost as good: Aaron Rodgers and the 15-1 Green Bay Packers of 2011. Peyton's signature win? He beat Rex Freaking Grossman.
- Eli's four playoff road wins are tied for most in NFL history. Peyton's had only two.
- Peyton has never thrown for as many yards as Eli did this season (4,933), even with more than half his games in domes.
- Eli's been more Clutch Cargo this season than Peyton ever has. His fifteen fourth-quarter TD passes broke the NFL record held by Johnny Unitas (1959) and—oh, wait!—Peyton Manning (2002).

Is that a revenge wedgie or what?

Can you imagine, Pops?

"I'm not going there," says Archie. "But I know there's nobody happier for Eli than Peyton. He's the biggest Eli fan in the world."

You might have a fight over that in the Giants' locker room now that Eli has led the Giants to five wins in their last six games.

"I think we've got the best QB in the NFL," says Giants receiver Hakeem Nicks. "Don't matter what his name is."

"This is probably the best he's ever played," says Archie, "because we [the Giants] haven't been able to run the ball like we did in past years. Plus, we had three changes in the offensive line [one move, two new players], and all the injuries."

Even former tormentor Cooper Manning, seven years older, has said he's never seen Eli play with such confidence.

"He's been so good in the last two minutes," Archie says, and he's right. Eli's five comeback wins this season were the most in the NFL, tied with the 49ers' Alex Smith and whoever it was quarterbacking the Denver Broncos.

You think if Eli makes it to the Super Bowl in Indianapolis, he'll call up Indy resident Peyton and ask, "Hey, Bud! You OK? You need tickets to the game?"

If Eli does end up with more rings than Peyton, it might be because he deserves it. The man watches more film than Roger Ebert.

"I don't know if I've ever come to work here and his car wasn't already in the lot," says tackle David Diehl. "He just outworks everybody. I was here when he walked in as a rookie, and to see his development in the eight years since then, it's amazing."

Diehl is so fond of Eli that when Eli takes off running, Diehl gets up and chases after him, even if the play is going to be dead by the time he gets there. "I'm Marty McSorley and he's Wayne Gretzky. Nothing better happen to him."

What's weird is, Eli doesn't even get the most press among New York QBs. The guy across town—the Jets' Mark Sanchez—still gets most of the back-page headlines. Now there's wild talk that if Peyton can get his tortured neck healthy, he could wind up replacing Sanchez next season. Lord, that's all Eli needs.

Marcia! Marcia! Marcia!

Anyway, as a little brother myself, the one that always had to get up and change the channel (pre-remote America), I say: Make him get up and chase you, kid.

So here's to Eli the Other, Eli the Overlooked, Eli the One Peyton Would Forget to Drop Off at Middle School Until He Was Locking Up His Car in the High School Parking Lot and Saw Him Sitting Sheepishly in the Backseat.

"He wouldn't speak up!" Peyton protests.

He just did.

Postscript: *After nine wonderful seasons and two Super Bowl wins, Eli screwed the pooch in 2013. He led the NFL in interceptions (26) the way Secretariat led the 1973 Belmont Stakes. And it led to this joke: "Did you hear about the joke Eli Manning told his teammates? It went over their heads."*

693 Reasons It's Tough
to Get an Ace

September 8, 2009

I got sick of reading the stories, is why I did it. I know it was wrong and unethical and even unholy, but I just couldn't stand the stories anymore.

A 5-year-old in Belleville, Illinois, sank a hole-in-one . . . A 102-year-old woman became the oldest ever to ace . . . A man in Bowling Green, Ohio, has now made holes-in-one both right- and left-handed.

Really? Because I've been playing since I was 13, and I'm 51 now and not hideous, and I've never made one righty, lefty, with a walker, a lollipop or anything in between. So maybe they can all kindly choke on a divot?

The one that made me snap was this one: 62-year-old Unni Haskell of St. Petersburg, Florida, made an ace a few months ago on the first swing she ever took on a course.

And that's when I lost it. I vowed to go to my local par-3 course and keep playing, round and round, like a rat after cheese, until I made a hole-in-one. I didn't care if it took me an hour, a week, a month.

With my 22-year-old son and caddie, Jake (he's made one—barefoot!), I arrived at the Golf Courses at Hyland Hills, in Westminster, Colorado, and set out on the dinky nine-hole North Course: 673 yards total.

"My dad's made five," said Hyland's director of golf, Todd Coover (seven). "One went off a tree. I kid you not!"

"How cool!" I lied, chewing through my lip.

The odds against making an ace are about 12,500 to 1. I guessed I'd played 50 rounds a year for 38 years. That's 7,600 par 3's. At that pace, I'd have my ace when I turned 75. Maybe. Unless I did the sensible thing: cheat.

I figured at ten shots a hole, nine holes a round, seven rounds a day, my ace would arrive in no more than eight days. I would be divorced, unemployed and fused at the T3 and T5 vertebrae, but I'd finally be a golfer.

My first shot missed. So did my second. In fact, my first 63 missed. My 64th, though, hit the pin and . . . rolled away. My 77th lipped out. "We'll be done by lunch!" yelled Jake, standing by the hole and pounding his baseball glove, ready to catch any shots that didn't have a chance.

But after three loops, I was 0-for-270. Many of them gloved.

After 5 hours 43 minutes—and five loops—I was fried like a fritter and 0-for-450, with two pins, two lip-outs and one O.B. (don't ask). Jake was looking like he wanted to be adopted. "We're really doing this again tomorrow?" he groaned.

You bet your inheritance we are.

Day 2: 20 more; 120 more; 200 more. Nothing. I repeated holes. I skipped holes. I hit twenty shots per hole. I tried not caring, caring too much, singing, one-handed, Happy Gilmore . . . all useless. The golf gods had spited me.

As my back spasmed and hands gnarled and Jake's eyes became shark-dead, I asked myself, "What if I never do it? Am I less of a person? Besides, Ben Hogan never had one, right?"

My self answered: (1) You'll feel like ferret droppings; (2) yes; and (3) Hogan had two.

And then, when all seemed hopeless, on my 694th shot of the quest, on the tiny 52-yard second, I hit a gorgeous little punch sand wedge that went straight as a Jonas Brother, landed exactly 11 feet from the pin and rolled directly and obediently into the cup like a happy little gopher off to bed.

Ho-lee hole-out!

Jake threw his glove about fifty feet high. I threw my sand wedge God knows where. We ran at each other like we were in a feminine hygiene TV ad. We collided in midair—me falling on my sore back and Jake falling on top of me. And it didn't even hurt.

I had done it. I had achieved the achievable. Climbed the world's smallest mountain. Slept with Madonna. It had taken 6 hours 23 minutes, over 500 ball-mark fixes and 12 Advil, but it was done. Suck on that, Unni Haskell.

To the pro shop to report the news!

"I hate to tell you this," Todd Coover whispered, "but it's not technically recognized by the PGA. Sorry." And I thought, Umm, Todd? I was hitting twenty balls per hole! On a golf course the size of a throw rug! What made you think I gave a mole's pimple about "official"?

The reaction from my friends was also less than congratulatory.

"A 50-yard ace?" e-mailed my pal the Vanilla Gorilla (two). "That's like a 150-foot putt."

Do I care? No. Am I going to tell people how I came to mine (one)? No. And what will I say when I read the next story about a legless 104-year-old blind nun who got her first hole-in-one Tuesday while a live wombat chewed on her clavicle?

"Damn! What took her so long?"

Postscript: *Like women who get pregnant the day after giving up on motherhood forever, you can predict what happened next. The next spring, during the traditional round we play on the road to Augusta, I made a real hole-in-one: 132 yards, gap wedge, flew in the hole. Suck on it, 104-year-old blind nuns.*

Thanks for the Memories

Thank you, Peyton Manning.

This might be the beginning of something better. Might be the end of everything good. But before we slog into what happens next, where you'll go, what you'll do, we owe you a thank-you for what you've done and who you've been.

So thank you, Peyton Manning, for never showing up in the VIP section of Cheerleaders, overserved and undermannered.

Thank you for never ending up on Court TV, or Page Six or with parts of somebody's nose on your knuckles.

It was trendy to make fun of your "Yes, sir"s and "No, sir"s and your 1950s haircut, but many of us secretly admired it.

You played a violent game and yet somehow held on to that Southern gentility. In the middle of the worst time of your life, you took the time to write a handwritten note of sympathy last week to Fox's Chris Myers upon the death of his son.

Thank you for watching more film than Martin Scorsese. Thank you for always being the last one to go home at night, for knowing more about what defenses were going to do than some of the players on those defenses themselves.

You came to a nowhere franchise and made it Somewhere. Greatness poured out of your fingers because you put in the hours and the study and the pain to let it. Two Super Bowls, 4 NFL MVPs, 11 Pro Bowls, eleven playoff seasons and more records than a used-CD store.

That Super Bowl win was classic you. Every day that whole week, you made your center, Jeff Saturday, spend an extra fifteen minutes snapping you balls you'd soaked in a bucket of water. "It might rain," you said. So when it did, and Chicago Bears quarterback Rex Grossman looked like he was throwing greased watermelons, you looked like you were throwing rocks.

Fourteen years in the league and the worst we can say about you is that you made a lot of castor-oil faces and your helmet left funny marks and one time you laid into your "idiot kicker." Fourteen years and you didn't sext anything, wreck anything or deck anybody.

You were a 10,000-watt bulb in a small city, and yet you never seemed to tire of it. If you did, you rarely showed it. There's a fan website—peytonmanning18.com/encounters.html—where everyday people tell how you were with them. It's hard to find a rotten one.

"Peyton was so nice and down to earth," one wrote. "He was just as polite and nice as I've always heard," wrote another. "He was getting ready to leave and wanted to take a picture with me and thank me for driving his golf cart," said a third. It's a lousy site if you're a cynic.

I have no idea how much time and money you have to give to a hospital to have it renamed in your honor, but they did that for you in Indianapolis. Peyton Manning Children's Hospital at St. Vincent. Says a lot.

How many times can one man change an entire city? Well, without you there's probably no Lucas Oil Stadium. Without Lucas Oil Stadium, there's no Super Bowl this year in Indy. Without the Super Bowl, there's no brand-new, drop-dead-gorgeous JW Marriott downtown. *Forbes* figures you improved the Colts' value by $233 million. Compared to that, $28 million to keep you doesn't seem like much, does it?

Thank you for showing up at podiums in your shoulder pads some nights because you know some of us had early deadlines. Thank you for making us laugh in all those ads. If there's ever been a funnier jock on *Saturday Night Live*, I'll keep a ham in my pants.

Thank you for showing up to work every day, every week, season after season. You started 208 straight games—through purple thumbs and black eyes and stomach flus that left you green. You get paid either way, so thanks.

Hell, you even tipped great. The other night, in North Carolina, you left an extra $200 on a $740 check that already had an 18 percent tip in it. According to my abacus, that's 100 percent class.

Lastly, thank you for the way you left. Always thought you'd go out as a Colt, and go out the way you wanted, but if it had to end this way, "I truly have enjoyed being your quarterback" is as good an exit line as I've heard. You made it sound like it was an elected position, an honor, a job where you knew people were depending on you. You were right.

You came to the line and changed the play 1,000 times, but you never changed your team, your city, your fans. Jim Irsay did all that for you Wednesday.

That would've gone down most guys' throats like a porcupine, but you took it and you smiled and you stood there with your arm around Irsay like he wasn't the one dumping you, like there wasn't a thing he could do about it.

That's grace. You had it in the huddle and you had it in the pocket and you had it in the end.

So, thank you, Peyton Manning. And bravo. You wore the horseshoe, but it was us who got lucky.

Postscript: *Manning ended up in my hometown, Denver, so I've come to know him even better. The things he does for people would amaze you. In the weeks after the Aurora theater shootings happened, Manning, unprompted, called some of the victims' families with condolences and wrote others. People get handwritten cards from him every week with his congratulations and encouragements. Everything matters to him, and it shines through in everything he does.*

Fights

(Columns That Got Me
in Hot Water)

A Call Kaepernick Should Make

January 30, 2013

Rae, my 23-year-old daughter, is adopted from Korea. Sometimes I look at her and feel for the woman who gave her up, who never got the joy of knowing her, raising her, watching her.

The 49ers' 25-year-old starting quarterback, Colin Kaepernick, is adopted, too. I wonder if he sometimes feels for the woman who gave him up, who didn't get the joy of knowing him and raising him.

That woman does get to watch him, though.

She'll watch him again this Sunday, as he plays in the Super Bowl against the Baltimore Ravens. Her name is Heidi Russo, a 44-year-old nurse from Thornton, Colorado. He's declined her requests to visit or talk. She accepts it, but she aches for more.

Wouldn't you? She was 19, unmarried and nearly broke when she gave him up. She cared for him for five weeks while she looked for an adopting couple who were (A) set for money, (B) had other kids and (C) loved sports. Heidi stands 6-foot-2, and the birth father, now absent, was also 6-2.

She picked another nurse, Teresa Kaepernick, and her husband,

Rick. They had one request: they wanted a boy. They had two kids already—son Kyle and daughter Devon. But they'd lost two sons to heart defects, Lance and Kent, who would be 34 and 32 now.

"I think about them every day," Teresa says. "What we went through. What they went through. They played a role in all of this."

And so on that early December day in 1987, in a Wisconsin attorney's office, four lives took wildly new turns.

"I'll never forget that day," says Teresa. "They brought him in an infant carrier and set him down. The birth mother [Russo] was there. I looked at her and she nodded, and I just picked him up out of the carrier. The minute I picked him up, I just cried. We gave her a big hug. And she needed a couple more minutes. And then we left."

Colin Kaepernick turned out to be an iron-willed, headstrong athletic tornado. He was so good at every sport that his family called him "Bo," after Bo Jackson. Still do. As he grew, the new mother would send the old one letters and pictures, until Russo finally asked her to stop. They were too painful.

"I couldn't move forward with my life," she recently told Denver TV station KDVR. (Russo did not return my phone calls.)

Russo sent Colin one last letter, for him to open at 18. Even after reading it, he had no interest in contact with her. A lot of adopted kids think if they so much as talk to their birth parents, it's a slap in the face to their adopted ones. They refuse out of a vague notion of respect.

"Is that how you feel?" I asked Kaepernick on Tuesday at Super Bowl media day. "That it would be disrespectful to meet with your birth mother?"

"No," Kaepernick said. "It's not really a respect thing. It's just—that's my family. That's it."

"But aren't you curious?"

"No."

That's odd, since many adopted kids are crazy curious about their birth parents, and their adopted ones.

"Why don't I look like you?" Rae would ask me. Finally, when she was 11, we flew to Korea and met the birth mom in what turned out to be a cloak-and-dagger adventure that I wrote about for *Time* magazine. Turned out the birth mother was a terrified 18-year-old girl when she gave Rae up. She didn't even tell her parents, just ran away to the city for three months.

But Colin Kaepernick never asked those questions. Not even when he was playing in a video arcade as a little boy, with his mother standing nearby, and a woman sneered, "People shouldn't just leave their kids in here all alone." Not even when he'd be standing next to his parents as they all checked into a hotel, only to have the clerk look at him and say, "And how can I help you, young man?"

Otherwise, "it all went really smooth," says Rick Kaepernick, vice president of operations for the Hilmar Cheese Company in Hilmar, California. "I know it's not usually that smooth with adoptions, but it was. Colin never had any adoption issues at all. The only difference is his skin is a little bit browner than ours."

The Kaepernicks have told Colin they'd have no problem with him speaking to Russo. They even met with her recently without Colin. But Colin hasn't budged on the issue. One of his friends told Yahoo Sports that Colin would think it's "treasonous" to meet with Russo.

But it's not. It's healthy. It's healing. It's natural.

More than that, it's important. When that 11-year-old version of Rae finally got to meet her birth mother, even though it was only for twenty minutes, she glowed. Her roots were no longer a mystery. She finally knew where she came from.

Your parents are your parents forever. Nothing can ever change that.

But you can't imagine what it would mean, how deeply it would be felt, for a woman with regrets and doubts to once again hold her child, even for five seconds. A meeting like that could fill two hearts.

Last year, Rae went back to Seoul to see her birth mother again, for a month. She found out she had three half siblings, too. One half-sister just made the Korean Junior Olympic gymnastics team. They all Facebook, e-mail and text.

I know my daughter is living a wonderful life in America, one that an 18-year-old Korean mother could never have given a secret daughter. So I'm happy Rae has let her into that life. In fact, I'm delighted.

What better way to pay her back?

Postscript: *This piece outraged all kinds of people, especially adoptees who accused me of trying to run the kid's life. I wasn't. I was only offering advice from someone who's been there. Kaepernick said publicly I had no business writing it and any talk about his birth mom is insulting to his parents. And yet Heidi and Teresa continue to have a good relationship. Heidi started a nonprofit to support birth moms called "Three Strands." "Birth moms have been shamed into silence for decades," she says. "And I'm on a journey to change that." Still, at press time, she had yet to speak to her birth son.*

Have the People Spoken?

September 18, 2013

I guess this is where I'm supposed to fall in line and do what every other American sportswriter is doing. I'm supposed to swear I won't ever write the words "Washington Redskins" anymore because it's racist and offensive and a slap in the face to all Native Americans who ever lived. Maybe it is.

I just don't know how I'll tell the athletes at Wellpinit (Washington) High School—where the student body is 91.2 percent Native American—that the "Redskins" name they wear proudly across their chests is insulting them. Because they have no idea.

"I've talked to our students, our parents and our community about this and nobody finds any offense at all in it," says Tim Ames, the superintendent of Wellpinit Schools. "'Redskins' is not an insult to our kids. 'Wagon burners' is an insult. 'Prairie n—s' is an insult. Those are very upsetting to our kids. But 'Redskins' is an honorable name we wear with pride. . . . In fact, I'd like to see somebody come up here and try to change it."

Boy, you try to help some people . . .

And it's not going to be easy telling the Kingston (Oklahoma) High School (57.7 percent Native American) Redskins that the name they've worn on their uniforms for 104 years has been a joke on them this whole time. Because they wear it with honor.

"We have two great tribes here," says Kingston assistant school superintendent Ron Whipkey, "the Chickasaw and the Choctaw. And not one member of those tribes has ever come to me or our school with a complaint. It is a prideful thing to them."

"It's a name that honors the people," says Kingston English teacher Brett Hayes, who is Choctaw. "The word 'Oklahoma' itself is Choctaw for 'red people.' The students here don't want it changed. To them, it seems like it's just people who have no connection with the Native American culture, people out there trying to draw attention to themselves.

"My kids are really afraid we're going to lose the Redskin name. They say to me, 'They're not going to take it from us, are they, Dad?'"

Too late. White America has spoken. You aren't offended, so we'll be offended for you.

Same story with the Red Mesa (Arizona) High School Redskins. They wear the name with fierce pride. They absolutely don't see it as an insult. But what do they know? The student body is only 99.3 percent Native American.

And even though an Annenberg Public Policy Center poll found that 90 percent of Native Americans were not offended by the Redskins name, and even though linguists say the "redskins" word was first used by Native Americans themselves, it doesn't matter. There's no stopping a wave of PC-ness when it gets rolling.

I mean, when media stars like *USA Today*'s Christine Brennan, a white woman from Ohio, and Peter King, a white man from Massachusetts, have jumped on a people's cause, there's no going back.

Besides, NFL commissioner Roger Goodell said last week that if "even one person is offended" on this issue, we need to "listen."

One person?

Got it. Guess we need to listen to people who are offended by the Kansas City Chiefs' name, too.

One person? I know an atheist who is offended by religious names like the New Orleans Saints and Los Angeles Angels of Anaheim. There are people who don't think Ole Miss should be the Rebels. People who lost family to Hurricanes. There are people who think Wizards promotes paganism. Shall we listen to all of them?

I guess so.

Edmundo Macedo, vice president of ESPN's Stats & Information Group, told ESPN ombudsman Robert Lipsyte that the term "Redskins" is abhorrent. "We would not accept anything similar as a team nickname if it were associated with any other ethnicity or any other race," Macedo said.

Oh, yes, we would.

In fact, ESPN and many other media companies cover the Notre Dame Fighting Irish, the Cleveland Indians and the Atlanta Braves without a single searing search of their social conscience.

Doesn't matter. The 81-year-old Washington Redskins name is falling, and everybody better get out of the way. For the majority of Native Americans who don't care, we'll care for them. For the Native Americans who haven't asked for help, we're glad to give it to them.

Trust us. We know what's best. We'll take this away for your own good, and put up barriers that protect you from ever being harmed again.

Kind of like a reservation.

Postscript: *Wow, did this column stir it up. Some people thought I should be fired. Some thought I should run for Congress. Three weeks after it came out, though, my wife's birth father (she was adopted at birth) said I'd misquoted him. I stand by the quotes, but I've removed them in this version out of respect for Bob. At press time, the name hadn't changed.*

Demoting Notre Dame

August 3, 2012

I once loved Notre Dame football.

My dad went to Notre Dame and flunked out and I still loved Notre Dame football. I loved Lindsey Nelson telling me "neither team advanced the ball so we move to further action in the fourth quarter" while my mom was yelling, "Get ready for Mass!"

But I grew up.

I don't love Notre Dame football anymore. Notre Dame football has been living a lie, as Lou Holtz likes to say. Outlined against a blue-gray October sky, nothing happened. The echoes are in REM sleep. It has failed to advance the ball.

If I told you about a team that had lost 10 of its last 12 bowl games, had dropped 9 of its last 10 to USC, had led the nation only in disappointment, you'd figure that team would be halfway down the Mountain West standings. But Notre Dame still gets perks and love from the NCAA and BCS as though the year is 1946.

I'm declaring an end to all that.

In Europe, if you play too much bad soccer for too many years, you get "relegated" to a lower division, moved down, demoted. It just happened to the Blackburn Rovers.

It needs to happen to Notre Dame football.

If Notre Dame isn't a factor this season—and it hasn't been a factor in almost twenty years—it's time to take it down a literal peg.

We can't demote Notre Dame from its conference—since it is far too noble to belong to any piddling conference—but we can demote it in stature.

From now on:

- Notre Dame no longer gets its own television deal with NBC.
- Notre Dame no longer gets to be the only school in the country with an inexplicable seat at the BCS decisions-making table.
- Notre Dame no longer gets its yearly undeserved hellahype in preseason rankings and preseason All-America teams.

In short, until Notre Dame football starts winning again, it's Rice to me.

That hurts your feelings? Watch *Rudy* 'til you feel better.

Can you explain to me how a team that hasn't won a national championship since 1988, a Heisman since 1987 or more than eight games its last five seasons still gets treated like the 1967 Green Bay Packers?

Notre Dame has won 86 games since the turn of this century. Oregon has won 111 games since then. TCU has won 119. Boise State has won 136. Do they have their own TV deals? Do they get to be the only school that sits with the BCS conference commissioners, deciding how a playoff is going to work?

Somebody needs to stick a pin in the still-inflated Golden Dome. Look, the ACC wants Notre Dame. Would die to have it. But word is, Notre Dame won't go if it has to share TV and gate revenue with the rest of the conference, like everybody else. The Irish people love to share. The Irish athletic department? Not so much.

If college football won't put its foot down and force Notre Dame to join a conference—as every other sport at Notre Dame has—then the least it can do is stop paying it a bowl bonus of $1.3 million when it DOESN'T go to a bowl game. That's right: Notre Dame gets a $1.3 million bowl bonus simply for dressing up the stupid leprechaun.

I hear what the Domers are saying. They're saying, "Notre Dame doesn't have to be in a conference. Notre Dame is unlike any other football power. Notre Dame is a national brand."

Sure, and girls are still wearing leg warmers.

Notre Dame is not a national brand any more than USC, Alabama or Stanford. A national brand? What would its slogan be, "Dominating Navy just about every year"? What kind of national brand loses to freaking Tulsa (2010)?

Please, NCAA and BCS, stop leaping to attention every time caller ID says it's Notre Dame. The Irish haven't finished in the top 20 in any poll in five years. They can leave a message.

When did I quit on Notre Dame? When it quit on itself.

Last season, against USC, the Irish were trailing by only two touchdowns, 31–17, with about seven minutes left when USC got the ball. But Notre Dame didn't use any of its time-outs, and it had a hatful of them. It let USC waste as much time as it wanted and never got the ball back. Good job. Good effort.

"They did give up," USC quarterback Matt Barkley told ESPN 710 radio in L.A. "I wouldn't have wanted to be on that sideline."

You are not royalty anymore, Notre Dame. Turn in your tiara.

When your NBC contract expires in 2015, do the right thing and don't renew. Lower some expectations until you can turn this thing around. And you're a Mars Rover trip from turning it around.

Wait, what? Coach Brian Kelly is the savior? Really? Because he looks to me like he's doing a very good impression of Bob Davie so far. He's opened with back-to-back 8-5 seasons. Wow. Give him a sitting ovation.

And with Kelly throwing the QB job up for grabs again, instead of just handing it to Tommy Rees once his one-game suspension is up, this season looks like 7-5 to me, with Ls to Michigan State, Michigan, Oklahoma, Pittsburgh, and you don't even want to know what USC will do to the Irish in the Coliseum. Cue the DentDoctor.com Bowl.

Somebody needs to make Notre Dame play by the same rules as everybody else. If there's anything we've learned from the Penn State mess, it's that nobody gets to live on a pedestal anymore.

You flunked, Notre Dame. Go back a grade.

Postscript: *Just my luck, the next season Notre Dame went from The Heap to The Hulk. Led by a very real linebacker (Manti Te'o) with a very fake girlfriend, they went undefeated right up to the USC game. I figured it was all a fluke, so I tweeted that if they did the impossible and beat USC, I'd "polish every helmet on campus." Yeah, well, about that...*

Notre Dame Fooled Us All

December 1, 2012

If you hate me, you'll be delighted to hear what happened last week.

First, I guaranteed undefeated Notre Dame wouldn't beat USC on November 24 in Los Angeles. I was sure of it. Flying across the country. Trojans with zero to lose. I was so sure, I tweeted:

> @ReillyRick
> No way Notre Dame beats USC tonight. If I'm wrong, I'll come to South Bend + polish every freaking helmet. I can't be wrong ALL year, can I?
> 6:33 PM—24 Nov 2012

Then USC coach Lane Kiffin decided to run approximately 473 halfback dives at the goal line straight into the Notre Dame line. Just to repeat: USC, a team whose best two players were wide receivers, kept trying to ram it through Notre Dame, a team with the best front seven in the country. Wished he'd have checked with Dad on that idea. The Irish won 22-13.

Minutes afterward, in the bedlam of the Irish locker room, Notre Dame co-captain DE Kapron Lewis-Moore couldn't wait to get to his phone so he could tweet this:

> Kapron Lewis-Moore @KLM_89
> @ReillyRick I'LL SEE YOU IN SOUTH BEND POLISHING OUR HELMETS!!! #EXTRASHINY
> 24 Nov 12

Me and my big mouth.

Which is how I happened to land in Chicago on Wednesday, which was inconvenient for my bag, which landed someplace else, which made me an hour behind schedule, which is why I drove like Brad Keselowski on 11 Rockstars up the Indiana Toll Road, which is why I suddenly had red-and-white state patrol lights in my rearview mirror.

Patrolman: License and registration.
Me: Yeah, sorry, officer. I was in such a hurry. See, I'm that ESPN guy that lost the bet? And has to come polish all the helmets at Notre Dame?
Patrolman: Oh, yeah! I heard of you!
Me (relieved): Right, right!
Patrolman: License and registration.

It wasn't just the tweet that made Domers so torqued. It was a column I'd written just before the season insisting Notre Dame's reputation far outkicked its performance ("It hasn't been a factor in almost twenty years") and how Notre Dame gets far more hype and perks than it deserves ("Somebody needs to stick a pin in the still-inflated Golden Dome") and how Notre Dame should save itself the weekly NBC embarrassment ("Do the right thing and don't renew").

Oops.

They wound up 12–0, No. 1 in the nation, and will now play Alabama in the BCS title game January 7 in Miami.

When I finally got to the equipment room, a bunch of gleeful players were waiting for me, especially Lewis-Moore, who opened his arms wide and hollered, "EXTRA SHINY!"

Then assistant equipment manager, Adam Myers, handed me a pair of scissors and a piece of shiny gold sticky paper. Turns out they don't polish the helmets at Notre Dame anymore. They patch them. They switched last October to a new kind of textured graphic helmet that's so shiny they look like miniature Golden Domes. When they get a gouge in them, you don't paint them, you apply a sticky gold bandage over it, the way you would on the skinned knee of a Trump.

Over the next three hours, every player who came in wanted to watch me do their helmet. Maybe they thought I'd spit in it.

But here's the weird thing: It was fun. It was an honor. This team will never be forgotten at Notre Dame, and saying that at a school with eleven national championships is a mouthful. Imagine: They went from unranked to No. 1 and finished up beating USC, a team that went from No. 1 to unranked.

Every player I met was not only cool about what an idiot I'd been, they all seemed to have stories.

I patched the helmet of center Mike Golic Jr., whose brother, Jake, plays tight end for the Irish and whose dad, Mike Golic, was so hacked off about the column, he nearly knocked out Mike Greenberg in the ESPN radio booth. "Oh, he was really mad," Golic Jr. said. "But not as mad as the time my mom took a hammer to Jake's cell phone in high school." Not a family you want to cross.

I patched the helmet of quarterback Everett Golson, who was benched, got a second chance, and became the surprise of the season. Golson plays all kinds of instruments, but piano and drums the best, not to mention defensive backfields. He's had only two interceptions in his last seven games.

I patched the helmet of center Braxston Cave, who grew up

eighteen minutes from Notre Dame and dreamed of wearing this helmet his whole life. He used to watch the managers painting the helmets on Friday nights with actual gold-leaf dust scraped off the actual Dome.

"You should see the first day we get our helmets," says Cave. "All the freshmen go running into the bathroom so they can take pictures of themselves."

At one point, there were five seniors around, pestering me to unscrew their face masks faster, or patch straighter or disinfect the inside better.

Me: OK, be honest. How many of you thought you'd be 12–0?
Them: [Silence. Shrugs.]
Me: OK, what do you guys think of being an undefeated underdog in the title game?
Them: [Laughter.]
Golic Jr.: They had us twelve and a half underdogs at Oklahoma.
Cave: And weren't we underdogs against Michigan State? [Yes—4.5 points.]
Lewis-Moore: And you said we were going to lose at USC.
Cave: And we won all those.
Golic Jr: So good. Let 'em. Bring it on.

True, a few students screamed &#%@s at me as I walked the campus for two days, but nothing I don't get at family reunions. I even spoke to a Journalism School class and nobody brought blow darts.

At one point, Notre Dame coach Brian Kelly walked by.

Me: Hey, Coach. I'd like to apologize. I was wrong about . . .
Kelly: Hold on. I don't read anything anybody writes. So we're good.

Anyway, the helmets you see atop the Irish in Miami will have been hand-patched by yours truly. Which is why they have no chance of winning.

"Thank God," Golic Jr. said. "If you started picking us now, we'd be screwed."

Postscript: *I learned my lesson. Before the Notre Dame–USC game the next season, I tweeted: "I absolutely guarantee USC will beat Notre Dame or I'll polish every helmet on the Juilliard Campus."*

Jimmer Grows Dimmer

March 25, 2011

So that's the end of Jimmermania. Saw it for myself. Caught the closing act. Not impressed.

Thanks to one of the worst performances of Jimmer Fredette's frabulous career—and a set of teammates who looked like pizza delivery guys—the BYU star took a hard fall in the Big Easy. BYU was bumped out of the Sweet Sixteen on Thursday, losing to Florida in a lopsided overtime, 83–74.

You can take off those "Romney-Fredette in 2012" T-shirts now.

Except for a stretch in the middle, when he was brilliant, Fredette was brutal.

Yes, he scored 32 points, but he took 29 shots to do it. He seemed to be wearing a blindfold from the 3-point arc—3-for-15. Plus, he committed six turnovers and wandered aimlessly through the lane on defense like Moses in the desert. I've seen dead people play better defense. At least they occasionally trip people.

If his last college game is what he's bringing to the NBA, then I'd say, in five years, he's got a really good chance to be your Provo-area Isuzu dealer.

Great kid, though. Polite, smart (good chess player, whiz at Sudoku), studies his Bible in hotel rooms. Maybe that was the problem. Fredette and the largely Mormon BYU Nation should've never been made to come to New Orleans. You can sin just by osmosis here.

You should have seen some of them on Bourbon Street, the freshly scrubbed Cougars fans, horrified to find themselves among the window strippers, the hurricane chuggers and the bead catchers.

Then again, some of the comparisons BYU fans were making about The Jimmer this week made you think they deserved it.

"He's a little Maravich," a guy in a BYU shirt told me.

No! No, he isn't! He's not within a mile of Mardi Gras floats of Maravich. Maravich could get his shot off from the bottom of a swimming pool. He could get 40 in handcuffs. He averaged 44 points a game in college (to Fredette's 28 this season), and that's without the 3-point shot. With it, studies of his game film have shown, he would have averaged over 55.

"He's better than Danny Ainge was," a lady in a Cougars sweatshirt told me.

No! No, he isn't! Ainge was Danny Clutch (remember his Sweet 16 drive in 1981). Fredette didn't have a single game-winning shot all year. Against Florida, he didn't score a single point in the game's final 8 minutes, or, for that matter, the first 13.

"I know from just watching him he's going to be a great NBA player," Oklahoma City Thunder point guard Russell Westbrook said.

No! No, he isn't!

Don't get me wrong. The Jimmer will make a modest living in the NBA. When he gets hot, he can drain them from the hotel coffee shop. He splits the double team as well as anybody in the league right now and he has a whole Santa bag of off-balance scoop shots with either hand. But until he shows more interest in defense than a blind man has in rainbows, he's going to spend most of his NBA life sitting on padded folding chairs.

To his credit, he'll have more help in the NBA than he had this season at BYU. His best rebounder, Brandon Davies, was thrown off the team for violating BYU's no-booze, no-sex, no-caffeine honor code, which meant it was pretty much Jimmer or nothing against the tall trees of Florida. He never came out once in the first forty-four minutes and had to fire up shots through the tiniest cracks of light allowed to him by the Gators. He wore out. He fired up two 3s from at least six feet behind the arc in the overtime and missed them both, badly. Then again, he had a cut in his chin that looked like something George Foreman had left and his calf was killing him. But when his teammates really needed him, at the end of regulation, on defense, Jimmer really hit the dimmer.

Florida missed a trey with twenty-four seconds to go and Fredette's man, Erving Walker, who stands only 5-6, beat him to the long rebound. It wasn't hard. Fredette was nowhere to be found. I'm not even sure Fredette knew who his man was the entire night. Florida wound up with a reset and the last shot.

"If we'd have gotten it, we'd have had about eight seconds left differential," Fredette said. "I'd have had the ball in my hands at the end."

Note to Jimmer: To get the ball, one must occasionally check one's man and/or box said man out. One did neither.

"The weird thing is, [his defense] has gotten progressively worse over the year," says Fredette's own teammate, Nick Martineau. "From the start, he's never really been accountable to it, but it's just gotten looser as the year's gone on. But he can play defense. He really can. He'll definitely tighten it up for the NBA."

He'd better.

"I just want to take a couple weeks off and then start getting ready to try to make an NBA team," said the man who probably will be voted about five Player of the Year Awards. "That's my dream, to make an NBA team."

Fine. That he can do. But you think this barely 6-2 kid with no speed and YMCA hops can be the next Maravich or Ainge or Westbrook?

Fredette about it.

Postscript: *I wrote this column at the Sweet 16 when a fan came up to me and showed me a huge re-creation of the Sistine Chapel ceiling—only with Jimmer's face replacing Adam's. That was the last straw. People accused me of being anti-Mormon, anti-Christian and anti-BYU. Then Jimmer started his first game in the NBA. So I had to write this . . .*

Nobody's Perfect

December 22, 2011

It takes me sixteen minutes to do Eight Minute Abs.

I have a time-share in Pyongyang.

I once asked the ship's captain what time the midnight brunch was.

But this is the first time my tiny brain has cost me $5,000.

Back in March, I said that BYU hoops star Jimmer Fredette wouldn't be a good NBA player. "In five years," I wrote, "he's got a really good chance to be your Provo-area Isuzu dealer."

I was so sure that I said if Fredette started even one game his rookie season, I'd give five grand to his favorite charity.

Well, Fredette's a rookie now with the Sacramento Kings and he finally started a game.

His first game.

He scored 21 points on 7-for-11 shooting, with 4 assists. And now it looks like he has a chance to become the Tim Tebow of the NBA.

Wanna buy an Isuzu?

Tuesday I handed him a check for $5,000 made out to the Fredette

Family Foundation, which helps families in New York, Utah and Sacramento.

In the check's memo line, I wrote: *Crow.*

"That's one thing that's different about you," says Steve Young, a BYU grad and longtime Jimmermaniac. "Most people have an opinion and stick with it for four or five years until they're proven wrong. You're wrong after the first game."

At least Fredette wasn't all I-told-you-so about it. He could've been.

"I wasn't really sure myself," concedes Fredette, who led the nation in scoring last season. "It depended on what team took me. I thought, 'What if I get stuck behind a great guard for eighty-two games?'"

Don't even try, kid. I was wrong as poodle sweaters.

I said he wouldn't be able to get off his shot in the NBA. So far, in two preseason games, he's averaged 16.5 points. He's been pyrotechnic from the wider NBA 3-point arc (67 percent). His handle is tighter than a coffeepot's. His rebounding and defense still have more holes than a Danielle Steel novel, but, all in all, he's been jaw-droppingly good.

"A lot of my friends and my family, they were mad about it [the article]," Fredette says. "They kept saying, 'That guy is going to have to pay!' But I really didn't read it, to be honest."

Touché.

I should've known Fredette would be fine in the NBA. This is a guy who can do anything, including a terrific jerk and a standing back flip, a trick taught to him by his petite blond fiancée, Whitney Wonnacott. He'll marry her on June 1 in Denver, once she's done cheerleading for BYU and graduated in broadcast journalism.

"So excited about that," says Fredette, who, like Tebow, has publicly stated he's a virgin. "Getting married is the most important decision I've ever made."

Does Fredette want kids?

"We'll wait a few years," he says.

If it's a boy, might I suggest Jimmest?

Anyhow, things are starting to shimmer for The Jimmer. In just over a week, the Kings have sold more than 1,000 Jimmer jerseys and now have two full-time employees affixing his name on the backs of blank ones to meet demand.

Plus, he's getting monster minutes from Kings coach Paul Westphal, who's a Fredette Freak already. The other day in practice, Jimmer was coming up to the hash mark—twenty-eight feet from the hoop—when Westphal hollered, "Shoot it!"

"Why not?" Westphal says. "Every time he shoots it, I think it's going in. It's beautiful and effortless."

"I like how much space there is in the NBA," Fredette says. "And if I get double-teamed, the guy I pass it to is an NBA player. He can hit shots."

His dad, Al, saw all this coming.

"Nobody ever thinks Jimmer can do what he does. I remember he was in the eighth grade. He was playing in a high school tournament. This one coach said something beforehand about the 'chubby kid being so slow.' Jimmer lit them up. Afterward, I walked by the guy and said, 'Hey, how'd you let that chubby kid beat you like that?'"

The chubby kid isn't chubby anymore, but he's still a little person in the NBA—6-foot-2 (maybe) and 195 pounds (sort of). He'll try to use that body to stop Kobe Bryant—Bryant's injured right wrist willing—and the Los Angeles Lakers in the Kings' opener the day after Christmas.

"I've never met him," Fredette says, "but I've always been a big fan."

Kid's got a lot to learn about trash talk . . .

. . . and defense. Can he score more than he gives up?

"That's what we're about to find out," Westphal says.

. . . and the rookie wall. He's going to be playing a lockout-shortened jailbreak season that will have him playing sixty-six games with only fifty-six days off. And, unlike BYU, the Kings want him to work both ends.

But seeing how he's playing on a Kings team that would love to put Tyreke Evans at shooting guard, Fredette may be the starting point guard before long.

Former ESPN NBA analyst and current Golden State Warriors coach Mark Jackson thinks Fredette could stick as a starter. He got his first pro look at The Jimmer in his Warriors' loss to the Kings on Tuesday night and declared, "The kid is going to be a very good pro. He can play. He's tough. He competes. You can see that."

Why didn't he tell me that $5,000 ago?

Postscript: *I still think I should get some of the $5,000 back. In his first three years in the league—through January 2014—Jimmer had started a whole seven games and averaged a shimmering 7.1 points per game.*

Commitment to Honesty

October 14, 2011

As you pass the casket at Maori funerals in New Zealand, you are encouraged to speak frankly to the dead man, sometimes even mentioning his faults right out loud.

With all due respect to his life and legacy, I think we need a funeral like that for recently departed Oakland Raiders owner Al Davis—a man I covered since I was 25.

Yes, Al Davis, 82, was a color-blind genius who changed the game. He was an original with guts and vision who "belongs on the pro football version of Mount Rushmore" (Adam Schefter, ESPN).

But somebody needs to come along and mention: He was about as warm as Rushmore granite, too. Utterly single-minded, he was a selfish egocentric who only liked you if you could help him. Mostly, Davis had all the charm of C. Montgomery Burns.

Yes, Al Davis's life should be celebrated. He was a maverick and an innovator, "the brains behind the AFL-NFL merger, the curator of the downfield passing game" (Bill Plaschke, *Los Angeles Times*).

But let's be sure to add: As ahead of the curve as he was in the

1970s and '80s, he was that far behind in the last two decades. Davis had three winning seasons in the last sixteen. He was exactly like those Members Only jackets he wore—fashionable once, dreadfully dated forever after.

Yes, Al Davis "was what all Raiders fans identified with" (SBNation.com).

And the rest of the league has had to live with them ever since. A Raiders jersey or jacket became gang uniform in Oakland and L.A. "The Black Hole" at Oakland games is about as disgusting a place as you can find. YouTube is lousy with guys in Raiders jerseys throwing haymakers. Now there's talk that Davis's oldest son, Mark, may sell the Raiders to Philip Anschutz, who would move the team to Los Angeles. After what happened at Dodger Stadium this year, you want to bring a thug element that would make Dodgers fans look like Our Gang? Better barricade I-5.

Yes, Al Davis had a "great eye for spotting talent" (SFExaminer .com), rescuing Jim Plunkett after the San Francisco 49ers waived him in 1977 and signing thirteen Hall of Famers.

He was also the guy who spent a first-overall choice on QB Ja-Marcus Russell, the most booming bust in NFL history. Yet Davis fired his coach, Lane Kiffin, for choking at having Russell crammed down his throat. Davis mocked Kiffin for wanting to draft WR Calvin Johnson instead. Today, Russell is out of football and Johnson leads the NFL in touchdowns.

Yes, Al Davis was "infallibly loyal to his players and officials: to be a Raider was to be a Raider for life" (AP).

Except when he'd turn on them. He hired a former Raiders assistant, Tom Cable, as head coach, then fired him in 2010, the sixth coach he'd fired in nine seasons. He fired Mike Shanahan and never paid the remaining $250,000 on his contract. He fired Kiffin after less than two seasons and tried to weasel out on what remained of Kiffin's $6 million deal. He benched Hall of Fame RB Marcus Allen for two years for no other reason than jealousy, inspiring fans to wear

"Free Marcus" T-shirts. Allen sued, then became the NFL Come-back Player of the Year in Kansas City. Prince of a guy, Al Davis.

Yes, Al Davis believed in "A Commitment to Excellence."

Yet he didn't demand it in himself. The facilities he put his teams in were among the shabbiest in the NFL. I covered the world-champ '83 L.A. Raiders at an abandoned elementary school in El Segundo. I can remember Howie Long changing out of his pads in a dilapidated classroom. The Raiders' current headquarters in Oakland would make a lovely Goodwill store. And yet Davis constantly complained about the stadiums he was given—the L.A. Coliseum and Oakland-Alameda Coliseum—to great profit. He suckered the city of Irwindale, California, out of $10 million with fake interest in moving his team there, then took $30 million from Oakland to come back.

Yes, Al Davis had "a deep love and passion for the game of football" (Oakland Raiders).

You sure couldn't tell in person. I sat in dozens of press boxes with Davis steaming in the back row, yelling, cussing and pounding his fists at the tiniest miscue. Even when he'd win, he looked miserable. I've known happier inmates.

Yes, Al Davis "made football a better game" (Mike Holmgren).

But not for everybody. He was as paranoid as a getaway driver. His PR staffs were routinely the most hamstrung in the league. Davis had no use for press or the fans they serviced. Once, at an AFC title game, a reporter he didn't recognize asked a question. Davis was livid. "Why should I talk to you?" he snarled. "I don't know where you're from! You could be from Florida! Or Afghanistan!" Perhaps Davis suspected the guy was as devious as he was. Once, as an assistant in San Diego, he posed as a reporter and asked a Buffalo Bill to diagram a play that had gone for a touchdown. He later used the play to score a touchdown—against Buffalo.

Yes, Al Davis's catchy "Just win, baby" became a mantra that transcended sports.

Just win, baby, no matter whom you trample to get there. The problem is, people take only so much trampling. In 1983, Davis could've had Stanford QB John Elway. Davis needed to work a three-way deal with Baltimore and Chicago, but the Bears despised him. So Broncos owner Edgar Kaiser, a man who knew less about football than Davis's housekeeper, snuck in at the last minute and got a player who would lead the team to five Super Bowls. Karma.

Yes, Al Davis could be "generous to a fault" (former Raider Warren Bankston). He took care of former Raiders who were hurting and even paid for the funeral of Kansas City Chief Derrick Thomas.

Yet after practices, Davis would routinely throw a towel down on the locker room floor and wait for somebody to clean his shoes. No please, no thank you. Just do it, baby. And grown men would.

Yes, Al Davis "bled silver and black" (CBS San Francisco).

Accent on the black.

Postscript: *Never got too much protest over the truth of this column, just the timing of it. "Couldn't you have waited until the body was cold?" Please. He lived cold.*

At Merion, Smaller May Not Be Better

June 13, 2013

Reason No. 317 we all love Merion but won't ever be coming back for another U.S. Open: Thomas Gravina came downstairs Thursday to find a bunch of golf pros eating muffins in his living room.

Because Merion is the size of a casserole dish, the Gravinas' kitchen, living room, dining room and library are now the U.S. Open Player Hospitality Center, which means he can walk in his front door nearly any time of the day and find Tiger Woods, Phil Mickelson or some other touring pro loitering around his house.

"I'm sitting there eating breakfast this morning with some guy's kid," says Mike Weir. "He was sitting on the couch, eating, oblivious to us even being there. Their dogs are running around. The guy's wife is coming in and out. We're watching *SportsCenter* and the kid changes over to the Golf Channel. I start to say, 'Hey, wait a minute, kid . . .' and then I realized, oh, yeah, this is his house."

The Gravinas' backyard? It houses the giant tent that is serving as the player locker room. Why can't they just use Merion's actual locker room? Because it's the size of a U-Store-It. (Reason No. 117.)

There's no room at Merion for anything beyond eighteen holes and a putting green, and even that gets tromped on by groups trying to get to the fourteenth tee. This course is so small you have to leave the property to sneeze.

David Martinelli's front yard looks like the scene of a daily tractor pull, since all the vans that drop off players at the fourteenth hole (yes, the fourteenth hole) drive over his lawn to do it. It's a hole now.

"People see what a wreck our yard is," says Christine Martinelli, David's wife, "and they're like, 'Oh, my God!' But, really, when you think about it, if somebody is going to wreck your grass, who else would you want fixing it than the USGA?"

All these people turned their lives upside down (for no money) so the USGA could shoehorn one last U.S. Open into this little jewel box. But this is getting ridiculous.

The Martinelli backyard is the Volunteer Hospitality tent. The neighbor's backyard and driveway is where the media interview the players. I have never interviewed U.S. Open combatants next to a kids' playhouse before.

There's so little parking, fans have to be bused in from eighteen miles away. They're calling 526-yard holes par 4's just to keep the red off the scoreboard. And yet the rest of the course is so short, they've had to make the fairways as narrow as sidewalks.

The whole thing is just . . . quirky, right?

"Quirky doesn't even begin to cover it," Jay Don Blake said Thursday.

How small is Merion?

Merion is so small that to get from the media center, which is near the sixteenth tee box (yes, the sixteenth), to the Martinelli Family Interview Area, vans go through a guy's gate, down his driveway and out the other side. (Reason No. 256.) One woman from the *Philadelphia Daily News* knocked on the people's door in hopes of using the restroom.

Merion is so small, only 25,000 people a day can come watch. At last year's Open, at Olympic in San Francisco, there were 40,000. That's 15,000 people who don't get to see it. The USGA will lose an estimated $10 million this week. (Reason No. 118.)

Merion is so small there is no decent practice area to speak of, so the players warm up right next to the Gravinas' house, at Merion's West Course, a mile away, or up to thirty minutes in traffic. (Reason No. 22.)

Can you imagine this in any other sport?

Announcer: Well, the Miami Heat seemed a little cold in this first quarter, possibly because they had to warm up at the Fort Lauderdale YMCA and then bus here.

And yet a very large space at Merion is mostly going to sit empty this week: the big interview room in the media tent.

Players won't be coming to be interviewed in it because to get to it requires Google Maps. Phil Mickelson, for instance, had a two-shot lead when he finished Thursday (after clearly earning a nomination for Father of the Year) and refused to come to the main interview room.

Why? Because he started on 11, finished on 10, had to walk another 1,000 yards to get to the Martinelli Family Scoring Tent and wasn't about to then get in a golf cart and ride fifteen minutes to get to the interview room before he navigated the congested one-mile van ride back to the Gravina Family Player Hospitality Area and Locker Room.

Are you starting to see the problem?

Look, Merion is like playing in your favorite grandmother's attic—the basket pins, the steep wooden staircases in the middle of holes, the giant rock walls that are in play. But it's a rotary dial phone. Ebbets Field was wonderful, too, but we had to give it up.

Trying to force a U.S. Open into the pillbox hat that is Merion is like trying to fit into the pants you wore in high school. We're splitting apart at the seams here.

So enjoy cuddly, furry, wonderful Merion for this one last week. Hopefully, after this, it goes the way of Old Yeller.

Postscript: *The day this posted—the Saturday of the Merion Open—I happened to be wearing a bright fuchsia golf shirt. I was standing on the seventeenth green, waiting for Mickelson to hit his tee shot. In the silence, some guy bellowed, "Hey, Rick! Why don't you write your next column on bad shirts?" Got a huge laugh. My face out-fuchsia-ed the shirt.*

Welcome to Tramplona

July 22, 2010

PAMPLONA, Spain—Ernest Hemingway made the running of the bulls legendary, but he never ran himself, and now I know why. It's an excellent way to die.

That thought occurred to me as I found myself trapped in a shop doorway, alone, while a 1,200-pound bull, three feet from me, sized me up as a possible hornament.

Of course, the bulls aren't the only way to die during the running of the bulls, which occurs from July 7 through 14 every year and really is something you should do once if you (A) aren't particularly bent on living a long life and (B) are comfortable drinking sangria by the barrel.

Another good way to end up dead is under the people behind you. Two thousand or more run now. Way, way, way too many people. I met ten guys who were doing it as part of a bachelor party. I saw a guy dressed as Elvis. I saw women with purses, their tears running their mascara as they realized what they'd gotten themselves into. I saw a group of people with a tour guide.

OK, if you're not gored, meet back at the hotel and have your bags ready.

The world now seems to think of the running of the bulls as some kind of cute tourist item to check off, like the Eiffel Tower or Anne Frank's house. I was standing in the town square, two minutes before the rocket went off to let us know the bulls were loose, when I had this actual conversation:

Spiky-haired British dude with his wide-eyed girlfriend: We've never done this before. Is this a good place to stand?

Me: Well, it depends on if you want to make it to Dead Man's Corner before the bulls.
British dude: Dead Man's Corner?
Me: Yeah, where the guy died last year?
British dude: Died?

But if you enjoy replacing your entire bloodstream with adrenaline and feeling rushes that leave you still tingling on the plane home, I Know What You'll Do Next Summer.

This chaos all started sometime in the fourteenth century, when a few mead-sopped men decided it was a thrill to sprint ahead of the bulls as they were being run the 928 yards from the pens at one end of town to the bullring at the other for the evening's bullfight. It was all part of the San Fermin festival that fascinated Hemingway. "All the carnivals I had ever seen paled down in comparison," he wrote.

If you go, take your oldest, whitest clothes, because strangers will douse you all night with sangria, make you drink nonstop until 6 a.m., leap from fountain tops into your arms, dance and sing and offer to make out with you. And that's all just something to do until the real madness begins.

The Sun Also Rises, but you better be up before it does if you want your chance to toy with death. Get yourself to the town hall square by 7 a.m., or the merciless Spanish cops will kick you out.

I watched the first day's run from a spot on the balcony I rented for 30 euros ($38). I stood up there and watched a guy get flattened like a tortilla on the cobblestones below. Welcome to Tramplona. And I knew I would be down there the next morning. The fear was starting to climb up my throat. Miguel, the old guy who'd rented me the balcony, declared, "This is my thirty-first running. It's not something you can explain with words. You must experience it to understand."

Me: What year did you start running?
Miguel: Oh, no. I have never run. I find it much more sensible
      to watch it from up here.

As the minutes bore down to 8 a.m. the next day, I was wishing to God I was more sensible. I huddled with a few hundred other morons, adjusting my little helmet cam and holding my rolled-up newspaper in hopes of achieving the one noble goal of any Pamplona runner: to swat a bull's ass. As we waited to hear that dreaded rocket, my brain screamed, "We could jump over that fence! It's right there!" I didn't. Maybe because I'd already expensed the flight over.

A big guy in a Red Sox T-shirt pointed to the corner behind us and said, "Don't run until you see the flashes of the cameras. Then you know they're coming." His name turned out to be Richard Pettito; he's a Daytona Beach, Florida, firefighter. "That's when you run like hell. I'll see you at the bullring. Good luck, man."

I swallowed hard and wished him the same. And that was when I noticed he was wearing a white lace skirt over his pants.

Just when you think you're being brave and valiant and Hemingwayesque, you realize you're taking advice from a guy in a skirt.

"Uh, Rich, what's up with the skirt?" I asked.

"Yeah, I try to wear something different every day. Helps me find myself in pictures later on."

I hurried to the little shop doorway I'd picked out the day before. I'd calculated that from there I could run with the bulls until they passed me just before Dead Man's Corner. Then I could follow them through it, assuming no bull had slid into the corner wall and was doubling back on us, confused and mad. But when I got to my spot, somebody had taken a crap in it. No joke. Fear 1, Man 0.

I moved down ten more feet and heard the rocket. In less than a minute, I saw the flash of the cameras. But I wasn't ready for what came next—hundreds of people sprinting dead at me, panicked, as though fleeing the Hindenburg. This was what I'd chosen to do? Purposely put myself inside a soccer riot?

On their heels were the bulls. That's when, for some reason, I decided not to run. I decided instead to keep everybody in my immediate vicinity from running. I leaned backward against the crowd, stuck my butt out and my arms wide, and kept half a dozen people from running, including me. I don't know why. Something paternal inside me screamed, "Protect yourself and all the kids in your minivan, you idiot! Those are live bulls coming down the street!" That's how this thing is. You lose your mind. After the bulls are gone, most runners are surprised to find themselves on top of fences and window ledges and police officers, having no idea how they got there. They're the smart ones. On this day alone, four would be gored and thirty-nine injured.

Finally, I took off for Dead Man's Corner, only to have the cops close the gate right in front of me. A man had been knocked cold by the bulls. Another man's scarf got wrapped around a bull's horns, and he was dragged under it for about twenty yards until the bull fell on top of the guy. We watched the medicos hustle the two guys out on stretchers. Not exactly motivation. The gates opened again, and we sprinted for the bullring.

But with about 300 yards to go, I heard from behind, *"Vámonos! Más toros!"* Let's go! More bulls! I turned to see three more coming. This time I was ready, stepped nimbly to the side without losing speed, leaned in—again risking the horns—and slapped one on the rump with my paper.

Victory was mine!

"Those were not bulls," Miguel said with a snort when I told him of my heroics. "Those were oxen. They are the sweepers. They come along later to help the stray bulls who have lost the way."

I was an oxen-moron. Vowing to reclaim my honor, I waited the next morning in the dreaded square, fear gripping me even tighter. Above me, a woman came out onto her balcony in her bathrobe, holding a mug of coffee.

Honey, do you want to see some human carnage before breakfast?

My mind was bent on swatting a fighting bull, not a clomping oxen, bent on redemption, bent on glory. Unfortunately, the rest of me was bent on leaving.

"You fool!" it said. "You already did this once! Why risk certain quadriplegia a second time?"

And I was just about to agree when . . . Rocket. Flashes. Bulls.

This time, I ran. And not next to the wall with the timid and the sane. I ran near the thundering bulls. OK, not as near as some of these idiots, but near enough. The closing speed of a bull is breathtaking, and they were closing fast. I angled closer. I reached out. I swatted.

I whiffed.

I dared closer. I swatted again. And hit! I angled back out of the way, tried another and hit again! Honor and bravery were mine! Suck on that, Miguel!

Later, though, when I looked at the pictures my wife took, I couldn't have been farther away. No wonder I whiffed. I looked like a guy reaching over a Volkswagen to put a quarter in a parking meter. Still . . .

Speeding around Dead Man's Corner, I raced with a hundred others, all cussing in different languages. I checked the helmet cam's angle only to discover—no helmet cam.

Somewhere in the madness and the panic and the pushing and elbowing and Heisman Trophy stiff-arming, it had been knocked off.

So now what? Double back against a rushing river of white-and-red humanity? Or forget it and sprint on to the glory of the bullring?

I doubled back. But there was no sea of humanity. The Dead Man's Corner gate had apparently closed behind me. More stretchers perhaps. Suddenly, I heard someone yell, *"Peligro!"* Danger!

And that's when I saw the stray fighting bull, muscled and black and snorting, thirty yards ahead of me, coming my way.

I ducked in the ten-inch-wide doorway. I tried the door. Stupido! Every door is locked during the running! The bull menaced closer. I looked above for something to grab on to and hoist myself up. Nothing.

Now he was ten feet from me and walking slowly toward me.

Where were the freaking sweeper oxen now?

Five feet.

I stayed still as a corpse, trying not to breathe, not to smell, not to exist.

Three.

He stared at me. A bead of sweat trickled down my nose into my mouth. If it was five seconds, it felt like five hours.

It suddenly became very clear to me how a doorway can become soiled.

Finally, he tore away after some other poor bastard.

The story in the next morning's paper said:

PAMPLONA, Spain (AP)—One man was gored and two others injured in a panic-filled third running of the bulls Friday at Spain's San Fermin festival that saw at least three people sent airborne by the beasts. One of the six bulls caused more chaos when he separated from the pack and prompted several minutes of fear as he charged runners and tried to break through wooden barriers separating onlookers from the bull run.

My God, it was horrifying, feral and glorious. I loved every moment of it.

I Also Vowed, in That Moment, That Every Year, for the Rest of My Life, No Matter What, I Would Do Everything in My Power to Never, Ever Be in Pamplona Again.

Postscript: *Like skydiving, donating a kidney and marrying Khloe Kardashian, running with the Bulls is something you only do once, so I've never been back. This is probably a good thing. In 2013, fifty runners were taken to the hospital.*

Gilt by Association

December 12, 2013

I'm so pumped up for next July in Cooperstown!

I can't wait to see who's going to be in the crowd at the Hall of Fame induction ceremony for new members Tony La Russa, Bobby Cox and Joe Torre.

Maybe Mark McGwire will show up? It might be as close as he'll ever get. La Russa managed him for fifteen seasons in both Oakland and St. Louis and says he never saw McGwire do a single steroid. Imagine that.

Maybe Alex Rodriguez will attend? He probably won't get in, either. Former New York Yankees skipper Torre says he didn't even notice A-Roid's alleged PED use in the four years he managed him. A-Roid's got plenty of time to go to Cooperstown. He's appealing a 211-game suspension for PEDs. Torre? No ban for him. In fact, he's an executive vice president of Major League Baseball now.

Maybe former Atlanta Braves manager Cox will look out in the crowd to see his old star Gary Sheffield. Probably not. Cox says he never saw all the PEDs Sheffield was taking when he had him right under his nose in the Atlanta clubhouse.

In all, the three managers being inducted oversaw at least thirty-four players who've been implicated as PED users and never noticed a thing wrong.

You could build a wing with the admitted and suspected drug cheats they won with: A-Rod, Roger Clemens (Torre), Jason Giambi (Torre and La Russa), McGwire, Jose Canseco (La Russa), Melky Cabrera (Torre and Cox), David Justice (Torre and Cox), Andy Pettitte (Torre), Manny Ramirez (Torre with the Dodgers) and Sheffield (Torre and Cox).

If we get really lucky, maybe disgraced HGH pitcher Darren Holmes will show up. He played under all three of them!

It's just another year in the Hall of Farce, where the codes of conduct shift like beach sand; where the rules for one set of men are ignored for another; where PED poppers can never enter, but the men who turned their backs to the cheating get gleaming, bronze plaques.

La Russa's slipping on the Hall of Fame jersey Monday is the sight that really tested my gag reflex. He did more for juicers than Jack LaLanne. He managed McGwire and Canseco—the Wright Brothers of the Druggie Era—for twenty-one combined seasons. He made millions on their pimpled backs, won his first World Series title on their syringes and built his thirty-three-year managing career on their artificially carved biceps.

Under La Russa, the Oakland clubhouse became a kind of leather-upholstered showroom for creams, rubs and injections that allowed players to work out harder, recover quicker and attack the game like a wolf in a hen house. It didn't change much in St. Louis, either, where he says he didn't notice what McGwire, Troy Glaus, Fernando Viña and Ryan Franklin were doing.

He spent eight hours a day around these guys, eight months a year, and yet he never saw a thing. Maybe he dressed in a different clubhouse?

But he goes into the HOF and those players never will. Maybe he can send them some Instagrams.

Hey, you think any of the three skips will mention how PEDs helped them get to that sunny afternoon in Cooperstown?

Oh, and I can't forget to thank Katalina at Tijuana Pharmacy for all her help. As my players always said, "We can't get cut without Kat!"

You won't even have to be in Cooperstown to smell the hypocrisy. Even the faintest scent of a rumor of PED use is enough to sink a player now.

Managers? Odorless.

Take Houston Astros great Craig Biggio. He had more than enough career to get in, and even though there isn't a stitch of evidence against him, the writers have kept him out because they have a niggling hunch he might've used.

Remember, kids: If you play the game under even a single cloud of suspicion, you're out. Manage it under one? Come on in and pull up a plaque!

Can you imagine this in any other sport? Do you think for a second Johan Bruyneel, the manager of all of Lance Armstrong's cheating, champion Tour de France teams, didn't know what was going on? You figure Bonnie and Clyde's driver just thought they were always running late?

Next month, the writers are expected to vote down McGwire for the eighth time and Clemens for the second time. They're right to do it. Those guys are tainted beyond any reasonable doubt, though Clemens still maintains innocence. But for the expansion error committee to let these three managers in—unanimously, no less—after winning hundreds of games with better chemistry is the gold standard of double standards.

If you believe they didn't know, then you'll fit perfectly in Dupers Town.

Postscript: *Because of this column, I can no longer eat lasagna in downtown St. Louis.*

Far

(Columns from Abroad)

Playing Soccer with Pablo Escobar

March 22, 2012

To make Oscar Pareja laugh, tell him that he'll be coaching a "tense" game this weekend for the Colorado Rapids of the MLS.

Pareja knows what tense is, and you're not within ten stadiums of it.

Twenty years ago, Oscar Pareja was the star and captain of Independiente Medellín in Colombia, in the time when murderous drug czar Pablo Escobar terrorized the country.

One day in 1991, Pareja got a message. Escobar would like him and six of his Independiente teammates to come to Escobar's one-man, government-built luxury prison—La Catedral—and play a game. Escobar wouldn't be watching. He'd be playing against them.

What happened next Pareja has never shared with any of his three kids, nor any of the players he's coached, nor any reporters.

He went. He had to. Declining Escobar's invitation would be tantamount to signing his death certificate. Escobar had ordered the murder of thousands—police captains, business owners and judges. The year before, he had ordered the executions of no fewer than three Colombian presidential candidates for not seeing things his way.

So Pareja said yes, even though it was the middle of the season. "Coach said practice was canceled," remembers Pareja, now 43. What else could the coach do? "For all we knew, we were partly owned by him [Escobar]."

La Catedral hung over Medellín like Olympus. It sat on a cool hill and was lavish—with Jacuzzis, a gym and a fully lit soccer field. From it, Escobar continued to carry on his billion-dollar cocaine business.

Pareja and his teammates were escorted into an ornate sitting room, where they waited, nervously, for the bloodiest man in Colombian history.

"There were fine couches in there," remembers Pareja. "And TVs. And they gave us snacks to eat. And then a bunch of bodyguards came into the room, and then [Escobar]. And it made me wonder, 'Who, exactly, is the prisoner here today?'"

Escobar, then 42, took a seat on the couch next to Pareja. He treated Pareja like a visiting god, calling him by his nickname, El Guapo.

"That day I can't forget," says Pareja, twenty years younger than his host. "He sat next to me talking about [soccer] with great passion and knowledge, for an hour. He knew everything. He said to me, 'Why do you yell at the refs so much, Guapo? We pay them. This does no good.'"

Eventually, the players were escorted to the prison soccer field, which was lit for the night. Escobar came out in sweat pants and a soccer jersey, and played left midfielder, "even though he was right-footed."

Pareja's teammate, Carlos Alvarez, had to guard him, a most delicate job. Guard him too lightly, and Escobar would feel disrespected. Guard him too closely, and Escobar would feel humiliated. Either way, it could mean his neck.

"Don't kick me," Escobar told Alvarez with a grin, "because [if you do] you will stay here with us."

"Carlos only pretended to guard him," Pareja remembers. "He never got the ball from him once."

There was only one ref—Escobar.

"He could actually play pretty well," says Pareja. "His guards, too."

The game lasted an hour and a half. The pros won, but the game was kept fairly close.

They were thanked and escorted out. They were invited back one more time for another game, also won by the pros, and without bloodshed.

"I think back now and consider all the things that could've happened to us inside those walls," says Pareja. "There were no police. No control. Anything could've happened. But it didn't."

It would soon enough. The next year, Escobar summoned four of his top lieutenants to La Catedral, where they were tortured and killed. That caused the Colombian government to insist Escobar be put in a regular prison. Instead, Escobar escaped.

"Not surprising," Pareja remembers. "All the guards were his people. It looked to me like he had easy access anywhere he wanted to go."

On December 2, 1993, the now-fugitive Escobar was fleeing on a roof in a Medellín neighborhood, talking to his son on a cell phone, when he was shot dead by Colombian National Police. They say he was wearing soccer shoes.

One of Pareja's teammates from his Independiente days would become involved with the drug cartels and wind up dead, too. Another teammate of Pareja's on the Colombian national team, Andres Escobar (no relation), was murdered in 1994 by drug czars after making an own goal against the U.S. that knocked Colombia out of the World Cup.

Pareja, though, made his own escape. He eventually signed with the Dallas Burn of the MLS, where he starred and then coached. He became the Rapids' coach in January.

He is twenty years from those days, and yet they haunt him to this day.

"We were numb to what was going on around us," he admits. "We didn't know. . . . We would win a game and suddenly there would be $8,000 bonus money for us. From who? We didn't know. We didn't ask. . . . I sat on a couch next to a man who did so, so much damage to my country. I sat with him . . . we were so naive."

Someday, when his MLS career is done, Pareja wants to go home to Medellín and cattle-ranch with his father.

"I want to bring my American friends back and show them, 'Here is the country I want you to see. We're not drugs and killers. We are good people from a beautiful land. The bad days are over.'"

Postscript: *One of Escobar's hit men, Jhon Jairo "Popeye" Velásquez Vásquez, was freed not long ago after only twenty-three years in prison, even though he's admitted he killed roughly 300 people. When you have to guesstimate the number of murders you've committed, you get your own circle of Hell. As for Pareja, he was still coaching Colorado at this writing, leading them to the playoffs despite having one of the youngest, cheapest teams in MLS.*

Are We Having Fun Yet?

March 15, 2010

Apparently, I may have inadvertently upset some of our Canadian friends with my recent column in which I pointed out that Vancouver is somewhat rainy, as evidenced by a mallard winning the women's moguls.

Many people thought I was making fun of this fine city, such as local resident Kev Holloway, who wrote: "Yeah, it's tough living in a city that's consistently voted as one of the best places to live. . . . Bitter much?"

And Pat Gibson, of Calgary, who wrote, "Are you sure you weren't in Michigan?"

So, as they say in Canada, sore-ee aboot that. I love Vancouver. I love rain. I love algae growing between my toes.

I am also sore-ee that:

- Vancouver's opening ceremonies were so boring that I wanted to jam my official Olympic drumstick into my brain and stir. Of course, Vancouver had to follow the greatest spectacle in theatrical history—the opening ceremonies of the Summer Games in Beijing in 2008—but, wow, most of it was duller than a Mennonite knitting workshop. Although I liked the Coca-Cola polar bear.

- The big, emotional moment—the lighting of the Official Olympic Giant Reefers—was botched. Only three of the Official Olympic Giant Reefers came up, and points are deducted for going for the quad and pulling only a triple. Although I did like torchbearer Wayne Gretzky being taken to the lighting of the Official Olympic Giant Outdoor Reefers in the back of a pickup truck. It was just him back there, holding on to a steel bar, riding through town. That is what's known as a Canadian limo.

- Vancouver officials tried to tell people that "3 billion people" watched the opening ceremonies. Three billion? No. Not possible, no way, nohow. Consider: There are around 6.8 billion people on Earth. Three billion is 44 percent of the world's population. Really? Forty-four percent of the world's population watched, when approximately 1.5 billion people live without electricity? When nearly 2.2 billion are children? No.

Huddling man by a dung fire in Mongolia: Whatchu doing tonight, Gorg?

Gorg: *Dude! Watching the opening ceremonies on TV! I'm all about k.d. lang!*

Huddling man: What's a TV?

- The Canadian team's promise to "own the podium" has not exactly come true yet. After the first weekend of competition, thirty medals were handed out, and only three went to Canadians. Perhaps Canada is leasing the podium out?

- Anyway, my apologies, Canada. You are a very kind people living in a beautiful country that has given the world many kinds of bacon. As soon as it stops raining, I would like to make up for it by awarding the following Canadian citizens gold in other disciplines:

- The Canadian Olympic women's hockey team, for beating Slovakia, 1–0. Slovakia beat Bulgaria, 82–0, almost two years ago in pre-Olympic qualifying. Eighty-two to nothing! Suck on that, Slovakia! How's it feel? Canuck women rule!

- The Canadian fans who wait more than four hours at Robson Square to ride a thirty-second zip line. And they wait happily! And they say "sore-ee" when they bump elbows accidentally! Do they realize they could build their own thirty-second zip-line ride in four hours?

- The guy who writes the messages that run on the front of the public buses here. About one-third of them come with a "SORRY" in huge letters, followed three seconds later by "OUT OF SERVICE." You know a country is polite when the buses apologize to you.

Really, do not blame Canada. Blame me. And for all the Canadians who now hate me, I offer up this story of vengeance, which involved me, my wife and accidental nudity:

We arrived in Vancouver to find our hotel had screwed up our reservation. We had nowhere to go, so the hotel allowed us to work out in the empty fitness room and shower there. But the women's shower didn't work, so my wife, Cynthia—a curvaceous blonde who would make a male figure skater drop his sequin gun—decided she'd shower in the men's locker room. "But there's no shower curtain in there," she told me. "So you have to watch the door."

Well, we were so alone in there, I never dreamed anybody would come in. Which is how I managed to miss the pool guy.

I heard a kind of muffled shriek, followed by the pool guy coming out of the men's locker room with a squeegee in his hand and a quarter grin on his face, followed thirty seconds later by my wife, furious, wrapped in a towel, tromping across the floor, leaving behind a stream of water and whispering/screaming at me: "I thought you were going to watch the door!"

OK, Canada. We're even.

Postscript: *I continue to hear about this column, and there's only so much crap I'm going to take from a neighboring country. Watch it, Canada. You don't want to ruin your chances of being our fifty-first state.*

These Olympics Are Unreal.
And That's ~~Not a Good Thing~~ Exactly How We Planned It

August 20, 2008

At the risk of offending the Chinese government censors, who seem to be everywhere, these Beijing Olympics are ~~fake~~ *a productive exercise.* They're the Fauxlympics. They make a Times Square Rolex look ~~real~~ *like a wise economic purchase.*

There is a building in downtown Beijing that is the perfect symbol of these Games. It's a monstrous edifice—takes up a whole city block—and it's beautiful and impressive.

Until you get up close, that is.

And that's when you see that it's ~~fake~~ *improved.* It's a façade on all sides. It's a computer-generated image of a building transposed onto giant sheets of vinyl, stretched tight. Behind the vinyl is the real building, going through a very slow constructive.

But the Chinese government saw it as ~~an eyesore~~ *not a harmonious image for the people,* so they put up a picture of a building, on all sides, complete with two businessmen standing at a window on one of the floors, chatting happily about the great city below.

Fake Guy No. 1: Do you think we'll ever leave this window?

Fake Guy No. 2: I hope so. I really gotta ~~pee~~ do my part to make the Beijing Olympics a shining example of Chinese solidarity!

But sham buildings are only the start. The Chinese government also stands ~~guilty~~ *unjustly accused by poisonous Western media* of:

- Having a darling little 9-year-old girl ~~lip sync~~ *interpret* "To the Motherland" during the Opening Ceremonies to the real voice of the ~~poor~~ little 7-year-old girl who was replaced at the last minute for having ~~crooked teeth~~ *laryngitis*. Good thing they weren't in charge of Michael Phelps.

- ~~Faking~~ *Digitizing* 28 of the 29 giant footprint fireworks that appeared to be marching toward the Bird's Nest Stadium during those same ceremonies. In reality, only one was real. NBC went along with the sham, with host Matt Lauer hinting only that it was "a cinematic device."

- Pretending to march in a child for each of China's *very difficult to find* 56 ethnic groups, when, in fact, they were all from one, the prevalent Han Chinese race.

- ~~Falsifying~~ *Updating* passports of three Chinese female gymnasts to make them seem 16 when previous documents and reports had them at 13 and 14. Sixteen happens to be the minimum Olympic age for competition. The Chinese team won the gold, leaving a ~~heartbroken~~ *elder* American team with the silver.

- Filling seats with mobs of "volunteer fans" to make venues look full when ~~they weren't~~ *parking problems delayed many*.

- Raising 10-foot-high "culture walls" along the marathon route to hide ~~slums~~ *charming indigenous areas*. So much for the Year of the Rat.

- ~~Throwing out, keeping out or arresting~~ *Repurposing* those considered "a threat to the success of the Olympics" including dissidents, migrants, homeless (some estimate up to two million in the years leading to the Games), even 2006 speed skating gold medalist and Darfur *(non-China related problem)* activist Joey Cheek.

- Putting up The Great Firewall, blocking Media Center access to websites on Taiwan, Tibet, Darfur *(non-China related problem)*, the Tiananmen Square ~~Revolt~~ *Incident*, Amnesty International and others, and red-flagging words like "democracy," "demonstrations" and *crazy-people group* "Falun Gong" in blogs, so that entries disappeared and pages weren't "found." Luckily, you could still find IOC president Jacques Rogge's promise from seven years ago promising "no censorship in Beijing."

- Presenting a city that is phony as Velveeta. Thanks to an even-odd license plate driving ban and massive factory closures, ~~pollution~~ *healthy mist* and ~~traffic~~ *industrious commuting of workers* that are only half as ~~bad~~ *active* as usual, if you can imagine that.

The Chinese government did everything but put up a giant fake blue sky. Wait. Actually, they sort of did. They sent up "rain rockets" in the days leading up to the Opening Ceremonies to drive off rain clouds, *which succeeded for the best result of the people's event.* And that was about the last anybody saw the sun for the ~~smog~~ *healthy mist*.

God knows what they've got planned for the Closing Ceremonies. A ~~fake~~ *Western-puppet* Dalai Lama doing a 3½ into a fake reflecting pool? *Dear* Leader Chinese President Hu Jintao ~~lip-synching~~ *gloriously interpreting* Lil Wayne? The two fake guys from the fake building leading the athletes under a fake rainbow?

This is what comes of the IOC ~~cashing in~~ *supplementing* its moral ideals with financial ones. You get an Olympics that pretends to be a nation's coming-out party in a new-found freedom and enlightened openness, and you wind up with ~~something as phony as Michael Jackson's nose~~ *the great Olympic leap forward.*

If I'm Phelps, I take those eight gold medals to a good jeweler, just to be sure.

Postscript: *China has not opened up much since the Olympics. After the* New York Times *ran a 2012 piece about the fabulous wealth accumulated by the relatives of then Chinese Prime Minister Wen Jiabao, its website was blocked, as was Bloomberg's. It's yet another reason why if you ever see me in China again, you'll know I've been* ~~kidnapped~~ *enlightened.*

The Escape Artist

May 7, 2011

As it turns out, there was one jam that Seve Ballesteros couldn't escape.

Ballesteros died early Saturday at 54, from complications of a cancerous brain tumor, but I'll never believe it. In twenty years covering him, I never saw a mess Seve couldn't get out of. He made birdies from parking lots, concession stands, bushes, trees, ditches, weeds you could lose an eighth-grader in, ponds, creeks, flower gardens and even women's purses. I saw him hit shots on his knees, on his tiptoes, stooped over, one-legged and one-armed. The man was 80 proof.

If you were within 100 kilometers of him, Seve was the one player you just couldn't miss. A typical morning conversation in the 1980s among golf writers went like this:

Me: Looks like Seve's out of it—11 back.

You: True, but it's Seve.

Me: Let's go.

You couldn't miss Seve, because (A) you never knew what he was going to do next, and (B) since he never hit any fairways, you'd be standing right next to him when he did it.

He could make birdie from under a Renault. He could make par from places where a lot of guys would require a chain saw.

"Someday," Ballesteros once said, "they'll play without fairways. Just rough and green. Then I'm sure I will have a very good chance."

He made bogeys that were more thrilling than some guys' eagles. But it wasn't so much what he did with the shot but what he did afterward—leaping, charging, punching unseen enemies in the sky.

Seve was Arnie with an accent. A conquistador in green pants. He was tan and handsome and raw. Emotion poured from his fingernails. He had so many urgent facial expressions, you'd have thought he was on trial.

You never knew what he'd say. Once he had one of his three brothers caddying for him and he hit an awful shot. He was sure he'd been given the wrong club, and he was hot.

"I am very, very angry!" he chirped at the poor guy. "But not at YOU! I do not blame YOU! No, I blame myself [long pause] for PICKING you as my caddie!"

I'll never forget the time we asked him how he managed to four-putt the sixteenth at the 1988 Masters, where he finished eleventh.

He shrugged and said, "I miss. I miss. I miss. I make."

Simple!

Practically born with a club in his hand, Seve had only a 3-iron for much of his childhood, and he'd play it out of anything. He learned to escape bunkers with that 3-iron, so you can imagine what a wizard he was with a sand wedge. He could get out of a silo with one.

We weren't the only ones who loved watching Seve. The greatest players in the world loved it, too.

I remember once Johnny Miller got paired with Seve when Miller was only playing part-time and Seve was still making balata-covered objects appear out of nowhere. It was a blustery day at the British

Open, yet Seve shot around even par. Miller couldn't stop talking about it.

"That was one of the most amazing rounds of golf I've ever seen," he gushed. "It was a clinic! If the wind was coming right to left, Seve would carve these perfect five-yard fades into it. If it was left to right, he'd carve gorgeous draws. The man is a master."

They loved him until they had to play against him, that is. He had such a blood thirst for match play, it seemed to be all he could do to keep from wrestling you on the first tee.

"I look into their eyes," he once said, "shake their hand, pat their back and wish them luck, but I am thinking, 'I am going to bury you.'"

He was an infamous gamesman. At Ryder Cups he was always followed by family members who would jingle the change in their pockets or suddenly come down with whooping cough when it was an American's turn to putt.

He'd stop at nothing to win. At the 1995 Ryder Cup, the American Tom Lehman was thumping Seve in singles and it was driving Seve mad. Lehman lagged a putt up to within six inches and then tapped in, out of turn. That happens approximately 500 times in a tournament, but Seve was suddenly irate. He called over a rules official and insisted Lehman replace his ball and mark it. After a heated debate, Lehman did exactly that.

The reason for all this?

"I wanted to use his mark as my line," Seve said.

Seve was a one-man plague of locusts on the United States. Not only did he revive European golf with his luminescent career, but he campaigned to get the Cup moved to other nations—like Spain—and then waged the most outrageous winning captainship there in Ryder Cup history in 1997.

He had certain greens mown—during the rounds!—without telling the U.S. side, so that only the European players would realize that the greens were twice as fast as all the others.

Any time there was a ruling to be made, he was there, barking at officials. He either had a turbo on his golf cart or jiggered the governor, because it was twice as fast as American captain Tom Kite's. Although maybe Kite's seemed slower because it was always bogged down by Michael Jordan or George Bush Sr.

Seve's glory days in golf ended the way you knew they would, *con el stupido* driver—going eighteen holes and hitting one or two fairways, shooting 75-75—150 on Thursday and Friday with fifty putts. He had the reverse yips and it was over. The Fun Meter was on Empty.

Severiano Ballesteros was the most distinctly original player I ever had the privilege to watch, and the most heart-stopping. He didn't hit a golf ball; he crashed into it. His swing had miles too much movement, but it echoed his beautiful mind, which gave him the greatest imagination for the game in history.

Who would've believed it? Trouble finally got Seve.

Life just got a little duller.

Postscript: *Ireland's David Feherty has a favorite story about Ballesteros. They were playing together at the Cannes Open and Feherty shanked his drive right. With the ball in flight, Seve—ever hyper—quickly put his tee in the ground to hit next. Except Feherty's ball hit a tree and ricocheted all the way back to them and another ten feet behind. Seve picked up his tee and said with perfect etiquette, "I'm sorry, you're still away."*

Carefree Jimenez
Enjoying the Ride

July 19, 2013

GULLANE, Scotland—Get ready. One of the best things in life approaches. Golf's Pleasure King—Miguel Angel Jimenez—has the Friday lead in the Open Championship, which means he's coming into the interview room.

"Hello!" he yells as he comes through the door. "I am here!"

He is a vision. He's 49, looks 59, and swings like 19. He is a plus-4 handicap, a size 42 belt, and a quadruple-A-rated interview. He is ultracomfortable in his own skin, which he seems to have borrowed from an alligator. He drives a Ferrari Maranello, favors Cuban Siglo VI cigars, and wears his tossed-salad orange hairdo in an awe-inspiring ponytail.

A fetching young Scottish woman, maybe 22 years old, turns his head. She works for the R&A. Jimenez offers her an unseen chair next to him on the stage.

"Please," he says, gesturing for her to sit down. He doesn't seem to care that his girlfriend, a very smoky Austrian named Susanne Styblo, is in the room. The woman smiles awkwardly. He grins. Susanne laughs.

The World's Most Interesting Man fears no challenge. He skis black diamonds. When he broke his leg doing it last year, a foolish reporter asked: "Will you give up skiing now?"

"Will you give up the things you enjoy in your life?" Jimenez asked.

First question:

How do you like your position, Miguel?

"To be atop the leaderboard, it's much nice, no?"

How are you leading the Open at 49 years old, Miguel?

"Why? I have not the right to do it? Only the young people can do it?"

Jimenez goes through life the way Kobayashi goes through hot dogs. He inhales it. He's been a high school dropout, a caddie, a soldier and a car mechanic. Now he's a millionaire. His swing is smooth, his life smoother.

"When you rush," he likes to say, "you cannot enjoy the food, the wine, the cigars, no?"

One night this week in Muirfield, he was seen heading back to the practice range after his round wearing aviator sunglasses, smoking a cigar and carrying a bottle of wine.

"Maybe he IS the coolest man alive," Keegan Bradley tweeted.

If Jimenez were to win this Open, he'd be the oldest to claim a major. He might also be the first person to win the Claret Jug who collects . . . claret.

Jimenez collects a lot of things, like fine, handmade Italian leather golf shoes by Italian shoemaker Gigi Nebuloni. He has fifty pairs. He has many cars, a few thousand bottles of wine, and a nice string of European Tour wins—nineteen in all.

What time will you go to bed tonight, Miguel?

"When I feel like it. And only after I smoke my cigar. Why, because I have the lead, now I must go to bed at ten? No, this is bulls—"

You look at him and your mind reels.

Is he wearing a gold Speedo underneath? Does he braid his chest hair? Each morning before his round, does he have a milk bath, followed by a snifter of brandy and twelve Aleve?

Jimenez has so much charisma it has to take its own car. He is constantly hugging fans and family. For the past couple of years at his hometown Andalucía Open, he's paid for many of the tournament expenses out of his own pocket.

He sweats neither the small stuff nor the big. In fact, he barely sweats at all. His bizarre and beautiful warm-up routine, which resembles a kind of teamster polka, has more than 200,000 hits on YouTube.

"There is maybe olive oil in my joints," he once said, "and drinking the nice Rioja wine and those things keeps me fit and flexible."

Maybe Rory McIlroy should try it?

One time, after Jimenez opened the 2009 Open Championship in Turnberry with a 64, someone asked him what he was thinking. "That it would be nice to have a little whiskey," he answered.

He really should do one of those Dos Equis ads.

Velvet-throated announcer over Jimenez hitting shots with a Cuban in his mouth:

"Par is whatever he shoots. When he wins, the town paints HIM. He once shot 63—with just his beard. He is . . . The Most Interesting Golfer in the World."

Fabulous, isn't it? Into the world of 6 percent body fat, joyless robo-golfers who work out ninety minutes a day, consult with their psychologists and eat no unsaturated fat comes a Spanish Buddha who not only isn't stressing about winning his first major, he may not even know he's in one.

How will you deal with the pressure of the lead, Miguel?

"When tomorrow is coming, when the sun is coming, I will deal with that thing."

If he won, it would be much nice, no?

Postscript: *Jimenez won the Hong Kong Open five months after this was written, making him, at 49, the oldest, chillest and most wrinkled player to ever win on the European Tour. I have no idea how he may have celebrated, but it certainly must've included nudity, a town square and a sable-lined rickshaw.*

Mickelson's Big Breakthrough

July 22, 2013

GULLANE, Scotland—Phil Mickelson wouldn't get out of bed.

It was the Tuesday after he'd blown the U.S. Open at Merion, and it had his wife a little worried. "Usually, he's good for a little mope and then he'll come out of it," Amy Mickelson remembers. "But this time, he hardly got out of bed for two days. He was a shell. It was the worst disappointment for him of any tournament, by far."

A sixth second-place finish at the Open will do that to a man.

Finally, on Wednesday, she dragged him out of bed for a pre-planned family trip to Montana: fly fishing, rafting, zip lining. Whatever happened in Montana put some zip back in Mickelson.

Next thing you knew, Mickelson was raging through Scotland like the Romans. His driver's license said 43, but his game said 33. He won the Scottish Open last week, then woke up Sunday at the Open Championship in Muirfield five shots back and feeling oddly joyous.

"I told him before the round, I thought even par or 1-over would win it," his coach, Butch Harmon, said. "But he said, 'I'm going lower than that.'"

In arguably his finest moment in striped pants, Mickelson passed nine guys, including Tiger Woods, with an unforgettable 66 to win. Suddenly he was hugging the Claret Jug in a giant family scrum on the eighteenth green. "That's your name," the kids kept saying, staring at the fresh engraving. "That's YOUR name!"

Phil was as Mickelstunned as anybody. Of all the majors he shouldn't win, this was No. 1. A guy who wants to hit flop shots off a sidewalk? Winning a links tournament? Preposterous.

It was so out of the blue that Mickelson and his caddy, Jim "Bones" Mackay, had to stand there by the scoring trailer for forty-seven minutes—from their last putt dropping to the moment Lee Westwood pulled yet another disappointment out of the hole—to get their goodies: Mickelson his trophy and Bones his eighteenth hole flag. And in between, you couldn't help but notice the look on Woods's face as he trudged by them into the trailer to sign yet another losing major scorecard. Talk about a buzzkill day. You think you're going to kickstart your sagging career, and instead, your chief rival kick-starts his.

Majors since 2008? Phil 2, Tiger 0.

"The guy is playing the best golf of his life," said a tearful Bones, who's looped Phil for twenty-one years. "I don't care how old you say he is, this is the best he's ever played."

But how can he be? At 43?

"Why shouldn't I?" Mickelson says. "I'm in better shape than I've ever been. I'm more flexible. My diet is better. . . . Why can't I?"

He can, I guess, especially when you consider that he now has a huge, world-class practice facility in his San Diego backyard that he designed and built himself. It features six greens made of every type of grass in the world he puts on, bunkers of every stripe and a grounds crew of six that jumps at his slightest whim. Before Merion, for instance, he asked them to take the greens up to Merion speed, which was just slightly faster than the hood of a 1989 Chrysler.

"That practice facility has made a world of difference," says Harmon. Says Amy, "Now he can practice at home a lot more. Even if he only has a spare fifteen or twenty minutes, he can go out there in his flip-flops and hit shots."

There's more:

1. "I'm putting better than I ever have in my life," he says.

And 2. He's found a 3-wood, made by Callaway, that's flying longer and straighter than many commercial flights. "Not since I found the Ping L-wedge, when I was 14, has one club altered my career like this [Callaway] 3-wood. I just hit bullets with it."

But mostly, it's his Silly Putty resiliency. Nothing seems to quench his thirst. Not the $44 million a year he makes in endorsements, not his arthritis, and not Merion.

"Being so down after the U.S. Open," Mickelson said afterward, his hand never leaving the trophy, "to come back and use that as motivation, to use it as a springboard . . . that feels amazing."

That's not just talk. "He's as motivated right now as he was when I met him in college," says Amy.

Says Bones, "I kid him. I say, 'You'll be the 60-year-old guy on the putting green at Augusta, telling people he thinks he's got a chance.'"

So how long can Phil 2.0 last? And how great can he get?

Well, for Lefty, there's only one wrong to right: the U.S Open. If he could finally knock one down, it would make him the sixth player to win all four majors, along with Gene Sarazen, Ben Hogan, Gary Player, Jack Nicklaus and Woods. It's his measure of the all-time greats. But his table has only three legs. "That last leg has been a hard one for me," Mickelson said in the understatement of the year. He won't quit on it until three days after they bury him. If that.

"He used to tell me he'd retire at 40," Amy said, bathed in the last of the Scottish light. "Now I don't think he has any idea. He just lives for today. He waits to see where life takes him. I'm just looking forward to the ride."

If it's anything like Muirfield, so should we all.

Postscript: *Of the seventy-five-something majors I've covered, this one ranks third on the Golf Goose Bump Grade: 1. Jack Nicklaus wins the 1986 Masters at 46. 2. Tiger Woods wins the 2008 U.S. Open on a broken leg. 3. Phil's Phabulous Phinish. 4. Larry Mize chips in at the 1988 Masters to beat no less than Seve Ballesteros and Greg Norman. 5. Tom Watson comes one bad-bounce 8-iron from winning the British Open at 59, which is a good thing, because that would've been nearly unwritable.*

World Cup Buzz Kill

June 15, 2010

Here are the top ten most annoying things about watching the World Cup already:

1. That pesky cerebrum-blowing incessant buzzing sound coming from the TV set. "Babe, something's wrong with the TV," my wife said Saturday. But there wasn't anything wrong. It was the dreaded vuvuzelas, the yard-long plastic horns (voo-*voo*-zellas) that South African fans blow all the time, without rhyme or reason, when something is happening and when it's not (it's usually not), during time-outs and time-ins, during halftime and at the breakfast table, and while they're on the bus and while doing their taxes, until you just want to stab two fondue forks deep into your ears and stir. They never stop. It's like having a desk in the center cubicle at American Bee, Inc. They sound like 80,000 yaks getting sick. They are the leading cause of Tylenol sales in the world today.

2. The embarrassing photographer bibs the guys on the bench have to wear during the game. They're very purple and dorky. My God, who knew you could make a World Cup team and be made to look like a geek? Hey, are you on the American national soccer squad or do you throw bags for Northwest Airlines?

3. The Twinkie-fingered gloves goalkeepers wear. No wonder the English goalkeeper allowed that easy shot to give America a 1–1 tie in the Group C opener. You couldn't stop a beach ball with those big goofy things. What, is Hamburger Helper a sponsor? Why must they be so huge? Doesn't Roger Rabbit need them back? And where do the batteries go? How are goal-keepers expected to hang on to the ball with them on? And is it difficult to play goalie while also taking things out of the oven?

4. The godforsaken vuvuzelas! Make them stop! One of the charms of soccer is the singing that fans do. There is always loads of singing and chanting because every game is 1-nil, so there's plenty of time for singing and chanting. Soccer fans sing and chant inane hilarious things like "We are from Norway! We came on a plane! And we are very drunk!" But we don't get to hear the singing and the chanting because of the horrible, hideous, heinous vuvuzelas! My God, they should take them into the mountainous caves region of Pakistan and play them until Osama bin Laden comes running out, screaming, "OK, OK! I give!"

5. All the faking. I haven't seen this much bad theater since I saw former "*American Idol* competitor" Ace Young starring in *Hair* on Broadway. These guys collapse as though they've just caught a javelin in the groin every time an opponent so much as asks them for the time. These guys make Paul Pierce look sin-cere. Sell it somewhere else, Sven. We live in the U.S., where hockey players pop their eye back into their socket without missing a shift. This will be the new rule when I'm made president of FIFA: If you stay on the ground longer than 30 seconds, you're out of the game; 45, you are taken directly to the nearest hospital; 60, you get a telethon.

6. The yellow cards. I love the way the refs come running up to the player as though he has just taken out a chain saw and sawed somebody's hand off. The ref looks very stern and upset. And then all the ref does is snap his little yellow piece of paper out of his shirt pocket and stick it in the offender's face, as though the little yellow card has some kind of superpower. As if to say, "Ha! you are powerless against my little yellow piece of paper, which shows your less-than-average marks from third grade!" I'd love to see that in the middle of an NBA fight. Can you imagine seeing some ref come running up to Rasheed Wallace after laying out Carmelo Anthony with a roundhouse right and sticking that yellow card right in his face? He'd soon be digesting it through his ear hole.

7. The ties. In the NFL in the past ten years, there have been two ties. As of Tuesday morning, in the first eleven games of this World Cup, there have been five ties. You will not see more ties at a JCPenney's Father's Day sale. I hate ties. Doesn't anybody want to win in this sport? All these ties are about as exciting as a Jonas Brothers roundtable on sex.

8. The World Cup itself. Really? All this running and vuvuzela-ing and pulling off shirts for that trophy? It looks like somebody soldered it together in their basement—after drinking a handle of Jack Daniel's. It looks like something you'd use to prop open your Tuff Shed door during spring cleaning. It's gold and small and looks like somebody accidentally melted it somewhere along the way. I mean, there IS chocolate in the middle of that thing, right? Maybe I just don't get it.

9. Stoppage time. Why can't we know how much time is left? Why must it be such a mystery? Whose idea was this? Why do only the refs get to know? Wouldn't it be more exciting if we all knew? You tell me which is more exciting:

A. "Ten seconds left now! Kaka needs to get a shot off here or it's over! Five seconds! Kaka wheeling! Two seconds! There's the shot! And . . ."

B. "Well, the ref should be calling this game shortly. A minute or two. Maybe more. Actually, I don't know. Nigel, do you know? Kaka seems confused. He's dribbling. Wait. Now he's stopped to examine a small scab and, well, that's it. The ref says it's over. I guess that's it, then."

All we get is B. Somebody needs to put some stoppage to stoppage time.

10. The vuvuzelas from eardrum-hellas! Don't tell me it's discrimination to want them to stop. Don't tell me it's an essential part of South African culture. If it is, it's an annoying part of their culture. Yes, I know that centuries ago, the vuvuzelas were made from animal horns to call the village elders in for a meeting. And I'll bet you five wildebeests that when the elders finally got to the meeting they said, "Would you STOP already with the blowing? You're making me crazy!" I've been to Africa four times. They do some of the most beautiful singing you can imagine. At the World Cup, I'm hearing no singing. I'm hearing no chanting. I'm hearing 80,000 kazoos on steroids.

But it still sounds better than Ace Young.

Postscript: *Pogs, Pokémon and the Pet Rock. None of them came and went as fast as the hideous vuvuzela. It was banned from many soccer federations after its ear-aching performance in South Africa. Even Wimbledon banned it. For the 2014 World Cup in Brazil, you will hear the green-and-yellow caxirola, a plastic invention that sounds a little like maracas. Bring Tylenol.*

Fixes

(In Which I Try to Fix Everything)

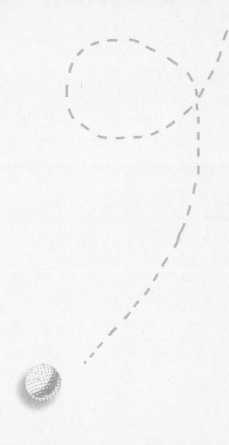

Rush to Rush

March 3, 2010

Listen, you Froyo freaks, you face-painters, you hoopheads of higher learning: Before you rush the court, storm the court, wreck the court . . . rush your butts back to your seats while I explain something.

You're doing it WAY too much.

This isn't karaoke Tuesdays. It's not a scheduled event. True rushing the court happens to a school once every twenty years or so. It should be, "Oh, there's Professor Krumpke. Let's have him tell us about the time he rushed the court." It's like walking down the aisle: If you do it more than twice in your life, you're doing it wrong.

It's spontaneous, like a flash flood. It's unpredictable, like Publishers Clearing House showing up at your front door. It's as unstoppable as a sneeze and just as unplanned. It carries you away like a tornado. You suddenly find yourself on top of the rim and have no idea how you got there.

You people are treating it like it's your weekly Spanish lab. Or poker night. You can't e-mail about it ahead of time. It'd be like penciling into your calendar "Make out with Halle Berry tonight after winning Oscar." And it can't be something to do just to get on TV. You wanna be on TV, go bother Matt Lauer.

I'm talking to you, Indiana. You rushed the court this season after beating Minnesota. Minnesota? Really? How is beating Minnesota cause for unrestrainable joy? It's like pantsing the chess club.

I'm talking to you, South Carolina. You RTC'd after beating Kentucky both this season and in 2005. It's supposed to be "Hats in the air! War's over!" Not "I really want a picture next to John Wall!"

I'm talking to you, Illinois. You RTC'd when you beat No. 5 Michigan State this year. Even Illinois legend Dee Brown was cringing. He tweeted: "No no no no! . . . We are Illinois! Winning should be normal."

Sorry, Dee. Illinois has a new motto: "We are Illinois! We really like to pregame!"

I'm definitely talking to you, Wake Forest. You RTC'd when you beat North Carolina last season. They were third in the nation. You were fourth. What's going to make you storm the floor next? New nets?

This has got to stop. Therefore, here are the Ironclad and Unbreakable Rushing-the-Court Rules. From now on, you CANNOT rush the court if . . .

- You've won an NCAA title in the past twenty years.
- You've been in the Final Four in the past five years.
- The team you just beat is not in the top three.
- Or is ranked within fifteen rungs of you. (Somebody do the math for Wake.)
- Or is really a football school. This includes Florida, Texas and Ohio State. Get over it.
- You've beaten this same team in the past five years.
- You won the stupid game by more than 10 points. There is no such thing as a PRTC (Premeditated Rush the Court).

- You're a university and you just beat a college.
- Coach K comes to your coach's clinic.
- You have a dead-mortal-lock lottery pick on your team.
- Your team has appeared in a recent "One Shining Moment."

I don't want to hear "It was a signature win!" I'm not signing off on it. I don't want to hear "It was the first time we've beaten a top-10 RPI team in six seasons." If it's a stat your mother wouldn't know, forget it. Nor will I stand for "It clinched our spot in the NCAA Tournament." Big deal. Sixty-five teams make it. It's like making the white pages. Cheer from your seat.

Now, we understand here at the Court of Court Rushing that there are occasionally unusual circumstances. Therefore, here are the Official Amendments to the Ironclad and Unbendable Rushing-the-Court Rules. You can rush the court if:

- Your arena is closing down forever after the game. That will happen this week at Freedom Hall in Louisville and Mac Court in Oregon. Fine. Dig up the boards, too. Take the chairs. Knock yourselves out.
- Something stupidly wonderful happens, like a ninety-foot David Blaine Special goes in or an air ball bounces off the ref's head to win your conference. Fine.
- You are Wisconsin-Milwaukee and you are 0-37 against your cross-city rival Marquette. When you win, you should rush the court, then City Hall, then the Miller factory.
- It's the first time you've beaten your archrival in ten years or more, plus one of the following: (1) they still have your goat, (2) they stole and painted your best physics professor or (3) they're going to end up making PILES more cash than you.
- Jihadists have kidnapped your power forward and are holding him captive near the key.

Finally, if you are in compliance with the Ironclad and Unbreakable Rules, make sure at least three of you hoist the center. Otherwise you'll drop him, causing him to rip a rotator cuff and, consequently, miss the rest of the year. Then people will egg your dorm room until you graduate, which will be never because every professor will hate you, too.

Now, get out there and remain seated!

Postscript: *It just gets worse. Recently, a University of North Carolina student got whacked out of his wheelchair during a court rush and was about to be trampled when a player picked him up and carried him out. In Boulder, a University of Colorado player hurt his shoulder in the melee and missed games. Write it down: Something really bad is coming.*

Don't Get Me to the Geek

May 27, 2009

Good, James Harrison. Please do retire. Make good on your threats and go drive a truck like your father did. And if you have as many head-ons in that job as you do in this one, heaven help you.

Harrison, the Pittsburgh Steelers hired headhunter, is talking about quitting after being fined $75,000 for using his helmet to knock not just one Cleveland Brown out of the game, but two, then issued words that were even uglier than his deeds:

"I don't want to see anyone injured," Harrison said, "but I'm not opposed to hurting anyone."

I'm sorry?

"There's a difference. When you're injured, you can't play. But when you're hurt, you can shake it off and come back, maybe a few plays later or the next game. I try to hurt people."

Harrison does more than try. He purposely lowered his head into two Browns wide receivers—Josh Cribbs and Mohamed Massaquoi—sending them off to the "How many fingers am I holding up?" guy.

Both men went for tests Monday, and it was uncertain whether either will play any time soon.

No problem, says Dr. Feelbad.

"A hit like that geeks you up," Harrison said. "It geeks everybody up—especially when you find out that the guy is not really hurt—he's just sleeping. He's knocked out, but he's going to be OK."

It didn't geek Patti Drake up. She was a kind of surrogate mom for Cribbs at Kent State, where he was, believe it or not, a teammate of Harrison's.

"It sickened me," she says.

You know what would geek me up? Harrison out of the game. Because as much as I abhor the way he plays, I don't want the day to come, ten years from now, when he starts suffering depression and slurred speech and all the other goodies that come with these massive crashes. Because no amount of sleeping is going to make everything OK then.

God knows how Harrison would've reacted if the NFL had done what it should've, which is to bench him for two games, one for each player he appeared to try to decapitate. If we can have a rule that a player who suffers a concussion can't go in for the rest of the game, why can't we have the same rule for players who hand them out?

The second to be suspended should be the refs in that Steelers-Browns game. Neither of Harrison's hits was flagged, even though both were purposely helmet-to-helmet and the second one, the assault on Massaquoi, was the blatant lighting up of a defenseless player. If the refs had flagged the first, we might not have had to watch the second.

And what does all this say about us? The Romans used to pack the Coliseum to watch barbarism and cruelty, a spectacle that dehumanized the fans as well as the combatants. Are we starting to become those fans?

New England's Brandon Meriweather head-butted Baltimore Ravens tight end Todd Heap in a shot so cheap and disgusting that you wanted to switch over to baseball.

Atlanta cornerback Dunta Robinson human-missiled Philly wide receiver DeSean Jackson so hard that both men were left concussed and sprawled out on the field as if they'd been leveled by a daisy cutter.

By the way, if you're counting, that's five Eagles who've been concussed this season. Hey, who wants to make the season two games longer?

All in all, seven players left games Sunday with brain injuries. It was the kind of Sunday that makes you wonder what kind of person you are for sitting there watching.

Watching men turn other men's cerebellums into oatmeal is starting to bring up the bile. We now know what these collisions can mean later in life. We know because the NFL is telling us. We know because we heard about what the battered brains of Hall of Famer Mike Webster and Terry Long looked like. Oh, yeah, they were Steelers, too, weren't they?

Steelers coach Mike Tomlin defended Harrison, saying he's a "model" for young players to imitate. Oh, yeah, he's a peach. Fined $5,000 for slamming Vince Young into the ground. Fined $5,000 for unnecessary brutality against a Cincinnati Bengal. Had to go to anger management and undergo psychiatric counseling after being charged with assault on his girlfriend. Owned a pit bull that bit his son, the boy's mom and his masseuse. When's he running for Congress?

Helmet-to-helmet hits involve two helmets. But when somebody asked Harrison whether he was worried about the long-term effects on his own brain, he scoffed. "That's the risk you take," he said.

Which demands the question: What brain?

Postscript: *In its entire history, the NFL has suspended only one (1) player for one (1) game for a helmet-to-helmet hit: Harrison, in 2013. Anything else is couch-cushion change to these guys.*

Rewriting History

June 26, 2013

Somewhere, LeBron James is wringing the champagne out of his T-shirt, bathed in the adoration of the nation, which declares him the greatest living basketball player, an improvement on Michael Jordan, Gandhi and possibly Alexander the Great.

But let's play "Let's Say" for just one tick of the clock, shall we?

Let's Say . . . that James's teammate, Ray Allen, doesn't drain that death-defying, Game 6–tying, desperation twenty-five-foot heave from the corner with five seconds left while the world unravels around him.

Then . . . everything changes. Then . . . NBA history changes. Then . . . it's Tim Duncan whose hamper smells like champagne this morning. Then . . . it's Tony Parker with a cigar in his mouth and three rings on his dresser. Which means . . . it's LeBron James being mounted and pinned like a butterfly by the sports world, which uses a magnifying glass to figure out why he's such a choking dog.

Just like that.

Fair or not, the legacies of athletes—unlike politicians or artists or musicians—flit and spin in the wind, like a canary feather. They turn in the tiniest breeze, twist on the simplest decision, float on a tea-spoonful of luck. And yet when that feather finally lands, it lands with a thud that echoes forever.

For instance . . .

Let's Say . . . the most perfectly catchable spiral ever doesn't go through the mitts of New England Patriots cornerback Asante Samuel with 1:18 left in the 2008 Super Bowl against the New York Giants.

Then . . . Eli Manning isn't still on the field for the next play and doesn't escape the jailbreak coming at him, doesn't throw up a bomb to David Tyree, whose special Velcro helmet doesn't snag the ball, which doesn't give the Giants a first down and lead to the game-winning touchdown to Plaxico Burress four plays later. Which means . . . the Patriots become the first 19-0 team in NFL history, two better than the 1972 Dolphins. Then . . . Tom Brady has his fourth Lombardi Trophy in six years. Then . . . the two Mannings each have only one ring and Thanksgivings are a lot less chilly.

Let's Say . . . A massive snowstorm doesn't hit Minnesota in 1948, just as John Wooden, the young head coach of Indiana State, is waiting on a call from the University of Minnesota, which will tell him whether or not it's going to agree to his terms and offer him its head-coaching job. Wooden, a devout man of his word, has told Minnesota if he doesn't hear from it by 6 p.m., he'll take a call from UCLA at 7 and accept its job, if offered. But his wife, Nell, doesn't want to move to Hollywood. She wants to stay closer to home.

Then . . . the phone lines in Minnesota wouldn't have been knocked out, the call would've gone through, and Wooden becomes the Maestro of Minneapolis. Which means . . . UCLA is a baseball school today.

Let's Say . . . Tiger Woods's too-perfect wedge into the fifteenth green on Friday of the 2013 Masters doesn't hit the bottom of the flagstick. Let's say it's one inch to the right and checks up nicely, rather than ricochets into Rae's Creek, which is as lousy a break as a man is going to get next to hitting a fire hydrant.

Then . . . he doesn't lose his mind and take a drop not prescribed in any rule book anywhere, which leads to a 2-shot penalty the next day. Then . . . he makes a birdie 4 on that hole (he got the replacement wedge shot up and down, you'll recall) instead of a snowman 8, which means he makes the play-off with Adam Scott and Angel Cabrera, whom he picks off like sweater lint. (He's 16-4 in playoffs, after all.) Which means . . . the golf world is buzzing like a caffeinated hive wondering if he can win the Grand Slam this year instead of asking if he'll ever win another major, as (cough, cough) SOME writers have lately.

Let's Say . . . it's 1956 and the son of seven-time NBA All-Star and Boston Celtics forward Easy Ed Macauley isn't sick back home in St. Louis. Let's Say . . . Macauley doesn't beg Celtics GM Red Auerbach to trade him to the St. Louis Hawks so he can be near him.

Then . . . Auerbach never trades his best player to the Hawks for their new draft pick, University of San Francisco center Bill Russell. Which means . . . Russell wins St. Louis those eleven rings instead of Boston, making St. Louis Basketball Heaven, not Beantown. Which means . . . thirteen years later, when Bill Simmons is born, the Celtics are a Sominex franchise and Simmons develops an overwhelming passion for horticulture.

Let's Say . . . the silver dollar that's flipping through the air in 1970, fresh off the thumb of NFL commissioner Pete Rozelle, takes just one more half a turn. Let's Say . . . it comes up heads, just as Chicago Bears executive Ed McCaskey calls it.

Then . . . it's the sorry 1-13 Bears who get the No. 1 draft pick, not the sorry 1-13 Pittsburgh Steelers. Then . . . the Bears use that pick on Terry Bradshaw, the All-Everything QB out of Louisiana Tech. Which means . . . the Bears win four of the next six Super Bowls and the Steelers remain the front-office bunglers they've always been, the team that cut Johnny Unitas, that could've drafted Jim Brown, that couldn't spell cat if you spotted them the "c" and the "a."

Let's Say . . . the most famous air ball in history—Dereck Whittenburg's last-second, twenty-five-foot, 3-point try in the 1983 NCAA title game—travels just six more inches. Let's Say . . . it bounces off the front of the rim, instead of settling into the hands of teammate Lorenzo Charles, who can't catch it and dunk it at the buzzer to win the title for 6-seeded North Carolina State.

Then . . . Jim Valvano doesn't run around the court looking for somebody to hug. Which means . . . he doesn't become the most huggable college basketball coach ever. Which means . . . he isn't a national celebrity when he contracts cancer ten years later, and he's probably not at the ESPYs to give his unforgettable never-quit speech, and the $100 million the V Foundation for Cancer Research has raised on the strength of that speech doesn't exist.

And lastly . . .

Let's Say . . . the wife of the assistant sports editor at the Boulder (Colorado) *Daily Camera* isn't working next to me in the teller line at National State Bank in 1978. Let's Say . . . she doesn't finally buckle under my six months of badgering and go home and tell her husband that the 20-year-old kid he'd anonymously judged as the winner of the state high school sportswriting contest two years before is bugging her every day to give the editor his phone number. Let's Say . . . that editor doesn't then call me the next day and offer me a job typing up girls' volleyball scores from 10 p.m. to 2 a.m. every night. *Then . . . you wouldn't have had to read any of this.*

Postscript: *And don't even get me started on how the world would be different if the punch hole for Al Gore's name on the 2000 Palm Beach County, Florida, election ballot had been directly across from his name instead of one down.*

A Different Call of Duty

December 19, 2012

You know who's as heartsick as you at the thought of a classroom full of murdered first-graders in Newtown, Connecticut?

Hunters.

Target shooters.

NRA members.

Some of them look at photos of the Bushmaster .223 semiautomatic rifle Adam Lanza used to leave twenty-six students and staff members at the Sandy Hook Elementary School in pools of blood—the kind anybody could buy at many stores for less than $900—and it twists their stomachs.

"A gun like that is not for deer hunting," says Stephen Czaja of Tarpon Springs, Florida, an NRA member. "That looks like a gun Schwarzenegger would carry, not a hunter."

Doug Goodman, another hunter from Cicero, Indiana, became an NRA member at age 12, but quit. He doesn't want the NRA protecting assault weapons in the name of his favorite sport.

"I hear this [NRA CEO and executive vice president Wayne]

LaPierre talking about how government wants to come and take our firearms," Goodman says. "That's insane. These are weapons of war they're talking about right now. These are mass-killing weapons. If I get three pulls of the trigger at a pheasant and I can't hit it, the pheasant wins."

Jeff Johnson of St. Paul, Minnesota, hunts waterfowl with a semiautomatic shotgun, but he'd gladly give it up to end this parade of caskets.

"Put the picture of [murdered first-grader] Emilie Parker next to my semiauto shotgun and pick one," he writes. "Put [murdered 6-year-old] Benjamin Wheeler's hopes and dreams against me not having to move my forearm six inches and pick one."

Hunters, target shooters, NRA members: I'm happy for you to keep your single-shot rifles and revolvers. But your right to get thrills by firing off Halo-style rounds ends at my mall, my cineplex, my local schools.

Nearly every double-digit mass murder in this country was made easier by semiautomatic guns that use high-capacity clips: Columbine (13), the Washington, D.C., sniper (10), Virginia Tech (32), Aurora (12), and now Newtown (27), just to name a few.

Enough.

Both Dwyane Wade and LeBron James of the Miami Heat wrote "Newtown, CT" on their shoes for a recent game against the Wizards. Each of them has a 5-year-old. Honoring the dead is noble. Making laws to protect the living is better.

There was a moment of silence at every NFL game this weekend. That's fine. But speaking up for gun sanity would be even better.

Something has to change, and that includes the mind-set of some people in Newtown itself.

For one thing, it's the home of the National Shooting Sports Foundation, the second-largest pro-gun lobbying agency in America— behind the NRA—and a tireless fighter for your right to hunt with assault weapons and high-cap magazines. It's easy to find. It's three miles from Sandy Hook Elementary School. (The foundation did not return my calls.)

For another, Newtown has two shooting ranges. Problem is, there's a waiting list to use them. That's probably why, in the past year, a bunch of unofficial shooting ranges have popped up on private property in the area, where gun fans have been firing away at targets with semiautomatic weapons. There are reports of people firing at propane tanks, just to watch them explode, according to the *New York Times*.

Yet when the noise complaints went way up, along with the terrified calls to 911, the town ordinance committee had hearings about it this summer, and a crowd including a spokesman from the NSSF showed up to squash any new ordinances. In the minutes of that meeting report, the NSSF spokesman said: "No safety concerns exist."

Didn't turn out safe for a 52-year-old Newtown mother of two named Nancy Lanza, who had a collection of guns, including a Bushmaster semi. She loved taking her son, Adam, to the ranges to practice, according to friends. Then, on Friday, Adam turned one of her own guns on her, according to police, killing her in her own bed.

So Newtown will have to wait for the next meeting to try again. Me, I'm sick of waiting.

The day of the Columbine shootings, I waited to hear if the three kids of three of my softball buddies were still alive. We played on the field right next to that high school. It was dinnertime before we knew they'd sprinted to safety.

The day of the Aurora shootings, I waited for three hours to hear if my son, Kellen, was still alive. He works in Aurora. My God, what if he was there? My fingers trembled reading the text: "I'm fine!"

The day of the Newtown shootings, I waited to hear if the daughter of my main feature producer at ESPN was all right. Turns out she goes to a different school.

My nerves are frayed, my patience gauze-thin. It's changed me. It's changed the country. And I'm sick of waiting for the laws to change.

Look, there will always be madmen. But why do we insist on making mass murder so easy for them? Adam Lanza killed every person he aimed at but two, and in an estimated eight minutes or less. We'll never stop people from going crazy, but we need to make it harder for them to murder rooms full of our kids when they do.

I know you love hunting and target shooting. But don't you see? The hunted—the targets—have become us.

Postscript: *In the 12 months after the Newtown massacre, there were 29 more school shootings in America, killing 27 more people.*

Football Getting
Harder to Watch

November 6, 2013

The NFL is asking viewers to write in and tell it, "Why do YOU love football?"

This is my answer:

I used to.

I used to love football the way German shepherds love sirloin. I'd sit in the press box and insist the window stay open—even on down-coat days—just so I could hear the sound of two men colliding at full speed. It thrilled me. And I'd wonder: Who does that?

Now I hear that sound and wonder how soon it will be before they can't remember where they parked, their sons' middle names, or where their families went last summer on vacation.

I see too much sorrow and ugliness to love football like I used to.

I watch Indianapolis quarterback Andrew Luck take a brutal lick now and I think of former Packers quarterback Brett Favre, who told a Washington radio show the other day he can't remember most of his daughter's soccer games. "That's a little bit scary to me," Favre said. ". . . That put a little fear in me." He's 44 years old.

I watch New England tight end Rob Gronkowski get up from wreck after wreck, and I think of former Colts tight end Ben Utecht, who said the other day he couldn't remember being at a friend's wedding until the friend showed him the photo album. See, you were a groomsman. And you sang, remember? He's 32 years old.

I watch Minnesota running back Adrian Peterson fling himself into crashing whirlpools of men and I think of former Cowboys running back Tony Dorsett, who said he sometimes finds himself driving on a highway and can't remember where he's going. "I'm just hoping and praying I can find a way to cut it off at the pass," Dorsett said recently. He's 59 years old.

I see too much sorrow and ugliness now to love football like I used to.

I read the filthy and racist transcript of voice mails between one Miami Dolphin and another and am told bullying is "part of the culture." Or lack thereof. I read about players like the late Chiefs LB Jovan Belcher, twisted inside his violent life, and yet not one NFL team has a full-time psychiatrist on staff.

I read the suicide obits of former Bears defensive back Dave Duerson, age 50, and former Chargers linebacker Junior Seau, 43, and I can't help but notice Buffalo Bills owner Ralph Wilson is 95, San Diego Chargers owner Alex Spanos 90, and Detroit Lions owner William Clay Ford 88. Good for them. They were lucky enough to get in on the luxury-box side of the business, not the pine box.

Now the guilt gnaws at me a little as I watch.

I covered former Broncos defensive end Karl Mecklenburg. Now he takes a photo of the front of his hotel in the morning so he can find his way back at night. I covered former Dolphins wide receiver Mark Duper. Now he has constant ringing in his ears. I covered former Bears quarterback Jim McMahon and used to giggle at the way he'd score a touchdown and then joyously butt heads with teammates at ten miles an hour. Now he has two teammates who have committed suicide and admits he's thought of it himself.

I realize the NFL handed over $765 million in a lawsuit settlement to cover the more than 4,500 players who say playing in their league damaged their brains, but that blood money doesn't assuage my small sense of shame—it only thickens it. I was entertained by so many of these men—made my own living off it—and now I realize some of them paid for my entertainment with their lives.

One time, I was standing on a street corner in Mexico City when I saw a man breathe a huge swath of fire for tips from cars. He'd fill his mouth with lighter fluid, flick a Bic lighter in front of his mouth and exhale a river of flames that lit up the shiny car hoods. I stood there for thirty minutes, watching him. Tipped him myself. But when I told my host about it, he said, "Don't you know all those fire-breathers get throat cancer from that? All of them."

The difference now is, our fire-breathers do it on our big screens.

I have heard about guys who wake up dizzy, with headaches every morning, and yet they still strap that helmet on and go out there.

Who does that?

This is the game I've spent thirty-six years glamorizing. These are the men I've spent five decades lionizing. And it turns out I was part of the problem. Howard Cosell stopped covering boxing when his conscience wouldn't allow it, and yet I go on. I'm addicted.

In Caesar's day, they filled the 50,000-seat Roman Coliseum to watch gladiators compete. These gladiators trained at special schools. They knew the risk. The glory and the money was worth it to them. If the gladiators weren't dead at the end of the fight, the emperor looked to the crowd to help him decide: Had the losing fighter fought hard enough to please the people? If he hadn't, the emperor would give a thumbs-down, and the victor would immediately stick his sword into the neck of his opponent.

We are all still in that Coliseum. We are still being entertained by men willfully destroying each other. It's just that now, the sword comes later.

Postscript: *The day this piece came out, Dorsett announced he'd been diagnosed with CTE.*

Play Ball! Really, Play Ball!

July 3, 2012

Things that nobody reads in America today:

The online mumbo jumbo before you check the little "I Agree" box.

Kate Upton's résumé.

Major League Baseball's "Pace of Play Procedures."

Not that baseball games don't have a pace. They do: snails escaping a freezer.

It's clear no MLB player or umpire has ever read the procedures, or else how do you explain what I witnessed Sunday, when I sat down to do something really stupid—watch an entire televised MLB game without the aid of a DVR?

Cincinnati and San Francisco was a three-hour-and-fourteen-minute can-somebody-please-stick-two-forks-in-my-eyes snore-a-palooza. Like a Swedish movie, it might have been decent if somebody had cut ninety minutes out of it. I'd rather have watched eyebrows grow. And I should have known better.

Consider: There were 280 pitches thrown, and after 170 of them, the hitter got out of the batter's box and did . . . absolutely nothing.

Mostly, hitters delayed the proceedings to kick imaginary dirt off their cleats, meditate, and un-Velcro and re-Velcro their batting gloves, despite the fact that most of the time, they hadn't even swung.

Buster Posey of the Giants, the Man Who Wrecked Your Dinner Reservations, has this habit of coming to the box, stopping outside it and unfastening and refastening his gloves before his FIRST SWING!

I knew I was in trouble in the first inning when the Reds' Brandon Phillips stepped up. My notes on his five-pitch at bat:

Strike: steps out, examines the trademark of his bat at length.

Ball: steps out, grabs barrel of bat, seems to be talking to it.

Ball: steps out, takes three practice swings, taps corner of batter's box, steps one foot in, taps plate, places other foot in, stretches, fiddles, finally looks at pitcher, calls time-out! Does it all again.

Swing and a miss: steps way out, adjusts belt, adjusts jersey, addresses barrel again.

Grounds out to short.

Apparently, the bat didn't listen.

By the way, the average number of seconds per pitch this game: 31:34. Thirty-one seconds per pitch? This is not a misprint. Do you realize people can solve an entire Rubik's Cube in 22 seconds?

All of this, of course, is in direct violation of MLB's "Pace of Play Procedures" (hah!), which state: "Umpires will not grant time for batters to step out of the box if to do so would unnecessarily delay the game."

Unnecessarily delay the game? The only delay these hitters knew was unnecessary. And when they weren't doing that, the pitchers were lollygagging behind the mound, re-rubbing pre-rubbed baseballs or gazing up to identify cloud animals.

New rule: Umpires who don't order batters back into the box within twelve seconds—because the rules state that a pitcher must throw the ball within twelve seconds of receiving it—will get the room at the hotel next to the newlyweds.

There's also this amusing passage in the "Pace of Play Procedures" (hah!): "When given permission to leave the batter's box under Rule 6.02, batters may not step more than 3 feet from the batter's box."

Who-eee! That's rich. These guys wandered away from the box like 2-year-olds at a petting zoo. Six times they left the dirt circle around the plate altogether. Left the entire circle!

And by the way, this nonsense about there's only a two-minute, ten-second TV break between half innings? Bull feathers. Only once did the break between half innings take 2:10 or less. The rest of the time, it was miles over. The break before the top of the fifth was four minutes and twelve seconds! Where did everybody go? Out to feed their meters?

There were more ways to waste time in this game than in a month of Teamsters meetings.

There were fourteen attempts by pitchers to pick off runners, not one of them even coming close. Most of them resembled somebody tossing a turkey to a coworker.

New rule: Pitchers get two pickoff attempts per runner. For every one after that, the umpire adds a ball to the hitter's count.

Four times the hitter, after going through his Art Carney routine, got in the box, decided the pitcher was messing with him, and called time-out.

Twice the pitcher wanted a time-out.

Five times the catcher called time-out to go out to the mound to discuss, what? Obamacare?

Four times the pitching coach wanted time. That's fifteen time-outs in a game that didn't even have a clock. Can you imagine if Tom Brady could call a time-out anytime he wanted? You'd be in Foxborough long enough to vote.

And explain to me why a reliever who's been warming up in the bullpen for five minutes still needs eight pitches to warm up on the mound. Do field goal kickers get eight practice kicks? Dumb.

Like tennis grunts, all this crud is just a lot of bad habits that only serve to annoy the very people MLB is supposedly trying to captivate—the fans. It doesn't sell more TV ads, doesn't get the game done before the kids have to go to bed, doesn't do anything but make your thumb hit the CHNL UP button sooner.

This game was mercifully won by the Giants, 4–3, on their last at bat, when Reds right fielder Jay Bruce botched an easy fly ball.

Three hours and fourteen minutes, 170 step-outs, and three double-shot macchiatos for that?

Please, I beg of you, bring on the NFL.

Postscript: *The average time for a baseball game went up again in 2013—to two hours, 58.9 minutes. The three-hour average baseball game will soon be upon us. Bring a pillow.*

Fearlessness

(Tales of Strength)

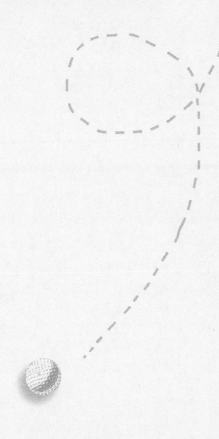

Some NFL Dreams Never Die

May 30, 2012

It's not every day that the Washington Redskins call up a man convicted of rape and ask him if he'd agree to a one-day workout, but it happened Tuesday.

Oh, and the Kansas City Chiefs called Tuesday, too. And the Miami Dolphins. And they were three days behind the Seattle Seahawks, who will work him out on June 7.

Why are all these NFL teams eager to check out a convicted sex offender, a man who served five years in prison and wore a GPS ankle bracelet for another five?

Because Brian Banks didn't do it.

A judge in Long Beach, California, threw out his kidnapping and rape conviction last week after looking at a videotape of his accuser admitting she lied. After ten years, he was suddenly a free and innocent man.

"My mouth hurts from smiling so much," Banks told me Tuesday night. "Unbelievable."

Banks was 16 in 2002, the bluest of blue chips out of Long Beach

Poly High School, an NFL feeder if there ever was one. He'd already been offered a full-ride scholarship at USC by then coach Pete Carroll.

But on a summer day that year, he and a girl named Wanetta Gibson decided to go make out in a stairwell at school. When they came out, she accused him of rape.

No semen traces in the rape kit. No witnesses. And yet Banks's attorney insisted he cop a plea, saying his size, age and race would mean a sure conviction of forty-plus years. He said no, no, a hundred times no, and finally, reluctantly, yes.

Banks got six years. He served sixty-two months.

When he got out, he had to wear a GPS ankle bracelet at all times. He had to register as a convicted sex felon. Couldn't go near schools, parks or zoos. Couldn't get a job. He was lucky to get a few hours a week unloading docks.

What did Gibson get? A $750,000 settlement from the school.

But then, last year, a chunk of luck fell from the stars. Out of the blue, Gibson, then 24, sent Banks a Facebook friend request.

Banks slammed the laptop cover down and jumped out of his chair. Was somebody playing a joke on him?

He looked again. Amazing. Gibson had typed, "Let's let bygones be bygones."

Easy for her to say. She didn't watch ten years of her life go by.

"She was adamant about meeting me," Banks says. "I asked my brother [Freddy], 'What should I do?' He said, 'Whatever you do, make sure you play chess, not checkers.'"

Banks's first move: to get everything she said on tape. He hired a private investigator and met Gibson in the man's office, where every conversation was secretly videotaped. The tape recorded Gibson saying, clearly, "No, he did not rape me."

Was he nervous she wouldn't say it?

"I didn't have to get her to say anything," Banks said. "She came into the room expressing herself. She even came back the next day. The investigator asked her again, point blank. 'Did Brian rape you?' 'No.' 'Did he kidnap you?' 'No.'"

And why would Gibson meet with Banks in the first place? Was it a trap? Was it guilt? No. Banks thinks Gibson—are you ready for this?—was hoping to get back together.

"You read the texts and that's the only conclusion you come to," says a source who worked on the case. "She seems absolutely clue-free about what she did to him."

Getting evidence is one thing, getting your rape conviction flipped is another. Banks called the California Innocence Project in San Diego. They agreed to help. It was the first time they'd taken a case of a man already out of prison.

"As soon as we met him, we had no doubt," says Justin Brooks, the lead attorney. "We could see this was a kid who had a big future ahead of him, one that had been lost."

On Thursday, May 24, in a Long Beach courtroom, Banks got his future back.

What's the first thing he did, besides cry at the courtroom table? Snipped off the stupid ankle bracelet, the scarlet letter of our age. "Oh, man, when that thing came off?" Banks says. "There are no words."

Then he went with Brooks's wife and kids to a place he couldn't have gone the day before—SeaWorld.

"It's so crazy to go from being labeled a monster to seeing your phone light up with all this support and offers and love," he said. "It's, really, a little hard to get used to."

And what does Banks want most now? Retribution? Revenge? Gibson's head on a serving platter? No. He's not even demanding Gibson give the money back. While he is suing the state for $100 for each day he was falsely imprisoned, what he wants back most is football.

Thanks to the best Tuesday of his life, he has now got a chance at it.

None of the four teams are offering any guarantees for a spot in training camp, nor is Banks asking for any.

"I'll make 'em happy," says Banks, who's been training nonstop since October. "After all I've been through these last ten years, I can still do some things that will impress you."

Like . . . deadlift 545 pounds, box-jump 55 inches flat-footed, broad-jump 10-plus feet and run a 4.6 40, all at 6-foot-2 and 245 pounds. NFL trainer Gavin MacMillan, who has volunteered to train Banks for free, says he has a shot. "You see him run and you can see why USC wanted him."

And if the NFL doesn't pan out? Banks already has all kinds of job offers. One of them is to "work in the front office and explore other sports opportunities" for the Arizona Diamondbacks.

"I about fell out of my seat when I read that one," Banks said.

I don't know about you, but I can't remember another story that made me want to alternately punch something and hug something like this one. The way Banks has handled himself, without bitterness or bile, with grace and guts, makes you wish he were running the U.S. Senate. If it were me, I'd be stomping around, waving lawsuits and screaming, "I TOLD you I didn't do it!!!"

"I know my story makes people angry at first," Banks says. "That's where I was, too, at first. But where would it have gotten me to stay mad for ten years? It's like when you're a little kid and you cry about having to clean your room. You can cry and cry, but it doesn't get your room cleaned."

Brian Banks's room is clean again. His heart is spotless. He's holding on to nothing but his dreams. He lost a full decade of his life and now all he wants in exchange is an NFL jersey.

C'mon, Miami Dolphins. Who's had more "Hard Knocks" than Brian Banks?

Postscript: *I think this is my favorite story in the book. Talk about letting go? Banks lives for the present, never the past. He made it to the Atlanta Falcons 2013 camp and actually recorded two tackles in a preseason game, but was released in the final cut. He still hopes to play in the NFL. Ms. Gibson, meanwhile, was ordered to pay $2.6 million to the Long Beach school district. At press time, her whereabouts were unknown.*

Chuck Pagano Stays Strong

November 7, 2012

You want to talk about the speech, but I want to talk about the man.

In my hometown of Boulder, Colorado, the Paganos were our Kennedys.

They were all charmers—with biceps. I used to cover the dad, Sam Pagano, a high school coaching legend who picked off state football championships like a cop shooting carnival bottles. His All-State sons, Chuck and John, could flatten silos. Hell, their paperboy could've run for mayor and won.

They were the best our town had to offer. That's why it seemed impossible, that 1979 day, when tragedy moved into their house.

Chuck and John's sister, Cathy, was dead at 22. Killed in a Jeep accident in California. Cathy, the bubbly one. Cathy, the one who showed up with a chocolate cake for her dad after every game.

"I remember Chuck driving home from college, getting out of the car and just sort of collapsing into my parents' arms," says John, now 45.

The Pagano family picked themselves up and started leading

again. The two boys became fine coaches in college and the NFL. John became the defensive coordinator of the San Diego Chargers. This season, Chuck Pagano became head coach of the Indianapolis Colts. Everybody from Boulder nodded and said, "Seems about right."

And then, late this September, tragedy knocked again.

Chuck's wife, Tina, was on the phone telling the Pagano's her husband would have to stop coaching and fight a dangerous form of leukemia, right away.

"I could hear Tina's voice, but I went blank," Chuck's mom, Diana, remembers. "And I thought, just for a second, 'I can't take this much pain again.'"

In San Diego, John flinched at the news. "When you bury a sister, man, that's something nobody wants to go through. And then, when you get the word [on Chuck], it's something you just can't imagine."

But Chuck, 52, had three things going for him to stay alive: (1) With luck and grit and chemo, this kind of leukemia is curable; (2) he'd gotten a break with an early bye week to get some stubborn bruises checked out and caught it early; and (3) Chuck himself.

Chuck Pagano has always been as unstoppable as the wind and twice as unpredictable. In the first grade, his teacher called Diana and asked if she could tie him to his chair to settle him down. "Sure," Diana said, "as long as I can come down there and tie you to yours." He'll turn left when you think he's going right. But there's always a reason. The man could motivate a tree sloth.

"Coach Pagano's an inspiration," says Colts QB Andrew Luck, who just shaved his head in solidarity, along with more than twenty teammates. "I love him. We all do." No wonder every Colts player wears a "Chuckstrong" T-shirt during pregame warm-ups.

But a constant chemo drip and twenty-five days in one hospital bed will get down even a 5,000-hour energy drink like Chuck. So when his brother flew in from San Diego on a rare day off two weeks ago to spend ten hours with him, he had his own motivational speech to give him.

"Listen," John said before he left. "Anybody comes in that door, you show strength, you show grit and you show them how you're gonna whip this thing. 'Cause you are."

And so it was that when Pagano crawled out of bed, got cleaned up and walked into the Colts' locker room after their win Sunday over the Miami Dolphins, you knew he was going to say something to put a lump in your throat the size of a grapefruit.

"He wasn't really supposed to talk after the game," says a Colts staffer. "His doctor wanted him to stay in a confined space with not a lot of contact with people, to avoid germs. But next thing you knew . . ."

. . . he was in among his players. He took off his hat for the first time and revealed his hairless head. In high school, he and his Fairview High School teammates used to shave their heads as a vow to beat one rival or another, but this time, it revealed something I'd never seen in a Pagano before: frailty.

Until he started speaking, that is, and then he was as Chuck as ever. With a cracked voice and glistening eyes, he vowed to his men that he'd live "to see two more daughters dance at their weddings" and to "hoist the Lombardi [Trophy] with you guys."

I cried watching it. His parents cried. Watch the video. Even the player behind him in the video cried.

"He just blows me away," his dad says. "He's such a leader, such a coach, such a man."

"He is reaching another place," says his mom. "He's got information coming from high places. I put Cathy in charge of all that."

"That's Chuck," John says. "He inspires me every day."

He starts another round of chemo this week, and it's going to clothesline him, just like the first round. He'll be flat enough to slide under the door. But I know Paganos, and they don't stay down long.

He knows cancer turns things upside down. You have to get sick to get better. Bet you he's back on the sideline by mid-December.

The question is, can his family take the stress of that?

"I can," Diana insists. "I'm Chuckstrong."

Postscript: *One Monday night in San Diego, I saw Pagano's parents walking to the Chargers' game against the Colts—Chuck's offense against John's defense. They looked like they were on their way to double hernias. Unlike with the Manning family—where Eli and Peyton never go nose-to-nose—there was no escaping it. One brother would make the other miserable. Turns out John's Chargers won. "There's no happy ending in a game like this," Sam told me. Oh, yes, there is. At this writing, Chuck remains cancer free.*

Toughest Fan You'll Ever Meet

August 23, 2010

Ask yourself whether you'd do this: Leave home. Walk 20 minutes to the train station. Take a 70-minute train ride to Penn Station in New York City. Weave for 10 minutes over to the subway station. Take a half-hour D train ride to Yankee Stadium. Navigate the vendors and chaos to get to your seat.

Now ask yourself: Would you do all that blind?

Jane Lang does it, accompanied at most games by only her Seeing Eye golden retriever, Clipper. Thirty times a year. At 67 years old.

Which is why she was so gobsmacked Tuesday when she set out from her home in Morris Plains, New Jersey, only to find Yankees manager Joe Girardi and four current and former Yankees waiting on her doorstep.

They didn't have a limo. They didn't have a fleet of Suburbans. They had only sneakers. They were going to make the journey with her.

"Oh my God!" Jane said.

"We think you're amazing," Girardi said.

"Follow me," Clipper seemed to say.

You have to understand what a two-hour, one-way journey to a baseball game takes for somebody like Jane. She's been blind since birth, and these trips have not always turned out well. Once, some kids decided it would be fun to spin her around a few dozen times. Another time, she fell onto the subway tracks and was nearly killed. But ever since she got a guide dog, she's been intrepid.

The whole bizarre troupe—Jane, Clipper, the Yankees, their security guys, the PR men and the media—paraded past the florist, Tony's pizza parlor and the little barbershop where one of the customers came out to wave and holler at Jane with the apron still around his neck.

Jane and Clipper walk at we-just-robbed-a-bank speed, which caused current Yankees pitching star Joba Chamberlain to holler, "Hey! Slow down!"

Soon Yankees fans figured out what was going on and joined in, along with nearly everybody in town. By the time they reached the train station, it looked as though Clipper were leading a marching band.

They crammed aboard the train, whereupon ex–Yankees star Tino Martinez slumped into his seat. "I can't imagine doing this," he said. Girardi, who was sitting next to Jane, said, "She's amazing. We should've done this blindfolded to give us an even better idea of what it's like."

Pah! You think this is hard? Wait 'til they'd see the next leg—Penn Station and the streets of Manhattan. It's mind-melting to watch Jane and Clipper make their way down the clogged streets of Manhattan—Clipper, taking cues from Jane, weaving her through a maze of street vendors, suits, iPhone zombies, boxes, bums, secretaries and scaffolding.

"And we complain about a little traffic on the Deegan [Expressway]," Girardi mused, shaking his head.

Usually, when Jane finally gets to the D train and takes her seat, she feels for eight pieces of candy in her right pocket. Every time the train stops, she transfers one piece into the opposite pocket. When there's one piece of candy left, she knows the next stop is Yankee Stadium. No need this time. The very people she was traveling to see were telling her it was time to get off.

Once Jane and Clipper reached Gate 6—two and a half hours from start to finish—Girardi and the players took over. They introduced her to former Yankees star Paul O'Neill, who let her feel his face. She touched it the way a sculptor would. They let her hold Babe Ruth's bat, Joe DiMaggio's hat, the 2000 World Series trophy. She felt the monuments. When she got to Mickey Mantle's face, she said, "He looks tired."

You don't know the half of it, lady.

They introduced her to Mariano Rivera and Derek Jeter, who let her feel his famous mug. And once, when there was finally nobody talking to her, she crouched down and felt the infield grass as though it were finely spun silk.

Imagine. She had learned the game as a girl, when her father had set up a checkerboard like a baseball field and guided her hands over it. She's been in love with baseball ever since. Now she was getting a guided, one-woman tour of the very heart of it.

"I'm the luckiest person in the world," she purred. "I always have known there were three different things I always wanted: a house with a roof that didn't leak, someone to love me and kids. And now I got this. It's the utmost frosting, you know what I mean? I'll never get sick of this frosting!"

Tuesday was just one day of the Yankees' Hope Week, a genius idea dreamed up by their public relations extraordinaire, Jason Zillo, who seems to have an addiction to helping people in ways nobody has thought of before. The Yankees gave $10,000 in Jane's honor to The Seeing Eye Inc., a place in Morristown, New Jersey, that trains guide dogs.

Still, the day was Jane's, and strong, young millionaires kept coming up to her, praising her guts, skills and moxie. To which Jane would only shrug and say, "This is just my way of being free and living in the world the way it is."

And as she stood there relishing the moment, it made a person think that the world the way it is can be awfully sweet.

Postscript: *Jane and Clipper are still intrepid. In 2013, the pair went to more Yankee games than ever. She says people still come up to her and tell her they saw the story about her. "No doubt," she says, "it was the best day of my life."*

Just Killing It

August 22, 2013

It should take you about three minutes to read this.

That's how long the worst of Jerry Kill's epileptic seizures last—arms and legs spasming, eyes rolling up, jaw clenching.

Imagine that for these three minutes. Imagine every muscle of your body firing out of control and there's nothing you can do about it.

"You feel like you were in a car wreck afterwards," says Kill, the University of Minnesota football coach. "I've never seen a seizure. And I don't want to see one."

But 50,000-plus fans, and a regional television audience, did see one on September 10, 2011, when Kill went down with seconds to go in a home loss to New Mexico State, Kill's home debut for the Golden Gophers.

As he lay there, the only sound you could hear was his two daughters—and some of his players—crying.

"I don't feel bad for me," says Kill, soon to be 52. "I feel bad for my wife, my kids and the people who have to watch it. . . . You wake up and find out 50,000 people watched you. It's kind of embarrassing."

Nobody knows why this started happening to Kill at 43. Maybe genetics. Maybe football concussions. Maybe the bad car accident he had once. But it did. He was on the sideline as the Southern Illinois coach in 2005 when he suddenly hit the turf and began shaking uncontrollably.

"I freaked out," says his wife, Rebecca. "I didn't know what to do. Now I know. You don't do anything except make the area around them safe. You don't reach in their mouth and pull out their tongue. And you don't panic. If I panic, everybody in the stadium panics."

And yet that seizure might have saved Kill's life. During tests afterward, doctors found cancer in his kidney and took it out—but not until after the season.

"I didn't have time for cancer," Kill says. "I was coaching."

Kill hates to take time off work.

"The only time he misses work is when he's laid out in the hospital and doesn't know he's missed work," Rebecca says. "Even with cancer. He did his surgery when they were on a break, and yet he recruited a kid that night!"

Kill loves a good comeback. He has turned around programs at Saginaw Valley State, Southern Illinois, Northern Illinois. Now he's trying it in Minneapolis, where he had six wins and a bowl game last year, his second season.

"It's impossible not to give your very best for him," says Gophers safety Brock Vereen, brother of New England Patriots RB Shane Vereen. "This guy has battled through cancer, epilepsy. He could have a seizure at any moment. Who am I to complain about being tired?"

"He's got to be one of the toughest guys in America," says punter and holder Peter Mortell, who sees Kill every day during special-teams practice. "I'd guess he's had upwards of fifty seizures that no one's ever heard about in the past year. And yet he still comes to work before everyone else in the morning and is the last one to leave at night."

Grand mal seizures, tiny frozen-moment seizures, Kill has every kind. He is ashamed of none of them. Ask him any question about epilepsy and he'll answer it.

How many seizures this year alone?

"Hard to know. I'd say twenty over the last two years."

Kill never even used to utter the word "epilepsy" until he got hate e-mails after a seizure in the postgame after the Northwestern game last season. One writer called him a "freak." One tweet encouraged Minnesota to "fire the flopper."

He decided to fight back, in the name of the 2.8 million American epileptics who couldn't. He went on the radio and shook again, this time with anger.

"Jerry Kill has epileptic seizures. . . ." he began. "I've been battling the same thing for ten years. . . . But at the same time, during that ten-year period, as a staff and as a head coach, we've won a helluva lot of football games. . . . [I've had people e-mail me that] 'We got a freak coaching the Minnesota Gophers.' . . . I'm not a freak, and neither are [others with the same disease]. . . . I'm gonna work my tail end off for the people who have the same situation I have."

And then he did. He began speaking out for the Epilepsy Foundation of Minnesota. One practice, he brought a group of young kids with epilepsy to meet with the team.

"Guys, I want you to look," he said. "These are my people. These kids are just like me. This is who I am." Then he asked what the kids wanted to be when they grew up, going up to each kid. One little girl wanted to be a Minnesota cheerleader. One wanted to be an NFL player. To each of them, he said, "Well, you can. Epilepsy won't stop you from doing it."

Some of the kids were smiling. Some of their parents were crying. Some of the players were grinning.

Says Vereen: "That's a moment I'll walk away from the university with. It was humbling."

Kill used to refuse to talk about his epilepsy, but now he can kid about it. This year, coming back from a long recruiting trip, he was riding shotgun with his strength coach, Eric Klein. "Kleiner," he said. "I'm gonna fall asleep now. But if I start to have a seizure, you just push me out on the road and let it happen, OK?"

He's not allowed to drive, of course. He has to depend on Rebecca to get to work in the morning and his coaches to take him home at night. Sometimes, he feels so bad about asking that he'll just walk the five miles home instead.

"I got two goals in life," he says. "Just two. One is to see all the people in the state of Minnesota proud of their Minnesota Gophers football program again. And two is to drive again. I just want to drive my truck, my elbow out the window, listening to country music."

Thanks to the nearby Mayo Clinic, it might happen. An epilepsy specialist there heard about Kill's condition and left him a message: "I can help you." He has. Kill has been eating right, taking long walks in the late afternoon and taking the right medicines. If he can get to six months without a single seizure, the doctors say he can have his truck keys back.

"Man, I'd really love that," he says.

You don't meet many men like Kill, a simple and good man who has more right than any of us to complain, feel sorry for himself and ditch work, yet he never does.

So here's to Jerry Kill and long drives on the road, long drives on the football field and a long career standing on the sideline at Minnesota. And, someday, may a certain little girl be standing in a cheerleader uniform with him.

Postscript: *It all couldn't have gone any worse for Jerry Kill after this ran. Instead of getting better, he got worse. He had so many seizures during games in the 2013 season—five—that he wound up coaching the entire second half of the season from the press box. And yet the Gophers went 8-4 in the regular season, their best record in ten years. Afterward, Kill said he has no plans to quit. Driving his truck, though, seemed a million miles away.*

Commuting to Staples Center
with Kobe Bryant

April 14, 2009

It's 49 miles from Kobe Bryant's house in Orange County to Staples Center, and yet, even in a Ferrari, it takes him 10 hours and 16 minutes.

What takes him so long? You're about to ride shotgun and find out:

7:15 a.m. Nearly $140 into a cab ride from my place, a security gate opens at the end of a very swank cul-de-sac to reveal Kobe Bryant, father of two, standing in front of seven vehicles—the Ferrari, the Range Rover, the Escalade, the Bentley Coupe, the two-door plastic Fred Flintstone car, the training-wheels bike and the tricycle smashed into a bush.

"You ready to go?" he asks. "I hate to be late."

I have a bag and nowhere to put it, since the Ferrari is basically a 503-horsepower engine with two seats. So he takes two helmets out of the trunk and puts the bag in.

Helmets for a car? Uh-oh.

7:21 a.m. I immediately spill my coffee in the $300,000-plus Ferrari, but how was I supposed to know he'd demonstrate its 0 to 60 mph in 3.1 seconds right at the very moment I was about to sip my delicious venti mochaccino?

Trying to wipe up the puddle with my sock without him noticing and trying to be heard over the Ferrari's throaty roar, I nearly yell my interview:

Me: Why are we leaving so early for a 6:30 Clippers game?

Bryant: Game day. Lots to do.

Me: Why does a Los Angeles Laker live clear down in Weeds suburbia?

Bryant: It's peaceful. It's a better place to bring up kids. Nice people down here.

Me: What's the fastest you've ever driven this thing?

Bryant: We're about to find out.

Me (to self): Did I ever complete my will?

Of course, the eleven-time All-Star doesn't always drive to work. Sometimes he has one of his off-duty, armed, Lakers-provided police officers take him in a customized van so he can watch scouting DVDs and ice his feet and knees. (He ices them for twenty minutes three times a day. The man spends more time in ice than Ted Williams.) Occasionally, though, he charters a helicopter. "Sometimes, there's just things you cannot miss," he says.

Like?

"Like my daughter's soccer game. Because what if I miss her first goal?"

Can't say I ever choppered into one of my daughter's soccer games, but still.

Bryant, 30, has been known to get up earlier than many barn owls to conduct his famously brutal workouts. One time, Larry Drew II— who now plays at North Carolina—asked to shadow him on one.

"OK," Kobe said. "Pick you up at 3:30."

But 3:30 came and went and Kobe never showed. Then, at 3:30 the next morning, he was ringing Drew's doorbell.

"You ready?" Kobe asked.

"I like to just get up and get it done," he explained to me, "then I'm back home and nobody's even up. Haven't missed a thing."

7:30 a.m. Bryant pulls the yellow Ferrari up to a massive O.C. health club and leaves it. This will happen many times today, leaving the car right in front of buildings. Gods do not park.

Today is a Sunday, and it's bothering him that he'll have to miss coloring with his girls—6 and 2—watching Ariel in *The Little Mermaid* for the 1,003rd time with his girls and going to Disneyland with the girls. But he's obsessed with winning the 2009 NBA title, which means he's committed to his boys. He wants to be as chiseled as possible for the coming playoff pounding. That's why it's no surprise we're met by Tim Grover, Michael Jordan's genius strength and conditioning coach.

Grover puts Bryant through a game-day workout like I've never seen. (Warning: If you don't want to feel like a complete jelly-filled donut, don't read this next part.) Among a dozen other drills, Bryant does suicide push-ups. At the top of the push-up, he launches himself off the mat so hard that both his feet come off the ground and his hands slap his pecs. He does three sets of seven of these. This makes me turn away and whimper softly.

8:35 a.m. Bryant wheels the asphalt-eating Ferrari onto the I-405 north and begins answering my questions about this remarkable comeback he's making in America, in basketball and in his life, which would be fascinating if it weren't for the 70-mph circus going on all around us.

People are pulling up next to us and waving. And screaming. And taking pictures with their cell phones. And honking. And craning back in their seats to see. And not watching the road. And getting too damn close. And Kobe doesn't seem to see any of it.

"Life is really good now," he's saying.

Kobe! Kill'em tonight! Yeeeeaaahhh bbbboy!

"And it's funny. A lot of these companies who dumped us during the [sexual assault] trial [in which all charges were dropped] are calling us now asking us to come back. And I just kind of smile and go, 'No. No, thanks, homie. We're good.' But that hurt, dude. To just be dropped like that. It hurt."

The guy in the Toyota Tundra is signaling that he wants an autograph.

"But my wife and I, we toughed it out. She and I, we got through it. We're going to be celebrating our . . ."

Two morons are motioning to me that they'd like Kobe to get off at the next exit and take a picture with them.

". . . eight-year anniversary together. And when I think about how I almost lost it, the family and everything . . ."

I can read their lips: "Dude! Please?!"

". . . I'm just very thankful, and blessed. It was really close there for a while."

Even a *Weekly Shopper* reporter would follow that answer up with "What do you mean?" But a knucklehead in a Ford truck is trying to cut in front of us so his buddy can take a picture out of the back window, so I ask, "Do you ever wreck on this commute?"

"No," he says with a grin, "but one time, this one guy was looking back and hit the guy in front of him. Not hard or anything, but he definitely hit the guy. It was kinda funny."

With all that chaos, I can't really vouch for the accuracy of all this, but I'm pretty sure Bryant says:

- He's taken up golf. Played Pelican Hill the other day with Maris Valainis, who played Jimmy Chitwood in *Hoosiers*.
- If I weren't in the car, he'd be listening to Lil Wayne, Jay Z or Biggie Smalls.
- He loves marketing and advertising. In fact, he conceived and wrote a Carl's Jr. poster, which featured Jerry West, Kareem Abdul-Jabbar and himself, and the slogan: "They Who Endure, Conquer."

- He and his wife, Vanessa, have no nannies.
- Most sports talk radio makes him nauseous.
- He's addicted to Discovery Channel, loves to spear fish and reads *New York Times* columnist Thomas Friedman.
- He has no plans to opt out of his contract at the end of this season, but "you can never absolutely say no, right?"
- His daughters speak a mix of English, Spanish and Italian.
- He'd like to have a boy.

Forty minutes, 37 missed quotes and 118 gawkers later, we've gone the 43 miles from the health club in O.C. to the Lakers' practice facility in El Segundo, right near LAX, for shootaround. He pulls up to the spot in front of the door, gets out of the car and doesn't lock it. It's all I can do to not get on my knees and kiss the ground.

12:03 p.m. After his two hours of shooting and stretching, we're off to a downtown hotel, where Kobe will ice, shower, sleep, eat (it's always the same: chicken, rice and broccoli), watch scouting DVDs and make calls until it's time to go. This time we're following one of the off-duty cops, who's driving the gray van.

"Why are we following the cop?" I ask.

"Because I need my jug to ice," he says.

"So why don't we take it ourselves?" I ask.

"Won't fit."

Do you love it? His ice jug gets a police escort.

"What if you can't sleep at the hotel?" I ask as he lead-foots it up the 110 north. "What do you do? Walk around downtown L.A.?"

He laughs and looks at me like I just landed from the planet Nimrod.

"Uh, no. I can't walk around L.A. There are fans and then there are LAKER fans. LAKER fans are, like, ten times more into it than regular fans."

Example: One time, he met a man who had the exact same tattoos as him. Literally, the exact same tattoos, down to the size, color, font, style, even the names of his daughters, his wife, the Bible verses, the crown, everything. And this was in Ohio.

"I mean, what do you say to something like that?" he says, still amazed. "I'm like, 'Wow.' And then I whispered to my security guy, 'Get his Social Security, OK?'"

12:14 p.m. Four security guards are waiting for us at the hotel. We leave the Ferrari AND the van out front, go through a side entrance, up a freight elevator, to a suite that's waiting for him. What does he pay for use of the suite for a full season? Zippo! "I just take care of them with playoff tickets."

Does the man ever see the inside of his wallet?

5:03 p.m. I get a call on the phone in my room and it's the cop, sounding urgent. "Mr. Reilly? Kobe is going to need to leave in exactly one minute. He was mistaken as to the start of tonight's game. Can you be expedited down here immediately?"

"Uh, well, yeah, I can expedite."

"Good. Much appreciated. Kobe doesn't like to be late."

So I've heard.

Turns out he thought it was a 7:30 start. It's actually a 6:30 start. "I'm such an idiot," he admits. "I do this all the time."

The drive to Staples is going to be a very expedited three minutes, so I have a lot of ground to make up.

How bad do you want this title?

"Beyond your comprehension," he says. "I'm obsessed. It keeps me awake at night."

Can this team do it?

"Yeah, we can do it. We're better equipped this time. Last time [in the finals], we ran into a buzz saw. That Celtics team was hungry. And not just hungry, but full of hungry veterans."

How long do you want to play?

"I'd love to play until I'm 40, but I'm not sure anybody would want me then. Put it this way: I'll play as long as they'll let me."

As a couple in a red Hyundai shrieks, "Kobe! Kobe! Take care of us tonight!" he turns into the players' gate, where a guy with a mirror on a pole checks under the Ferrari for bombs. I'm terrified what they'll find.

Excuse me, Mr. Bryant? There seems to be mochaccino leaking from your car?

He pulls it right up front, hops out, and immediately there's a still photographer and a Minicam taking our picture as we walk. I try to get away, but he yanks me back into the shot. "Just mean mug it," he whispers. He wears the expression of a mafia don on the way to a trial. I try it, but I can't pull it off. I look like a man suffering upper gastrointestinal blockage.

I try to say good-bye and thanks, but he's on the phone to his daughters, going, "Ciao, bella!" as he walks into the locker room.

It's 5:31 p.m. The Kobe Kommute is over. He's still got the game to go. (The Lakers will defeat the Clippers, 88–85, with Bryant scoring 18 points on 5-for-15 shooting—proving that, occasionally, Kobe DOES miss things.) As for me, I'm so exhausted, there's only one thing I want to do.

Go somewhere quiet and watch Ariel.

Postscript: *When Bryant ripped his Achilles' in April of 2013 and experts said he wouldn't be ready until after the 2014 All-Star break, I nearly spit out my Lucky Charms. "All-Star break?" I said aloud. "He'll be back by New Year's Eve!" I was wrong, of course. He was back just after Hanukkah.*

George vs. the Dragon

March 15, 2010

DAY 17

Tuesday, March 9, 7:30 a.m.—Denver Nuggets coach George Karl pops in his mouthpiece and puts on his helmet and braces himself for a brutal fifteen minutes, but this isn't football. This is cancer radiation.

We're in Denver's Swedish Medical Center. The helmet is actually a white, hard-mesh mask that fits to every contour of Karl's big bucket head. It has red crosses all over it, like a hockey goalie's. He lays his 283 pounds on the table and the technicians clamp the mask on hard. How Karl breathes I'll never know. They secure his limbs and ask him to hold a blue plastic donut so no part of him moves. He looks like Hannibal Lecter about to get fried.

"It makes you a little claustrophobic," the 58-year-old coach tries to say through the mask. "But what are you gonna do? Leave?" Coaching the wildly talented but wildly uneven Nuggets is hard enough, let alone doing it with throat and neck cancer, but that's what Karl is trying to do. Everybody tells him it's not possible, and today, maybe he's starting to believe them.

With only three of his torturous six weeks of treatment done, and the inside of his mouth looking like he just took 100 bites out of a lava-hot pizza slice, and his head throbbing and his eyes hollow, Karl looks like a guy who should be on a stretcher, not an NBA bench.

"George, this is only going to get harder," a nurse tells him. "You're not going to feel like working." Clearly, she's never met George Karl.

Suddenly, the huge gray machine whirs like a giant Transformer, turning sideways, first this side, then that, as though it's trying to decide how to eat him. Then it zaps his throat and neck lymph nodes, ravaging them. It gives him a radish-red rash that's covering his face, chest and back. I know. He shows me. He shows me many things I don't want to see. He's doing it because he wants people to know exactly what it's like. Wants to take the fear and mystery out of it for people.

"The rash is a good sign," says the technician. "It shows the radiation is working."

"Mine's not bad," Karl mumbles, hardly able to talk. "There's a guy in here who can't even lay his head on a pillow."

Karl absorbs the machine's worst for fifteen minutes every weekday, except on Wednesdays, when he does it for thirty.

Then he goes to work.

8:15 a.m.—The coach with the seventh-most wins in NBA history is having a glass of water and looking at film of the Minnesota Timberwolves ahead of the game the next night.

But we're not in his office. And the water just went into his stomach through a tube in his gut. And the hose from the liter bag of Erbitux, a cancer drug, dripping into his left arm hangs over the laptop he's trying to watch film on. And we're not in his office, we're at the Swedish chemo lab. This is the one day of the week he adds dripping to the zapping. You fight the dragon any way they tell you.

If there was a DL for coaches, Karl would be the first five names on it. He's not going to get on the team plane this afternoon for Minnesota. He won't coach them there. For a controllisimo like Karl, that's torture.

"I woke up today thinking of all the things that could go wrong," he tries to say through a mouth that sounds like it's full of rock salt. "Actually, I didn't really wake up. I didn't hardly go to sleep. Couldn't."

I don't know how your Monday was, but this was Karl's: He'd coached the Nuggets to a 12-point win over Portland the night before. Didn't hit the sack until 1. Got up at 5. Was at the hospital by 6. Had surgery at 6:30 to put in the stomach tube that, coming soon, will be the only way he'll eat. Out of surgery at 7. Radiation at 8. Home by 10. Nap. Then started working on preparing for the Minnesota game.

His doctors have called his cancer "treatable," but as a prostate cancer survivor from 2005, he knows there's no guaranteed contract with the dragon. Still, he refuses to play the victim card. "Nothing I do is painful," he tells the press. But the players know he's lying. They hear him say less every day. It's getting harder to hear him. He almost never yells now. And when you have a team with divas like J. R. Smith and Kenyon Martin, that's hard to believe.

"I don't think all the guys know what he's going through," says Nuggets point guard Chauncey Billups, "but I do. [Billups's mom is a cancer survivor.] We've had a lot of talks. I tell him, 'Take care of yourself. Don't worry so much about us.' But he's stubborn. He's been really inspirational for us."

9:05 a.m.—The oncology nurse asks Karl if there's anything she can do for him.

"Well," he tries to say. "I just think there ought to be somebody all the patients can just beat the crap out of. It's competitive for me. I get so mad, I just want to deck somebody."

They can't give him that, but they've given him all kinds of drugs for the pain he's going through. ("On a 1-to-10 scale of the most painful cancer treatments," says Karl's hematologist, Dr. David Trevarthen, "this is about a 9.") But Karl won't take the drugs, even though the pain is kicking his butt by about 40 points right now.

"Have you put on the [morphine] patch?" the nurse asks.

"No," Karl says.

"You will."

10:25 a.m.—Karl keeps looking at the science-fair project going on under his shirt. "I gotta get something to cover my tube," he says to nobody. "Can't let people see my tube when I'm coaching."

11:15 a.m.—The Erbitux bag is exhausted and so is Karl. He looks like a man who's lost a fight with a wheat thresher.

"I can't go to practice," he whispers, changing the day's plan. "I don't want the players to see the rash. That'll get them thinking negatively."

For only the second time in six seasons, Karl won't coach the Nuggets for a road game. And now he won't even be able to say goodbye. Assistant Adrian Dantley will take over. Get used to it.

Karl gets up to walk out. Nauseous, he grabs the wall as he turns the corner.

DAY 18

Wednesday, March 10, 7:05 a.m.—When Karl comes into the radiation room, he looks like a different guy. Somebody made a switch. This one seems rested. This one is smiling. This one can talk.

"The patch," he says, grinning. "I feel great."

The nurse rolls her eyes.

Karl was going to catch up with the team in Memphis in two days, coach them there, then coach again in Houston on Monday night. "But, man, I'm feeling so good, I might fly to Minnesota today!"

The Transformer will talk him out of that.

7:35 a.m.—Freshly zapped, Karl gets a visit from his oncologist, Dr. Marshall Davis, who comes in wearing a stocking cap. He's got cancer, too—testicular.

The doc is a Nuggets freak and he knows there's something secondary at stake here, beyond saving George Karl's life—getting him back on the bench. "I think this could finally be the year we win it all," the doc says.

Karl doesn't fight him. "When we play right, I don't think there's anybody in the league who wants to play us."

Bonded, the two of them plot out the schedule: Three more weeks of treatment. The worst three weeks. Then at least three—if not four—weeks of utter exhaustion. Then—and only then—might he be able to coach again. That puts them at about April 26.

"When does it get intense?" Dr. Davis asks.

"April 20," says Karl (though the playoffs actually start April 17). Could be a problem.

For anybody else.

"I hope my team is ready," Karl says. "I hope I'm ready."

8:30 a.m.—By his car, I ask Karl if he's scared to die.

"I'm scared every day," he says. "Scared all the time. But my kids, my family, my staff, they keep me thinking positive."

Anything good coming from all this?

"Oh, yeah. Lots. Sometimes, I feel the sunshine on my face and I just stop and think, 'Damn, this feels good.' I never used to think about sunshine, you know?"

He fairly beams saying it.

Guess there's more than one way to radiate.

Postscript: *Karl was Coach of the Year for the 2012–2013 season, which didn't keep him from getting pink-slipped that year anyway. At this writing, he's an analyst for ESPN. All of which matters zero, compared to the news that he remains cancer free.*

The Biggest Patriots Fan

October 16, 2013

His birth certificate says 16. His face says 80. His body says size 6. His mind says 35. His medical diagnosis says, "Failure to thrive," but that's a lie. Few people you'll ever meet fail to thrive like Sam Berns.

Ask Robert Kraft, owner of the New England Patriots.

"I get to meet a lot of people in my life," Kraft says. "But I've never met anyone quite like Sam. I love that kid."

Sam has progeria, which ages him at eight times the normal rate. Even though he's a junior at Foxborough (Massachusetts) High School, he looks like a tiny old man. And yet he play drums in the marching band, umps baseball games, wears his Eagle Scout badge, invents things, makes straight A's, talks like an after-dinner speaker, and is trying to decide whether to go to MIT or Harvard in two years.

Pray that he lives that long.

When Sam was 2, his parents were told that he probably wouldn't make it past 13, the usual life expectancy for the one in 4 million kids born with progeria. They were told that he would be a living time lapse. His skin would wrinkle, his eyesight would fade, his hair would go, his nose would beak, his head would swell, his face would shrink and there would be nothing he could do about it. There's no cure.

But Sam's parents—Dr. Scott Berns and Dr. Leslie Gordon—didn't listen. If nobody was coming to the rescue, why couldn't they?

They started a foundation and, after years of work, helped identify the gene mutation that causes the disease and the first experimental treatment for it, lonafarnib. But with Sam's time running out, they need money—$4 million—to figure out through clinical trial if it's a cure. That's where Kraft enters.

Kraft read about Sam in the *Foxboro Reporter*. This is a man who watches young men perform astonishing athletic feats with their bodies. This is a man who still grieves his wife, Myra, who died two years ago at 68. In Sam, he must've seen a tragic meld—a young man dying of old age.

He invited him to a Sunday practice, just before the Patriots' September 29 game in Atlanta, and liked him so much he decided to donate $1,000 for every year Sam had been alive.

But then Sam mentioned his birthday was October 23. Now the donation had to be $17,000. "Smart businessman," Kraft grinned.

And that was just the start of Kraft falling in love with a young man trapped in a senior citizen's body.

Kraft: "Who's your favorite player? I'll introduce you."

Sam: "Oh, I could never pick just one player. Football is a team sport."

So Kraft introduced him to the entire team. He met Tom Brady. He met Bill Belichick. Everybody. They gathered around and made Sam look even tinier. Then Sam gave the whole team a speech, telling them how they could strategically beat Atlanta and quarterback Matt Ryan. "Make Matty Ryan feel uncomfortable . . . so he throws an interception and we get the ball back. And drive it in."

The players and coaches stood there scratching their heads at this little old boy who sounded suddenly like Vince Lombardi.

"You're looking at him and these 300-pound guys are coming at him and he's got such a calm demeanor," Kraft says. "We need to keep him alive. We need to keep him strong and healthy."

And maybe they need to hire him as a coach. The Patriots rattled the Falcons, 30–23.

"I should've had him at the Cincinnati game," Kraft moans.

The soup thickened. Sam invited Kraft to a screening of a documentary—*Life According to Sam*—that airs on HBO on October 21. The longer Kraft sat there watching it, the more his wallet itched. The more he learned about Sam, the more he gave. His donation went from $17,000 to $100,000 to $250,000, to, finally, a $500,000 matching donation. Now, that's a movie that can OPEN.

He couldn't help himself. "I'm looking at him and seeing how smart he is," Kraft remembers, "how passionate, how full of life. And I'm thinking of so many other friends I have who are just, 'Woe is me.' . . . I haven't been moved like this by someone in a long, long time."

I know what he means. I spoke to Sam for a half hour and felt as if I were talking to a U.S. senator.

Wait. I felt as if I were talking to somebody with much more sense, charm and polish than a U.S. senator.

"I was so inspired by Mr. Kraft," Sam says. "Maybe because we're alike in so many aspects. I'm extremely inspired by how he approaches things and who he is as a person . . . I am so grateful that he's given this initial push, this initial mobilization, to finding a cure and helping so many."

You know many 16-year-olds who talk like that? Or 66-year-olds?

At one point in the terrific HBO film, Sam says, "I didn't put myself in front of you for you to feel bad for me. You don't need to feel bad for me . . . I want you to get to know me. This is my life."

Where does he get the courage not to feel sorry for himself, or beg for it in others?

"Sometimes I do feel badly," he says. "When this happens, the first thing I do is accept the fact that I feel bad about it. The second thing I do is remember that most of the time I feel happy. And that's how I negotiate through that feeling and get past it."

See what I mean?

At one point, Kraft showed Sam, a Patriots fan since birth, the Patriots' three Super Bowl trophies. It filled Sam with awe and hope.

"Hopefully this run isn't quite over," Sam told me. "We're going to try to keep getting better and keep this going."

Do, Sam. Please do.

Postscript: *Thanks in part to readers, we easily topped Kraft's $500,000 matching grant. Then Sam celebrated his 17th birthday by going to Game 1 of the World Series at Fenway Park, where he got a standing O. The next month he dropped the puck at a Bruins game. The Pats were about to honor him at their January 12, 2014, playoff game when they got the news: Sam had died suddenly the night before.*

Fringe

(In Which I Leave the Sports Yard Without Permission)

Presidential Fantasy

October 20, 2008

I have the absolute worst fantasy league football partner. Just try to get the guy to return a call. Or a text. You need a damn court order.

He's Barack Obama. And, yeah, I guess he's busy, but why was I the one who had to fly to Dayton, get frisked and have bomb dogs drool on my bags just so I could meet him getting off his tricked-out, chartered 757? He can't meet a guy halfway?

I asked each candidate to be my running mate for one week in a fantasy league, just to see what kind of president he'd make—how he'd handle decisions under pressure and balance a budget.

Still, you talk about bossy. I thought he'd let the professional sportswriter do most of the picking while the wonk occasionally looked up from some Pakistan brief and nodded. Yeah, not exactly. When I got on his campaign bus, all three flat screens were tuned to ESPN. Obama was sitting in a black leather swivel chair, reading the paper. "Hey, man, I'll be with you in a second," he said. "I'm poring over the latest economic news." It was the *USA Today* NFL stats page.

He is taller, grayer and quicker to laugh than I expected. Moves sort of like an athlete—cool and smooth. "Now, you're the expert," he began. "And I'll gladly be the junior partner in this, but I really think we should take Drew Brees. He could have a big week. Oakland's secondary is a wreck."

Ohhhh, so that's how it's going to be. "Well, I like Carson Palmer," I said. "He's due for a big week, plus he plays in Ohio and I figure that's a state you need, so . . ."

He looked at me like I'd stuck my elbow in his soup. "Man, this is more important than politics!" he insisted. "This is football!"

This is a man who could potentially audit me forever. We paid $7.3M for Brees.

He wanted Clinton Portis. I wanted Adrian Peterson. We took Portis ($6.6M). He wanted Brandon Marshall. I wanted Bernard Berrian. We took Marshall ($5.7M).

Doesn't work well with others. Check.

Have to admit, though, he knows his stuff. Turns out, he played a little. He was a tight end in ninth grade until a coach told him to "trample" an opponent's back. He gave up football for hoops. In 2004, when Mike Ditka considered running against him for Senate, Obama—remembering how Ditka let William Perry score a Super Bowl TD instead of Walter Payton—said that "anybody who would give the ball to Refrigerator Perry instead of Sweetness doesn't have very good judgment." Ditka didn't run. "Too bad," Obama says. "We were hoping he would."

Likes to bait Hall of Famers. Check.

It took us thirty minutes to pick nine slots. The man was into it. I said I'd need to talk to him the following week about how we did.

"Cool," he said. "How's Tuesday?"

"Sorry," I said. "Getting married Tuesday."

He looked stunned. "Who'd marry you?"

Wise guy. Check.

We wound up in a dark tunnel under Fifth Third Field in Dayton for a campaign event. He was telling me a story about throwing out a first pitch when suddenly I heard over the PA system, ". . . the next president of the United States, Barack Obama!" He looked at me, said, "Gotta go!" and sprinted up some steps to a thunderclap of a roar.

Afterward, while signing books, he asked if I thought we'd win. "Win?" I said. "There's like a gazillion teams in this thing!"

He glared a hole in me. "You think we're just messing around?"

Then Sunday came. Man, did he get lucky. The guys he made us choose—Brees and Portis—went nuts. The guys I wanted, not so much. We finished 32,190th for the week. But wait! That put us in the 81.2 percentile, which means we beat four out of every five teams!

Of course, he already knew. Because, like so many Americans, he was checking the fantasy stats all day, even while he was supposed to be prepping for his final debate. He e-mailed to say he wished he had followed my advice on Berrian (who smoked Marshall), but he was "pumped up" about our numbers. And he congratulated the newlyweds.

I e-mailed back and said that if he wins this election, the ambassadorship to Tahiti would make a nice wedding present.

Postscript: *Ronald Reagan was once a sportscaster. Richard Nixon always wanted to be a sportswriter. But we've never had a president as tuned in to sports as Barack Obama. He's an admitted* SportsCenter *freak, relishes his Chicago teams and even has the audacity to fill out his March Madness bracket each year on ESPN, where he's finished in the top third of the millions who fill one out with him.*

How I'd Fix the Economy

July 1, 2009

This Great Recession is on us like a golf club head cover. Every direction you look, blackness. I meet people every day who are working twice as hard for half the pay in offices that would make a morgue look cheery.

It's tough. It's brutal. It's depressing. And that's just the break-room fridge.

But I have a solution. What offices need right now is a little bit of sports.

If there's one thing games teach us, it's to buck up, dig in and hold on. That's what we cherish about sports—the faith that no matter how bad things suck, eventually you're going to win. How else do you explain Cubs fans?

For instance, what if—like in hockey—the boss picked the three stars of the day? And those three people came out of their cubicles and did a little spin around the main lobby carpet while the other employees banged their staplers on their desks in approval?

What if the office had chest bumps and shaving-cream pies and everybody slapping the "Work Like a Champion Today" sign over the door on the way in?

And office chatter!

C'monKidHeyKidOnlyTakesOneBuyerKidOnlyTakesOneYouAndHer KidRightOnThe DottedLineKid.

What if every accounting office came with cheerleaders?

Two, Four, Six, Eight!
What Do We Depreciate?
Corporate-Owned Vehicles!

Everything we need to know about the economic recovery we learned in sports: Back each other up, hustle for everything and get it back one score at a time.

The office needs hotfoots and butt slaps and Gatorade showers. And a room where people can go and bust the bejesus out of a cheap toilet with a bat every once in a while, just to get it out of their system.

When a really great secretary hits 65 and has to go, why not retire her number?

Dolores Ginty, no one will ever use extension 3713 again. It's yours forever!

Like baseball, firms should have some political bigwig come and throw out the first pitch of the day.

Mrs. Finsterwald? This is Governor Bloom. How would you like to own a vacuum that could change your life?

Work needs Rings of Fame along the office walls and tailgating instead of lunchrooms. At the end of the day, everybody makes human tunnels for everybody else to run through. Orange slices now and again would be nice, too. When the big sales drive starts, guys should grow playoff beards and women should stop shaving their legs, and everybody should start wearing their Jason Giambi lucky gold lamé thong and refuse to take it off until we're back in the black.

There's nothing better in golf than a good caddie, right? So why can't businesspeople have them?

All right, Mr. Grey, here comes the big client and his wife. Don't forget, she's been on that Oreo diet, so tell her she looks like she lost some weight. And remember, he can't hear out of his left ear, so stay right. You TOTALLY got this!

Tiger Woods wears red on Sundays for low numbers. Businesspeople need to start wearing green on Fridays for cash. And if they sign the big deal, let's watch it again on instant replay!

Look, we Americans are as resilient as Slinkys. As a country, we are too young and bouncy to let this get us down much longer. This is a time to turn our hats around backward and bring out our rally monkeys and start rattling the window shades. Don't make fewer business trips, make more! Don't buy less stock, buy more! Every office needs an organist playing "Charge!"

Think like athletes. Write "No Prisoners" on the soles of your shoes. Ask each other for autographs. And at the end of the month, put together a "One Shining Moment" highlight reel. Then, somebody, pull out the softball cooler of beer.

Pretty soon, as sure as cops love donuts, this will turn around. And we'll be using sports stuff we never thought we'd use.

Hey, nobody talk to Achmed. He's made a sale on every call so far today! Don't jinx it!

When everybody gets their job back and unemployment in this country is once again under 5 percent, here's what I'll do: If you see me in a bar, I'll buy you a jigger of your favorite adult beverage. But you get only twenty-four seconds once I walk in.

After all, I've got a shot clock.

Postscript: *Unemployment is still nowhere near 5 percent, but a few fine Americans have nonetheless purchased me a free shot in anticipation.*

Playing for Pay

July 12, 2011

SANDWICH, England—For the 116th straight season, it looks as if American golf is going to get through another year without a labor stoppage. Arnold Palmers for everybody.

Not true in the NFL and the NBA—both are in lockouts now— but how we don't have one in golf I'll never know. If anybody should strike, it's golfers. They have the worst deal since the Winklevoss twins met Mark Zuckerberg.

Not one of them has a guaranteed contract. In golf, you're promised zilch. You play good, you eat good. You play bad and you're suddenly working behind your uncle's pharmacy counter.

Per diem? Please. In golf, "per diem" translates as "What my wife gives me in the morning."

Contract year? Every year is your contract year.

Disabled list? Get real. If you break your hand in golf, you'd better have Aflac.

You think if Tiger Woods played in the NBA he'd be limping around these past two years without a biweekly paycheck? Are you smoking oregano? In the NBA, he still would have made his many millions per year and the owner would help him wheelbarrow it to the bank.

Look at Greg Oden, the rarely dressed center for the NBA's Portland Trail Blazers. In four seasons, he has played eighty-two games. That's one season spread over four. If he were a golfer, he'd be in Columbus running a big and tall man's shop. But in the NBA, he has made $19.3 million. Nice work if you can get it.

Golf might look as though it's all cashmere and courtesy cars, but in reality, these guys get squat.

In golf, you pay for your own transportation, your own meals, your own medical, your own lodging. You think Tom Brady pays his own bill when he checks out of the Miami Four Seasons? Phil Mickelson does.

LeBron James can stink up the finals like six inches of Limburger cheese and he still gets his cash. In golf, if you come to a major and freeze, all you're going home with is an ulcer.

You wanna see a pro golfer laugh? Tell him that the NBA players are hacked off about possibly having their average salary of $6 million trimmed in this lockout. Do you know how many guys on the PGA Tour made that last year? One: Jim Furyk.

"It's hard to really imagine that kind of world," says Justin Leonard, who will play his nineteenth British Open here Thursday at Royal St. George's. "Guaranteed contracts, no matter what? The rookie salaries? Wow. I can't get my head around all that. That's my incentive to play! I'm kinda proud we start at zero every week."

The only tiny morsel golfers have negotiated for themselves is that every year on Tour, a set of 125 guys are promised a chance to make a living. This is not to be confused with promised a living. If you can get there, you have a tee time, but only half of you will be cashing a check.

"We do have one thing those guys don't," says Tom Watson, who has won the British Open five times. "We get to choose where we play. NBA players don't."

True, and when golfers choose not to play somewhere, they get murdered. Kenny Perry, for instance, got ripped for not playing the British Open for many years. But look at it from his wallet's POV:

- Two round-trip business-class tickets, Kentucky to London: $6,000
- Caddie for the week: $1,500
- Seven nights at the players' hotel: $6,000
- Twenty-one meals at that hotel, where the dollar is limper than the cucumber sandwiches: $2,100
- Transfers, tips, etc.: $750
- Total: $16,350

So, before Perry can break even, he has to beat half the best players in the world in a style of golf he hates.

Good luck!

Golfers have the worst job security this side of Naomi Campbell's assistants. These guys are out there on their own skill and their own guts and their own dime, and they deserve some credit for it. You get the yips or a sore back or an ungrateful putter, we'll see you on the Hooters Tour.

Remember Trevor Immelman? Good-looking kid? Won the 2008 Masters? If he were in the NFL, he'd have signed a five-year deal for $75 million. Instead, he goes out and can't find a fairway with a course map, makes $1.3 million over the next three years, and must be wishing he had gone on to optometry school.

But none of that is what would drive your basic American multi-millionaire team-sport union-backed jocks nuts.

What would drive them nuts is the part of golf's unspoken contract that says: You call your own fouls. On yourself. Even if nobody saw it. Can you imagine if guys called fouls on themselves in the NBA?

We'd still be waiting.

Postscript: *Actually got a nice note from PGA Tour Commissioner Tim Finchem on this one, which is amazing, since he mostly loathes me more than crabgrass.*

The Sins of the Father

July 13, 2012

What a fool I was.

In 1986, I spent a week in State College, Pennsylvania, research-ing a ten-page *Sports Illustrated* Sportsman of the Year piece on Joe Paterno.

It was supposed to be a secret, but one night the phone in my hotel room rang. It was a Penn State professor, calling out of the blue.

"Are you here to take part in hagiography?" he said.

"What's hagiography?" I asked.

"The study of saints," he said. "You're going to be just like the rest, aren't you? You're going to make Paterno out to be a saint. You don't know him. He'll do anything to win. What you media are doing is dangerous."

Jealous egghead, I figured.

What an idiot I was.

Twenty-five years later, when former Penn State defensive coordi-nator Jerry Sandusky was accused of a fifteen-year reign of pedophilia on young boys, I thought Paterno was too old and too addled to understand, too grandfatherly and Catholic to get that Sandusky was committing grisly crimes using Paterno's own football program as bait.

But I was wrong. Paterno knew. He knew all about it. He'd known for years. He knew and he followed it vigilantly.

That's all clear now after Penn State's own investigator, former FBI director Louis Freeh, came out Thursday and hung the whole disgusting canvas on a wall for us. Showed us the e-mails, read us the interviews, shined a black light on all of the lies they left behind. It cost $6.5 million and took eight months, and the truth it uncovered was 100 times uglier than the bills.

Paterno knew about a mother's cry that Sandusky had molested her son in 1998. Later, Paterno lied to a grand jury and said he didn't. Paterno and university president Graham Spanier and vice president Gary Schultz and athletic director Tim Curley all knew what kind of sick coach they had on the payroll in Sandusky. Schultz had pertinent questions. "Is this opening of pandora's box?" he wrote in personal notes on the case. "Other children?" "Sexual improprieties?"

It gets worse. According to Freeh, Spanier, Schultz and Curley were set to call child services on Sandusky in February 2001 until Paterno apparently talked them out of it. Curley wasn't "comfortable" going to child services after that talk with JoePa.

Yeah, that's the most important thing, your comfort.

What'd they do instead? Alerted nobody. Called nobody. And let Sandusky keep leading his horrific tours around campus. "Hey, want to see the showers?" That sentence alone ought to bring down the statue.

What a stooge I was.

I talked about Paterno's "true legacy" in all of this. Here's his true legacy: Paterno let a child molester go when he could've stopped him. He let him go and then lied to cover his sinister tracks. He let a rapist go to save his own recruiting successes and fund-raising pitches and big-fish-small-pond hide.

Here's legacy for you. Paterno's cowardice and ego and fears allowed Sandusky to molest at least eight more boys in the years after
that 1998 incident—Victims 1, 2, 3, 4, 5, 8, 9 and 10. Just to recap: By
not acting, a grown man failed to protect eight boys from years of
molestation, abuse and self-loathing, all to save his program the embarrassment. The mother of Victim 1 is "filled with hatred toward
Joe Paterno," the victim's lawyer says. "She just hates him, and reviles
him." Can you blame her?

What a sap I was.

I hope Penn State loses civil suits until the walls of the accounting
office cave in. I hope that Spanier, Schultz and Curley go to prison for
perjury. I hope the NCAA gives Penn State the death penalty it most
richly deserves. The worst scandal in college football history deserves
the worst penalty the NCAA can give. They gave it to SMU for winning without regard for morals. They should give it to Penn State for
the same thing. The only difference is, at Penn State they didn't pay
for it with Corvettes. They paid for it with lives.

What a chump I was.

I tweeted that, yes, Paterno should be fired, but that he was, overall, "a good and decent man." I was wrong. Good and decent men
don't do what Paterno did. Good and decent men protect kids, not
rapists. And to think "Paterno" comes from "father" in Italian.

This throws a can of black paint on anything anybody tells me
about Paterno from here on in. "No NCAA violations in all those
years." I believe it. He was great at hiding stuff. "He gave $4 million
to the library." In exchange for what? "He cared about kids away from
the football field." No, he didn't. Not all of them. Not when it really
mattered.

What a tool I was.

As Joe Paterno lay dying, I actually felt sorry for him. Little did I
know he was taking all of his dirty secrets to the grave. Nine days
before he died, he had the *Washington Post*'s Sally Jenkins in his
kitchen. He could've admitted it then. Could've tried a simple "I'm

sorry." But he didn't. Instead, he just lied deeper. Right to her face. Right to all of our faces.

That professor was right, all those years ago. I was engaging in hagiography. So was that school. So was that town. It was dangerous. Turns out it builds monsters.

Not all of them ended up in prison.

Postscript: *I've had very bad luck with my* Sports Illustrated *Sportsman of the Year profiles. I wrote Joe Paterno in 1986. The Sandusky cover-up threw sludge all over it. I wrote Lance Armstrong in 2002. He goes down in history as Pinocchio. But it's not just me.* SI *also gave the Sportsman of the Year covers to both Mark McGwire and Sammy Sosa in 2002. This sports thing, it's a dirty business.*

Remember the Children

November 2, 2011

This is not about Joe Paterno.

If these boys really were molested, groped and raped by a middle-aged ex–Penn State football coach, then whatever misjudgment Paterno made will be a single lit match compared to the bonfire these boys will walk in for years to come.

Many of them won't be able to trust. Won't be able to love. Won't be able to feel—nor trust or love themselves.

Don't feel sorry for Paterno. He's had his life. Feel sorry for these boys, because they may never get one.

Ask former NHL All-Star Theo Fleury, who has reached out on Twitter and radio to the alleged victims of Jerry Sandusky. Fleury was sexually molested once or twice a week for two years by his youth hockey coach, Graham James. It twisted Fleury so inside out that he numbed himself for years with booze, cocaine and strippers. He blew much of the $50 million he made in the NHL trying to forget. He'd entrusted his hockey dreams to a man who flayed open his soul for his own sexual perversions and left him hollow.

"I no longer had faith in myself or my own judgment," Fleury, 43, wrote in his book, *Playing With Fire*. "Once it's gone, how do you get it back? . . . I became a f—ing raging, alcoholic lunatic."

Ask former Red Wing, Flame and Bruin Sheldon Kennedy. He was sexually molested by James every Tuesday and Thursday night at parent-approved sleepovers at James's house from age 14 to 19. This snake even took Fleury and Kennedy to Disneyland, where he groped them, by turn, in a motel room. It left Kennedy so shamed and confused that suicide looked better to him than living with the guilt of it another day.

"You can't trust anybody afterwards," Kennedy said yesterday from Toronto, where he runs RespectGroupInc.com, an organization that teaches adults how to recognize abuse. "So you tend to live a very lonely life. You mask the horrible way you're feeling with sex and gambling and drugs. You put all these walls up. You keep saying, 'Why didn't I say anything? I must've done something wrong. I let him do it to me.'"

Imagine: One reported victim in the Penn State case, now 24, has been living with that kind of hole growing inside him since he made allegations against Sandusky in 1998—thirteen years ago. Those allegations never led to charges. That's thirteen years of not being believed, of knowing his alleged perpetrator was out there, volunteering at high schools and running his grisly camp "tours" of the shower room.

The horror of it makes you want to punch somebody. If Kennedy could talk to boys Sandusky might have abused who haven't come forward yet?

"Tell someone," says Kennedy, now 42. "Because people are going to believe you. People know it's not your fault."

No, this isn't about 84-year-old Joe Paterno not taking more steps that might have stopped it. It's about everybody not taking more steps that might have stopped it. Not parents, not teachers, not uncles, not friends, not counselors.

Imagine: Victim One, according to the Harrisburg (Pa.) *Patriot-News*, was often taken out of class by Sandusky to be further molested. Just taken out of school by somebody who wasn't his parent, with no questions asked, until his mother finally called the principal and asked her to check in to it. Later that day, the principal called back in tears. "You need to come down here right now."

According to a 1998 study on child sexual abuse by Boston University Medical School, one in six boys in America will be abused by age 16. For girls, it's one in four by the age of 14. Those "If you see something, say something" billboards shouldn't just be about terrorism. They may apply to sex abuse, too. Doesn't matter if it's your uncle, your longtime assistant coach, or your buddy. You HAVE to say something. And yet, precious few people have the guts to say anything at all.

"The fear is too strong," Kennedy says. "People don't know what to do. They think, 'Oh my god, how bad is this going to look? What are we going to do now that we've let this guy operate right under our noses? We better keep quiet.' But it can't work like that anymore."

Does Kennedy blame Paterno?

"Does he have grandkids? [Yes, 17.] How would he feel if it were one of his grandkids in that shower with the coach? What would he have done? Somehow, the perpetrator felt welcome at that school. We need systems in place that make perpetrators feel unwelcome."

What must those boys feel like, right now, as all this darkness gets played out in front of the camera lights?

"Probably second-guessing themselves," Kennedy says. "Coming forward doesn't get these boys any further ahead in life. It isn't easy. But it has to happen."

The road these boys are on now is endless and buckled and uphill. Some will hate their parents for not protecting them and hate themselves for hating them. They will hate the pervert for tricking them and hate themselves for being tricked. And just when they think this cruel and long legal process is over, it can start all over again.

Imagine: Kennedy's abuser, James, got three and a half years but was pardoned by the Canadian National Parole Board in 2007. Currently, he is out on bail, awaiting sentencing on nine more counts of sexual abuse and who knows how many more sinister trips to motel rooms.

If all these charges turn out to be true, though, soon he and Sandusky will both be going to prison—a place where, with any luck, they will feel most unwelcome.

Postscript: *It was all true, of course. Sandusky was found guilty of forty-five counts of child sexual abuse and was sentenced to thirty to sixty years. James remains a free man.*

Collins's Ex-Fiancée
Offers Support

April 30, 2013

So you were shocked to hear that 7-foot NBA center Jason Collins is gay? You should talk to Carolyn Moos. She was engaged to him.

Moos, a former Stanford and WNBA center, dated Collins for eight years and was to marry him in 2009 until he suddenly called it off with a month to go.

Then: hurt, confusion and embarrassment. Today: answers.

Collins told Moos last weekend over the phone before coming out, the first male active American team-sport pro athlete to do so, in a *Sports Illustrated* story Monday.

"I had to sit down," says Moos, now a personal trainer and nutritional consultant. "I was shocked. There's no words to really describe my reaction. . . . But this does alleviate some of the pain. . . . I'm so happy for him. He deserves to live the life he wants."

Nobody—not fiancées, not four years' worth of teammates at Stanford, not six teams' worth of NBA teammates—saw this coming.

Especially not Mike McDonald, a childhood friend and former

Stanford teammate. A month ago, Collins stopped by the McDonalds' home to see their new baby. For the past nine months, McDonald noticed Collins was more stressed than usual, wasn't quite his bubbly self.

"What are your plans for next season?" McDonald asked.

"Well," Collins said, "it's kinda up in the air right now, because I'm gay."

Pause. Blink. Look at wife. Look back at Collins.

"Yeah?" McDonald said.

"Yeah," Collins said.

"Well . . . congratulations!" McDonald said. Hugs all around. The baby in the middle somewhere.

Collins told McDonald he was planning to out himself. He told him he was ready to live his life in the open. When you're 7 feet tall, there are not a lot of places to hide. The closet must've felt very cramped.

"Nothing, ever, made me think he might be gay," McDonald says.

Not canceling a wedding with a month to go?

"Nope. He just said there was a lot of stuff going on, that he just couldn't go through with it. . . . I'm happy for him. He seemed relieved to tell his friends."

Collins is now the Jackie Robinson of gay athletes and, like Robinson, strong enough for the job. He's universally loved in the NBA. He's smart, funny and a wheelbarrow full of sunshine in the locker room. He only cares about defense, not scoring points, which is why he'll probably sign for one last season—his thirteenth—somewhere in the league this fall.

Playing everywhere from New Jersey to Memphis to Minnesota to Atlanta to Boston to Washington, he's got more friends than Jim Nantz. He couldn't tell them all ahead of time. One of those was Stanford teammate, Grizzlies teammate and buddy Casey Jacobsen, now playing in Germany.

"I was disappointed, I guess," says Jacobsen, 32. "I've always said that if I ever had a gay teammate, I'd hope he'd feel he could share that with me and know that he wouldn't be judged by me. . . . But I get it. He's in the spotlight now. And I'm so proud of him. If there was one guy to break down this barrier, he's the guy."

Jacobsen's entire team heard the news together in the locker room after practice Monday and it sparked a discussion about how the towel-snapping world of jocks would welcome a gay teammate.

"There were a few ignorant statements, of course," Jacobsen says. "Like, 'I don't know if I'd be comfortable with that.' And I said, 'You guys, you're fooling yourselves if you don't think you've already played with a gay teammate.' I knew I had. I just didn't know who. Turned out to be Jason."

This whole I-don't-know-if-I'm-comfortable argument about gay athletes is 99.9 percent fear and 0.1 percent reality. It's paranoia in high tops. A locker room is about the worst pickup place in the world. It's not like a gay teammate is going to come up to somebody in the team shower and go, "Hey, is this bar stool empty?" It stinks, everybody's exhausted, and the coach is usually yelling at you. And besides, who says you're his type?

"I don't think it'd be weird to have a gay roommate on the road," Jacobsen says. "I don't think it'd be weird to shower with a gay teammate. My ego is not so big that I think every gay man thinks I'm a catch."

If anything, feel glad for Jason Collins that it's all over. All the hiding, all the lies, all the secrets. He had to hurt some people to keep them, starting with the woman he promised to marry.

"I'd mapped out my life completely," recalls Moos, 34. "I knew I wanted to be married, wanted to have children, live in this city, send my kids to this school. . . . I invested eight years in something. . . . To be able to recover from that is not an easy process. . . . But I'm glad Jason can be his own person now. I'm glad he can walk in his own shoes."

Be happy for Jason Collins, the ultimate NBA free agent. He's an agent of change now. And he's finally free.

Postscript: *Collins signed with the New Jersey Nets in late February of 2014. But as things turn out, he wouldn't have been the first gay team-sport athlete anyway. Read on . . .*

Before Jason Collins

May 15, 2013

The world is throwing a parade for Jason Collins, the 7-foot free-agent NBA center who came out last month. He was hugged by Oprah, celebrated by *Good Morning America*, and congratulated by President Obama.

But nobody seems to remember baseball's Glenn Burke, who tried to come out nearly forty years ago and was stuffed back in.

"How's Jason Collins going to talk about being the first?" says Burke's agent, Abdul-Jalil al-Hakim. "Glenn Burke was the first. And he wasn't any free agent, either. He was in the lineup."

Glenn Burke was a barrel-chested jokester, a singing, dancing, one-man cabaret. His teammates called him King Kong. In high school, the 6-foot Burke could dunk two basketballs at once, in street shoes. He roamed center field for the Los Angeles Dodgers and the Oakland A's in the late 1970s.

Burke was the pulse of the clubhouse. He wore a red jock. He'd jump in the backs of pink Rolls-Royces after games. He invented the high five (with Dusty Baker). Oh, yes, he did.

He was as out as an athlete could be in the mid-1970s. It wasn't that he was flaunting it. It was that he couldn't keep it in.

"When we'd land at airports," remembers Davey Lopes, the Dodgers' second baseman, "there'd always be guys waiting for Glenn. We'd go our way and he'd go off on his merry way. We'd go to clubs and women would hand him their numbers. But he'd never call 'em. Didn't matter to us. We loved him."

In the famous 1977 Dodgers–Yankees World Series—starring Reggie Jackson, Thurman Munson, Steve Garvey and Ron Cey— only one rookie cracked either starting lineup: Glenn Burke.

"Nobody tripped that he was gay," says Burke's longtime pal Doug Harris, who produced the documentary *Out* about Burke in 2010. "The people who tripped off it were the Dodgers [management]. They didn't want to talk about it. He was trying to tell reporters, but they said they couldn't write that stuff."

The atmosphere in Burke's time was far more hostile to gays than it is in Jason Collins's time. Few gay characters in movies. No states where gay marriage was legal. "You couldn't put [anything] gay in an ad or anything," remembers al-Hakim. "That was a no-no. The reporters didn't want to write it. You couldn't go there."

Glenn Burke was so out that the Dodgers' front office finally called him in, laid a $75,000 check on the desk and offered to pay for his wedding if he'd just get married—soon.

Burke started laughing.

"I guess you mean to a woman, right?"

Then he walked out, without the check.

"Glenn told me he wasn't the first Dodger called in and presented a check," says childhood friend Vince Trahan. "They'd done it with gay players before. The difference was Glenn didn't take it."

None of this helped his career. Nor did palling around with Dodgers manager Tommy Lasorda's colorfully gay son, Spunky, according to Burke's 1995 autobiography, *Out at Home*.

But friends of Burke say they were never a couple, despite

what you've read. "Glenn never had an intimate relationship with Tommy's son," says Trahan. "He wasn't attracted to the real flamboyant types."

Didn't matter. Next thing Burke knew, early in the 1978 season, he was traded to pitiful Oakland, despite Lopes and others walking into the office of general manager Al Campanis to complain.

A year and a half later, during spring training, new A's manager Billy Martin greeted Burke by sitting his team down in center field, pointing to Burke and saying, "Boys, this is Glenn Burke. He's a faggot."

That's when everything stopped being so funny.

"In those days, a guy did one of two things when a friend was out," says Lopes, now the Dodgers' first-base coach. "He'd either support him, or the pendulum would swing the other way and he'd avoid him. A lot of ballplayers back then would stay away. Guys were afraid somebody would start saying the same thing about them."

Cue the movie montage: Catcalls from fans. Latino players mumbling "maricon," a gay slur in Spanish under their breath. Nobody within twenty feet of him in the showers.

Injured, he packed his bag for the minors—Utah, to be exact.

To a partying gay ballplayer from Berkeley, a minor league team in Utah is hell on earth. Twenty-five games into the 1980 season, Burke and his tortured .237 batting average retired, after only four years in the major leagues.

"Had he taken that check the Dodgers offered," says Trahan, "his career would've gone on and on. He could've relaxed and played great baseball. But he wasn't going to lie. He was going to be true to who he was."

He was welcomed into The Castro as a conquering hero. "They can't ever say now that a gay man can't play in the majors," he'd brag, "because I'm a gay man and I made it."

But soon enough, he stopped making it. He became depressed. He became a cocaine addict. Then homeless. Then he contracted AIDS.

He died in 1995, at 42. They buried King Kong in Oakland, under a small stone, grave No. 3171.

Jason Collins came out of the closet and was put on magazine covers. Glenn Burke came out and got covered up. The president never called.

"I'm happy for Jason Collins," says Trahan. "But he wasn't the first. He was the first in this new era, this new time of acceptance of gays, gay marriages, gays on TV, all that. He wasn't the first. He was just the first who was listened to."

You say Glenn Burke was born too soon, but that's not exactly right. The problem was all the people born without the courage to stand up for a friend, a colleague, an employee.

Yes, Jason Collins was courageous to come out. But if others back then had the guts Glenn Burke had, Collins wouldn't have needed courage at all.

Postscript: *When they make the movie of Glenn Burke's life—and they should—they need to point out that he was the first pro baseball player to also play college basketball at the same time.*

Let's Keep Rolling

September 6, 2011

The first battle in the renewed war against terrorism wasn't waged in Fallujah or Kandahar or Tikrit. It was held 32,000 feet above Pittsburgh, on September 11, 2001.

And it wasn't soldiers who led the battle.

It was four athletes, pushing a food cart.

United Flight 93 was supposed to go from Newark to San Francisco that Tuesday morning, but 31-year-old Jeremy Glick wasn't supposed to be on it.

He was supposed to go the day before, but a fire at Newark Airport forced him to re-book for the next day, one of the bloodiest in American history.

About forty-five minutes into the flight, four radical Islamic terrorists stormed the cockpit, sliced the throats of the pilots and took charge. They told the thirty-three passengers and seven crew members they were hijacking the plane and returning to Newark.

Glick, a muscular 1993 national collegiate judo champion, scampered back to the second-to-last row and called his wife, Lyz. It wasn't long before he and the others—talking to their families—realized that nobody was going back to Newark. They were on board a 150,000-pound missile, bound for some unthinkable end. The World Trade Center towers and the Pentagon had already been hit. What was 93 aimed for?

"We're going to rush the hijackers," Glick told Lyz.

Horrified, she pictured the hijackers having machine guns.

"No," Jeremy said. "Box cutters."

And Lyz says, "I was thinking, 'OK, Jeremy can handle a man with a knife, no problem. With him being so strong, and with his experience in martial arts and judo, he's going to unleash some terrible force. That's no match for him.'"

Mark Bingham, 31, was back there with Glick. He'd won two national club rugby titles with Cal-Berkeley. He was huge, fierce, funny and, incidentally, gay. He once wrestled a gun from a mugger. A knife wasn't going to scare him.

"I remember Mark and his buddies got thrown off an entire island once," says his dad, Jerry. "He told me, 'Dad, we lost the match, but we won the fight.' I know how he was. He'd have definitely been kickin' ass and takin' names."

The third was Oracle salesman Todd Beamer, 32, a former shortstop at Wheaton (Illinois) College, a basketball star, and a soccer player.

"I knew, when I saw what happened," says his dad, David, "that Todd would be part of that. Todd was not going to be sitting in his seat while somebody was trying to crash the plane."

The fourth was 38-year-old Tom Burnett, a former high school football star from Bloomington, Minnesota. These men became convinced that they had to stop the plane, even if they had to stop it with their lives.

"I know we're going to die," Burnett told his wife, Deena. "Some of us are going to do something about it."

There certainly were more passengers among the thirty-three on board who planned the insurrection and stormed the cockpit, but we know about these four. All of them jocks. All of them with the physical and mental training to rise up when all seems lost. This is the best guess of what they did:

"We're going to attack," Glick told Lyz. "I'm going to put the phone down. I love you. I'll be right back."

Lyz couldn't hold the line. What she was hearing was sending her body into convulsions. She handed the phone to her dad and walked into a different room.

Beamer revealed the same plan to the operator, Lisa Jefferson, who was sitting in a call center in Oak brook, Illinois. When it was time, he let the phone dangle so he could keep the line open in case he made it back alive. She heard Beamer say to the others, "Let's roll." It's a phrase that would later be stenciled on jet fighters, NASCAR rides and above locker room doors.

Using a food-service cart as a battering ram, the attackers raced up the aisle and smashed through the cockpit door. It was almost 10 a.m.

"My dad said first he heard a series of screams," Lyz recalls. "Then he heard another set of screams. Then it all sounded like a roller coaster, up and down. And then it just . . . [pause] . . . ended."

Officials believe that the terrorists, being buckled in, rocked the plane up and down violently, trying to fling the passengers against the ceiling. Excerpts of the cockpit voice recorder tape are chilling. (Words in parentheses are translated from the Arabic.)

09:58:52—Stay back.

09:58:55—In the cockpit.

09:58:57—In the cockpit.

09:58:57—(They want to get in here. Hold, hold from the inside. Hold from the inside. Hold.)

09:59:04—Hold the door.

09:59:09—Stop him.

09:59:11—Sit down.

09:59:15—Sit down.

09:59:16—Unintelligible.

09:59:17—(What?)

09:59:18—(There are some guys. All those guys.)

09:59:20—Let's get them.

09:59:25—Sit down.

09:59:29—(What?)

09:59:36—Unintelligible.

09:59:42—(Trust in Allah, and in him.)

09:59:45—Sit down.

09:59:47—Unintelligible.

09:59:53—Ahh.

10:00:06—(There is nothing.)

10:00:07—(Is that it? Shall we finish it off?)

10:00:08—(No. Not yet.)

10:00:09—(When they all come, we finish it off.)

10:00:11—(There is nothing.)

10:00:13—Unintelligible.

10:00:14—Ahh.

10:00:15—I'm injured.

10:00:16—Unintelligible.

10:00:21—Ahh.

10:00:22—(Oh Allah. Oh Allah. Oh gracious.)

10:00:25—In the cockpit. If we don't, we'll die.

10:00:29—(Up, down. Up, down, in the) cockpit.

10:00:33—(The) cockpit.

10:00:37—(Up, down. Saeed, up, down.)

10:00:42—Roll it.

10:00:55—Unintelligible.

10:00:59—(Allah is the greatest. Allah is the greatest.)

10:01:01—Unintelligible.

10:01:08—(Is that it? I mean, shall we pull it down?)

10:01:09—(Yes, put it in it, and pull it down.)

10:01:11—(Saeed.)

10:01:12—. . . engine . . .

10:01:16—(Cut off the oxygen.)

10:01:18—(Cut off the oxygen. Cut off the oxygen. Cut off the oxygen.)

10:01:37—Unintelligible.

10:01:41—(Up, down. Up, down.)

10:01:41—(What?)

10:01:42—(Up, down.)

10:01:42—Ahh.

10:01:59—Shut them off.

10:02:03—Shut them off.

10:02:14—Go.

10:02:16—Move.

10:02:17—Turn it up.

10:02:18—(Down, down.)

10:02:23—(Pull it down. Pull it down.)

10:02:25—Down. Push, push, push, push, push.

10:02:33—(Hey. Hey. Give it to me. Give it to me.)

10:02:35—(Give it to me. Give it to me. Give it to me.)

10:02:40—Unintelligible.

United Flight 93 dove into a remote field in southwestern Pennsylvania, near Shanksville, killing all aboard. People ten miles away said they felt the ground shake. It's believed the plane was headed for the U.S. Capitol in Washington, D.C.

"This was the first victory of the war," says David Beamer. "The Capitol dome still stands."

The hole left by the Boeing 757 was twenty-four feet wide and eighteen feet deep. But the hole it put in those left behind sometimes feels even bigger.

This may be why Todd Beamer's wife, Lisa, does not talk about 9/11 or Shanksville or "Let's roll." She is raising her three kids—13, 11 and 9—alone. She didn't remarry.

In Church Hill, Tennessee, Mark Bingham's dad doesn't need an anniversary to remember his son. He thinks about him every day.

"I haven't been right since," Jerry Bingham says, crying softly. "We work on it every day. You think you're gettin' through it, but you don't. You just don't. Not a day goes by that it's not on your mind, ever."

But not all his memories are painful. President Bush invited the Flight 93 families to the White House the week after 9/11. Afterward, the families were being escorted out the back way of the East Wing. They were surprised to turn a corner and see that 150 to 200 White House workers had lined up on either side of them. They were applauding.

"The dishwashers, the cooks, the maids, the busboys," says Bingham. "They were clapping for us. They were thanking us. It just tore me up. And we were all crying and hugging each other. I'll never forget it."

Lyz Glick refuses to forget, too. She's turned Jeremy's heroics into Jeremy's Heroes, a nonprofit organization that has helped thousands of young public school athletes who otherwise couldn't afford to train. "That's helped us to heal the most," she says.

What's also helped is something Jeremy said in her twenty-seven minutes with him on that phone call. "Whatever decisions you make in your life," he said, "I need you to be happy and I will respect any decisions that you make.'"

Lyz was married to her grief for so long. She would continually call Jeremy's cell phone, just to hear his voice, over and over. Fold his clothes. Relive the call and hope it was enough.

Finally, years later, she married Jeremy's best friend and best man, Jim Best. She has three kids—one by Jeremy, age 10, and two with Jim, 4 and 2.

Many of the families of the Flight 93 victims have stayed close. So close, in fact, twenty-four of them will run in the New York City Marathon in November as a team, led by the sister, Kiki, of one of the slain pilots, Leroy Homer, a former high school track star.

You might recognize them. They'll probably be wearing T-shirts that read: *They didn't quit. Neither will we.*

Over 50,000 mementos, gifts and testimonials have been left at the battle site in Shanksville. Kids leave their favorite stuffed animals. People write long, emotional thanks on everything from granite stones to paper plates. One Vietnam vet left his Purple Heart.

Many of the families will be there Saturday, September 10, for one final burial ceremony.

And yet ten years later, the memorial that was promised these forty people hasn't been delivered. The Flight 93 National Memorial is still $10 million short of completion. There is still no visitors' center to teach, no Tower of Voices to listen to, and no forty groves of trees to honor.

"I'm 69 years old," says David Beamer. "I'd like to see the thing get done in my lifetime. If you and everybody you know can make one little sacrifice—one hour of your income—we could get this done tomorrow."

I sent an hour's pay not just to honor the passengers of Flight 93 but also to thank them. My niece was working in the Capitol that day. This spring, she had her second baby.

To send your hour's pay, go to honorflight93.org.

The passengers aboard Flight 93 saved hundreds of lives—if not thousands—in thirty-five minutes. We've had ten years.

It's a hole we need to fill.

Postscript: *Maybe you'll be happy to know the goal was reached. The Flight 93 National Memorial in Shanksville is now open. It's free.*

Getting Right with Ray Lewis

December 20, 2013

The times I loathe myself the most are when I'm so cocksure of something, so bulletproof screwed-down certain, that I don't make room for the possibility that I might not be just wrong, I might be loud wrong.

Take, for instance, Ray Lewis.

Despised him. Didn't trust him. Didn't matter that I didn't know him.

Didn't care that he was a thirteen-time Pro Bowl linebacker. Never liked the dance. Never liked all of the God speeches. Remember what he said after last season's Super Bowl win? "When God is for you, who can be against you?" What did the 49ers do to piss off God? Never saw any reason a man needed black paint all over his face to play football. It's not faceblack. It's eyeblack.

So when ESPN announced in the offseason that he was joining us on the *Monday Night Countdown* crew? Stuck on the *Monday Night Football* bus with him? Hell on wheels.

I suppose, secretly, I was nervous. I'd criticized him plenty in his seventeen-year career. Is there anybody in America you'd want mad at you less than Ray Lewis?

And then we met.

Turns out I was a fool. Ray Lewis is not the man I thought he was. He is friendly, open and honest. He wants to laugh—at himself first and second, and maybe you third. If he's read the things I've written about him, he's not letting on.

You spend ten hours with a guy every Monday, you get to know him. He plays Words With Friends. He studies photography. His kids light up his phone.

He has his bodyguard—as though he needs one—pull soldiers, Marines and sailors out of the crowd, just to meet and thank them.

I've never been around anybody who pours passion out of his every cell like this man. Until Lewis came, we'd watch the game in the *MNF* bus. Now we watch the game and we watch Ray.

The yelling. The jumping out of the chair as if it were suddenly made of snakes. The trying to pull his face off with anguish. And this isn't even during a Ravens game. This is Vikings–Giants.

"Rick, man, that is BASIC!" "Oh, no! No, that's TERRIBLE!" "What's he doing!? Man, what is he DOING???"

The other night, he was in the stands watching his son play safety in a high school game. He's tried not to miss a single football game, volleyball game or dance recital of any of his six kids since he quit the NFL after last season. His son and his teammates were falling for the same trick over and over. Lewis's brain was about to fall out of his ears. Finally, he ran down, jumped the fence, gathered them up and explained what was happening.

He can't help but try to fix things. During one on-field postgame show, he saw how we all were freezing, and the next week he bought us all battery-powered heated gloves and heated vests. Wrapped them up and everything.

Right across from me, every Monday night, was one of the great leaders football has ever produced. So I started asking him questions.

After a big Jets fight: "Ever fight on the field, Ray?"

"No. Never. I always said, 'Meet me afterward. We'll deal with this then.' And they'd never show up. Except once. He came. He saw me walking toward him. He turned and walked the other way."

After Cowboys receiver Dez Bryant walked off the field because he didn't want cameras to catch him crying: "Ever cry on the field, Ray?"

"I used to. Used to get mad, too. But after losing in the 2006 play-offs [to Peyton Manning and the Colts], I was driving my family home, just mad. All of a sudden, my mom grabbed my arm and said, 'What's wrong with this car?' I didn't know what she was talking about. She said, 'Nobody's talking. Everybody's scared to say a word. That's because of YOU. You made everybody in this car miserable. I NEVER want to see you act this way again. You play the game, you do your very best, and when it's over, it's OVER.' That changed my life."

Maybe that's why, minutes after the Ravens lost in the 2011 AFC title game to the Patriots, Lewis gathered all of his disheartened teammates and barked: "Don't EVER drop your head when it comes to a loss, dog. Because there's too much PAIN outside of this that people are really going through . . . Let's understand who we are as men. Let's make somebody smile when we walk out of here."

After we saw a piece on a player who'd grown up without a father: "Has your father ever re-surfaced, Ray?"

"He did. I was 33. You only get one chance at life, man. You can be bitter and pissed off all you want, but time don't stop for nobody. I wanted to make sure he knew that I forgave him."

And two weeks ago, on December 7, Ray Lewis was the best man at his father's wedding in Tampa.

"He's a very sophisticated dude," says Steve Young, another bus citizen. "I would've loved to play with him."

I'm about as different from Ray Lewis as a man can get. He ascribes everything that happens to God's will. I ascribe none of it. He rarely drinks. I keep entire breweries in the black. He's a player at heart and I'm a writer at heart, and almost never do the twain mix. As he says, "I always thought writers were nothin' but dangerous."

And yet, somehow, we've become close. We laugh at our failures. Knuckle our successes. Help each other through. He is a good man. And maybe I'm not the man I thought I was for judging him.

There's no reason you should believe any of this, of course. No company is going to let you rip a fellow employee. So I guess I'm only writing it as a memo to myself:

Throwing a person under the bus is not nearly as fun as becoming friends *on* one.

Postscript: *You're thinking it, so we might as well get to it: Lewis pleaded guilty to obstruction of justice in connection with the murder of two men outside an Atlanta nightclub in 2000. He got twelve months' probation and was fined $250,000 by the NFL. When the Ravens won the Super Bowl the next season, Lewis was the MVP, but the traditional MVP "I'm going to Disney World!" line was given to QB Trent Dilfer, who now works with Ray and me on* Monday Night Countdown.

Where Everybody Knows
Your Name

August 24, 2012

Just as every Five Guys has the same menu and every Tyler Perry movie has the same plot, every gym in America has the same dozen people.

Look around! There's . . .

Grunting Too Much Weight Dropper Dude. He's rocking the Zubaz pants, Guns N' Roses T-shirt, Harley do-rag, weight belt and grip gloves. He comes in every day for two hours without fail because it's Chest, Arms and Neck Day, which he executes with barbells that he drops from four feet for full head-turning effect. He looks like Conan the Barbarian on top and Conan O'Brien below because every day is Chest, Arms and Neck Day.

1986 Man. He's the one with the Walkman, headphones the size of twenty-five-pound plates, Richard Simmons shorts and the Tom Selleck 'stache. He spends most of his hour warming up with various yoga poses in the corner, affording you views you never hoped to see. If you checked, he'd be listening to Phil Collins.

Unlimited Minutes Gal. She's the one on the treadmill walking 1.3 miles per hour while watching *Judge Judy*. Her makeup never runs and her brow never moistens as she says on her endless cell phone call, "Yeah, I'm like working out, you know? Yeah, like five times a week! Like, what are YOU, like, doing?" After an hour, she bounces home and jumps on the scale, crestfallen to see she still hasn't lost any weight.

Gallon Jug of Water Guy. He takes it with him to every station he goes to, along with his beach towel and remarkable hair shirt. He sweats like a priest in a bordello, leaving small ponds of goop on every bench. Sadly, the towel is applied only to himself.

Double-Parked Guy. He's the ripped dude who's always asking you, "Mind if I work in?" while tapping his foot as you finish your measly ninety-pound lat pulldowns. He's built himself a ten-stop circuit in his mind and allows himself only eight seconds between each station, and you have the nerve to get in the middle of it here at the 24 Hour Fitness he seems to own. You're seriously harshing his endorphin buzz.

Barbie Ball Babe. She's the one with the teased ponytail, bedazzled headband and enough makeup to stump an archaeologist. She's got page 6 of the Lululemon catalogue on, with matching sports water bottle, leg warmers, tight spandex pants and shiny sneakers that go with her colorful wrist sweatbands. Except the sweatbands aren't needed, since she never actually works out. Instead, she just sits on the exercise ball you were actually trying to use, talking to her friends on the elliptical who were hoping to actually work out.

Unnecessarily Nude Chatty Guy. He's the guy in the locker room who suddenly wants to talk to you about the Vikings buck naked and propping one foot on the bench you're trying to get dressed on. What's most distressing—as you try to focus on the wall thermostat—is that he has a perfectly good towel in his right hand. All you can think of is prunes.

Sunday *New York Times* Woman. This is the gal on the recumbent bike in her khakis, black socks and dress shoes who's pedaling in Super Slo-Mo while reading every section of the *New York Times* as though they contain a new chapter of the Bible. Her knowledge level of the Syrian civil war is sky high, as is her cholesterol. There's no point in hoping she'll get off soon, since she's got an untouched Sunday *Washington Post* on the floor next to her.

Tour de France Lance. He's the dude in your spin class wearing bike shorts, click-in shoes and a yellow Bimbo jersey, with two water bottles in the back pockets, absolutely killing it. You're thinking, "Why isn't this guy racing in the Giro d'Italia this week?" until you realize the tension knob is on 1.

Orbiting Satellite Guy. This is the older, portly gentleman who walks in wearing polyester slacks, a white undershirt, a belt that fastens just south of his clavicle and blindingly white New Balance running shoes. He makes one loop around the gym, looking at all the equipment, sighs once and walks out. Another New Year's resolution dashed on the rocks of reality.

On the Way to Work Stripper. She has just twenty minutes to get in some sit-ups and power lunges before her shift at Cheerleaders. These are also the twenty minutes when more cumulative weight gets lifted by males than the rest of the day combined. It's no use, of course. Her boyfriend is Grunting Too Much Weight Dropper Dude.

Annoying Twitter Guy. This is the 50-something guy who tweets every ten minutes during his one-hour workout, thinks of a column idea, asks his eleven Twitter followers for help and then neither thanks nor credits them.

Oh, wait, that's me. Never mind.

Postscript: *People sent in so many more. Spot Each Other on 110 Pound Bench Presses Buddies. Sit on the Weight Bench and Read* Muscle & Fitness *Instead of Create Muscle and Fitness Guy. And the most demoralizing one of all: Incredibly Ripped 65-Year-Old Guy. I hope his HGH supplier croaks.*

Feel

(People with Big Hearts)

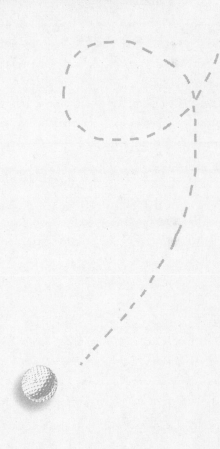

Eagles over Wolves in a Rout

February 14, 2011

Among the burdens of a married American male are to provide shelter, put food in the cupboards and occasionally sit through showings of *The View.*

Which is what my wife and I were doing last week when we saw something that made it hard to speak, much less drink our coffee.

A 13-year-old boy named Nadin Khoury told about how he'd been attacked by seven bigger schoolmates, kicked, beaten, dragged through the snow, stuffed into a tree and hung on a 7-foot spiked fence, all while adults watched.

The boy was only 5-foot-2, but he'd made up his mind to stand tall no matter how much of his pride bled out. As the brutal video played on a screen behind him, his collar stayed buttoned, his spine straight, but his bottom lip quivered.

"Next time maybe it could be somebody smaller than me," he said, loud and clear, like the Marine he wants to be someday. "Maybe next time, somebody could really get hurt."

That's when host Elisabeth Hasselbeck said, "There are some guys here who want to tell you just how brave you are."

From behind the curtain came three Philadelphia Eagles—All-World receiver DeSean Jackson, center Jamaal Jackson and guard Todd Herremans.

Khoury seemed at once shocked, overwhelmed and redeemed. Where once his chin stuck out as best it could, it now fell open in wonder. He looked like a kid who'd forgotten it was Christmas morning. He wept without wiping his tears. Jackson sat as close to him as possible, as if to make the two one. He praised the boy for his bravery and added, "Anytime ever you need us, I got two linemen right here."

Nadin's mom cried, Whoopi Goldberg cried, my wife cried and I cried.

Why would a superstar athlete up and fly to NYC from L.A. with one day's notice to support a kid he's never met?

Rewind four months:

Eighth-grader Nadin has just moved to the Philly suburb of Upper Darby with his sister. Their mom, Rebecca, had lost her Minnesota hotel-maid job. That makes him the strange new kid at Upper Darby High School. That makes him prey. Walking down a steep hill to catch the bus, kids start taunting him about his mother, an African refugee who fled bloody Liberia in 2000.

"They were calling her names," Khoury told me. "Talkin' about her 'booty.' I didn't want to hear that so I told them to stop. They pushed me down and dragged me down the hill. I got up and fought one of them. . . . The next day the other kids got on him about 'How you let a little kid beat you like that?' And I could see that it really made him mad. It bottled up in him until he was ready to explode."

The bullying gets worse. Alley ambushes. Pushes and slugs and draggings. And then comes the attack on January 11 by what Police Superintendent Michael Chitwood calls "a wolf pack." "I was afraid for my life," the boy recalls.

When one of the pack posts the video on YouTube, Nadin's mom has her proof and presses charges. The Upper Darby police ask if the family will bring the case public.

Rebecca thinks about the rebels in Liberia. Thinks about how they found her family hiding and dragged her father into the streets and murdered him there. Thinks about standing up to bullies, even the ones with AK-47s.

"I say to my son, 'Are you ready for this? This is not going to be little. This is going to be big.' And he says, 'Yes, Mommy.' And I say, 'Are you ashamed of anything?' And he says, 'No, Mommy.' So we do it."

The *Philadelphia Inquirer* writes a piece. A staffer at *The View* reads it. She finds out Jackson is Nadin's favorite player and reaches out to the Eagles. The Eagles call Jackson.

Jackson thinks of his childhood in South Central L.A. Thinks of the bullying that went on in his childhood, the kind that ends in mothers flung across coffins. Thinks of Desmond, his 13-year-old brother.

"He's a small guy, too," Jackson says. "Nadin reminded me of him. When I thought of kids doing that stuff to my little brother, man, that really got to me. Made me want to get my hands on those kids."

Next thing you know, Nadin is on a couch with his favorite NFL player at—and on—his side. Jackson takes the jersey he's wearing off his back, signs it and gives it to the kid. Then he gives him his cell phone number to back it up.

It only gets better from there.

Jackson starts an anti-bullying nonprofit—DeSean Jackson Against Bullying. The family receives Eagles tickets, 76ers tickets, jerseys, T-shirts.

The director of admissions at Valley Forge Military Academy, LaToro Yates, sees *The View*. He thinks of the bullies in his childhood. Thinks of the boys who terrorized him for the way he looked, the way he talked, the way he dressed.

Next thing you know, Nadin is being invited to the VFMA campus, where men like General Norman Schwarzkopf and J. D. Salinger and Arizona Cardinals wide receiver Larry Fitzgerald once walked.

"I admire this young man's courage," Yates says. "It takes courage just to come to school the next day. But to step up and go public with it to help other kids? Wow."

The academy is "working diligently to make the young man a cadet at Valley Forge Military Academy starting this fall," says Yates. Free.

The Upper Darby police, meanwhile, do a little dragging of their own. They walk into Nadin's school and drag the alleged attackers off in handcuffs. Eventually, charges were dropped against one, but the others will pay for their bullying of Nadin. Their cases and final charges are still pending.

The fear isn't entirely gone in Nadin's house—his mom still sleeps in the living room at night in case "somebody's coming to get my son," she says—but for Nadin, stepping up for others has been the best thing he's ever done for himself. He's already turned down $1,800 for the jersey. "I'm going to give it to my son and he'll give it to his son."

I keep thinking about why I cried that day. I think it's that when the biggest and fiercest and most famous of us takes time to stand up for the smallest of us, it makes me proud to be a sportswriter, proud to cover these athletes, these men.

But I'm prouder still when a young, poor boy like this stands up with no idea any help is coming.

(Oh, and a note to the wolf pack: If you think Eagles players shouldn't be messed with, wait until you meet the Marines.)

Postscript: *It wasn't just Jackson who believed in Nadin. The prestigious Wyncote Academy gave him a $150,000 scholarship through high school. Last I checked, Nadin was safe, unafraid and on track to realize his dream—becoming a Marine.*

I Believe in Tim Tebow

January 13, 2012

I've come to believe in Tim Tebow, but not for what he does on a football field, which is still three parts Dr. Jekyll and two parts Mr. Hyde.

No, I've come to believe in Tim Tebow for what he does off a football field, which is represent the best parts of us, the parts I want to be and so rarely am.

Who among us is this selfless?

Every week, Tebow picks out someone who is suffering, or who is dying, or who is injured. He flies these people and their families to the Broncos game, rents them a car, puts them up in a nice hotel, buys them dinner (usually at a Dave & Buster's), gets them and their families pregame passes, visits with them just before kickoff (!), gets them 30-yard-line tickets down low, visits with them after the game (sometimes for an hour), has them walk him to his car and sends them off with a basket of gifts.

Home or road, win or lose, hero or goat.

Remember last week, when the world was pulling its hair out in the hour after Tebow had stunned the Pittsburgh Steelers with an 80-yard OT touchdown pass to Demaryius Thomas in the playoffs? And Twitter was exploding with 9,420 tweets about Tebow per second? When an ESPN poll was naming him the most popular athlete in America?

Tebow was spending that hour talking to 16-year-old Bailey Knaub about her 73 surgeries so far and what TV shows she likes.

"Here he'd just played the game of his life," recalls Bailey's mother, Kathy, of Loveland, Colorado, "and the first thing he does after his press conference is come find Bailey and ask, 'Did you get anything to eat?' He acted like what he'd just done wasn't anything, like it was all about Bailey."

More than that, Tebow kept corralling people into the room for Bailey to meet. Hey, Demaryius, come in here a minute. Hey, Mr. Elway. Hey, Coach Fox.

Even though sometimes-fatal Wegener's granulomatosis has left Bailey with only one lung, the attention took her breath away.

"It was the best day of my life," she e-mailed. "It was a bright star among very gloomy and difficult days. Tim Tebow gave me the greatest gift I could ever imagine. He gave me the strength for the future. I know now that I can face any obstacle placed in front of me. Tim taught me to never give up because at the end of the day, today might seem bleak but it can't rain forever and tomorrow is a new day, with new promises."

I read that e-mail to Tebow, and he was honestly floored.

"Why me? Why should I inspire her?" he said. "I just don't feel, I don't know, adequate. Really, hearing her story inspires me."

It's not just NFL defenses that get Tebowed. It's high school girls who don't know whether they'll ever go to a prom. It's adults who can hardly stand. It's kids who will die soon.

For the game at Buffalo, it was Charlottesville, Virginia, blue-chip high school QB Jacob Rainey, who lost his leg after a freak tackle in a scrimmage. Tebow threw three interceptions in that Buffalo game and the Broncos were crushed, 40–14.

"He walked in and took a big sigh and said, 'Well, that didn't go as planned,'" Rainey remembers. "Where I'm from, people wonder how sincere and genuine he is. But I think he's the most genuine person I've ever met."

There's not an ounce of artifice or phoniness or Hollywood in this kid Tebow, and I've looked everywhere for it.

Take 9-year-old Zac Taylor, a child who lives in constant pain. Immediately after Tebow shocked the Chicago Bears with a 13–10 comeback win, Tebow spent an hour with Zac and his family. At one point, Zac, who has ten doctors, asked Tebow whether he has a secret prayer for hospital visits. Tebow whispered it in his ear. And because Tebow still needed to be checked out by the Broncos' team doctor, he took Zac in with him, but only after they had whispered it together.

And it's not always kids. Tom Driscoll, a 55-year-old who is dying of brain cancer at a hospice in Denver, was Tebow's guest for the Cincinnati game. "The doctors took some of my brain," Driscoll says, "so my short-term memory is kind of shot. But that day I'll never forget. Tim is such a good man."

This whole thing makes no football sense, of course. Most NFL players hardly talk to teammates before a game, much less visit with the sick and dying.

Isn't that a huge distraction?

"Just the opposite," Tebow says. "It's by far the best thing I do to get myself ready. Here you are, about to play a game that the world says is the most important thing in the world. Win and they praise you. Lose and they crush you. And here I have a chance to talk to the coolest, most courageous people. It puts it all into perspective. The game doesn't really matter. I mean, I'll give 100 percent of my heart to win it, but in the end, the thing I most want to do is not win championships or make a lot of money, it's to invest in people's lives, to make a difference."

So that's it. I've given up on him. I'm a 100 percent believer. Not in his arm. Not in his skills. I believe in his heart, his there-will-definitely-be-a-pony-under-the-tree optimism, the way his love pours into people, right up to their eyeballs, until they believe they can master the hopeless comeback, too.

Remember the QB who lost his leg, Jacob Rainey? He got his prosthetic leg a few weeks ago, and he wants to play high school football next season. Yes, tackle football. He'd be the first to do that on an above-the-knee amputation.

Hmmm. Wonder where he got that crazy idea?

"Tim told me to keep fighting, no matter what," Rainey says. "I am."

Postscript: *This was the most read opinion column on ESPN.com in 2012, shared more than 110,000 times on Facebook and tweeted more than 11,000 times. And after it ran, a truism hit me. When it comes to Tim Tebow, admire the man, not the game. Tiger Woods? Just the opposite.*

Take Your Pick

December 15, 2011

Tom is righty. Tim is lefty.

Tom is 34. Tim is 24.

Tom is second in passing yards among NFL starters this season. Tim is dead last.

Tom is third in completion percentage. Tim is dead last.

Tom has won five games in a row. Tim has won six.

Tom swears like a teamster who has stubbed his little toe. Tim says "Gosh!" and "Golly!" and calls reporters "Sir." (I hired a lip reader to monitor Tim in Week 13. The worst he said was an impassioned "Let's go!")

Tom has a QB rating of 106.0. Tim's is 83.9.

But in the fourth quarter, Tom's is 91.0 and Tim's is 99.6.

Tom is a national sex symbol who's had two children, one out of wedlock with a stunning actress and the other with his wife, a Brazilian supermodel. Tim is a national sexless symbol, a proud virgin.

Tom has won 77 percent of his games as a starter. Tim has won 73 percent.

Tom throws spirals that could slide into a mailbox from across a cul-de-sac. They nestle into receivers' arms like babies returned to new mothers. Tim throws chevrons of mallards. He has more overthrows than the Arab Spring.

Tom has the seventh-best-selling Fathead poster in the NFL this week. Tim has the best-selling one. And the second-best-selling one. And the tenth-best-selling one.

Tom is the ultimate pocket quarterback. He's as comfortable in it as Sarah Palin in mink. Tim treats the pocket as an electric chair. He bolts it like it's on fire.

Tom runs like he's wearing ski boots. Tim runs like he's wearing ACME jet packs. In his entire career, Tom has rushed for 697 yards. Tim could very well run for that many this season.

Tom has lost games this season scoring 31, 20 and 17 points. Tim has won games scoring 18, 17, 17, 16, and Tom is aided by the NFL's leading receiver, Wes Welker, and a touchdown-gobbling tight end, Rob Gronkowski. Tim is helped by God, according to his pastor, Wayne Henson. "God favors Tim for all his hard work," the pastor says.

Tom is in his twelfth season. Tim is in his second. Tom finished his second season with a passer rating of 86.5. Tim's passer rating is about the same, 83.9.

Tom was born in San Mateo, California, to an insurance consultant and has three siblings, all girls. Tim was born in Makati City, Philippines, to a Baptist missionary, and is the youngest of five.

Tom went to the prestigious Catholic high school Junipero Serra, where Barry Bonds and Lynn Swann went. Tim was homeschooled.

Tom was mostly unknown in college. He sat on the bench his first two years. Tim was one of the most famous college athletes in history, a cinch for the College Football Hall of Fame, winner of two national championships, claimer of one Heisman and finalist for two more.

Tom was a sixth-round draft pick. Tim was a first-rounder.

Tom did not start a game as a rookie. Tim did.

Tom has won three Super Bowls, two Super Bowl MVPs and two league MVPs. He owns the NFL regular-season records for TD passes, best TDs-to-interception ratio, consecutive home wins and consecutive playoff wins. Tim is a favorite of Skip Bayless.

Tom is Goliath. Tim is David. A 6-foot-3, 235-pound David who can bench 350 and flatten cornerbacks into peanut brittle.

Tom has twenty-four fourth-quarter comeback victories in his eleven years as a starter. Tim has six in, basically, one.

Tom has no jokes going around about him. Tim has this one: Tebow asks for an audience with the Pope, who grants it. Tebow flies to Rome and the Pope gives him a tour of the Vatican, the Sistine Chapel, everything. But it's Sunday morning and now the Pope needs to deliver Mass to the 50,000 people waiting in St. Peter's Square below his window. "Come with me to the window and see for yourself," the Pope says. The two of them go to the window. Down below, an Italian guy says to his buddy, "Hey, who's the guy in the pointy hat next to Tebow?"

Tom has made seventeen *Sports Illustrated* covers. Tim has eight, one more than Drew Brees.

Tom has nineteen books for sale about him on Amazon.com. Tim has six.

Tom is the namesake of the NFL's Brady Rule, which prohibits hitting QBs below the knees. Tim is the namesake behind the NCAA's Tebow Rule, regarding athletes wearing messages on their eyeblack.

Tom is on a greeting card. Tim is on a Christmas card.

Tom has been named his team's QB of the future. Tim has not.

Tom is 1-5 versus Tim's team. Tim has never played Tom's team.

Bradying is not an acknowledged English word, according to the Global Language Monitor. Tebowing is.

Both men would chew through a cement embankment to win a football game.

They play Sunday.

Who do you like?

Postscript: *In 2013, a Mayflower moving van full of starting QBs went down with injuries, and yet nobody wanted Tim Tebow. Traded by Denver, cut by the Jets, released by the Patriots. Since then, nothing. No CFL. No ads. No nothing. He remains the only Heisman Trophy QB to win an NFL playoff game as a starter. I still think he'll do great things, just without a helmet.*

Net Gain

August 6, 2013

CAMP NYARUGUSU, Tanzania—Freeze it:

Five thousand people are watching Golden State Warriors star Stephen Curry in midair, about to slam.

But something's upside down.

One man wears a Pittsburgh Steelers 2010 World Champions shirt, which is weird, since the Green Bay Packers actually won it. One woman wears a Connecticut Huskies 2011 Fiesta Bowl Champs hat, also odd, seeing as how Oklahoma crushed them.

Plus, the rim is bent two inches, the wooden backboard is tilting like a drunk and the court is red dirt. This is because we're in a refugee camp in Tanzania, where those preprinted losing Super Bowl T-shirts live. It's also a place where malaria thrives—62,000 cases of it last year among a population of 68,000.

Curry is here to try to fix that. But first he wants to show them his stuff.

Press play:

He soars, rises up (in jeans) with his right hand and dunks, nearly causing the rickety backboard to cough up its bolts.

Nobody claps. Nobody cheers. Instead, 10,000 eyes blink.

Curry looks at them. Shakes his head.

"They don't know how hard that was for me," he says with a shrug.

These refugees don't know dunks, nor do they know why a 25-year-old NBA star, coming off his breakout season, would fly more than 8,000 miles and twenty-four hours, risk malaria, typhoid and yellow fever, just to hang bed nets in their mud huts for the anti-malaria program Nothing But Nets. On his vacation.

"Man, for a huge American sports star," said Nothing But Nets director Chris Helfrich, "he sure doesn't act like it."

Coming to Africa wasn't easy for Curry. Today is his second anniversary and his wife, Ayesha, and his 1-year-old daughter, Riley, aren't here. So he's working on a poem to try to fill the gap. One stanza reads:

> *When I look at our daughter*
> *I'm beaming with pride*
> *She's the best example*
> *Of our love inside*

Standing near two goats in a dusty field, he reads it to her on his satellite phone. At the end, she's silent for thirty seconds. Curry wonders if the line has gone dead, but Ayesha is just overcome.

That feeling would come to Curry's throat, too, when he'd meet parents who left his mouth hanging open.

He'd meet a woman named Nabwamima, who's had four miscarriages due to malaria. "God bless you, Coory," she said.

He'd meet a 25-year-old woman named Machozi, whose name means "tear" and who's had malaria twenty times already. Her 6-month-old boy on her back is bloated and rust-colored from having it three times in the last three months.

He'd meet albino kids who had to flee their villages when chopping off albino limbs and grinding the bones into a "magic" dust suddenly became witch-doctor-approved good luck in 2009.

"This is exhausting," he said during one break. "Emotionally. You know?"

We know.

Very few of these people he's helping had ever even heard of him. They don't know he broke the NBA record this year for most 3-pointers in a single season (272), or that he scored 54 points in a single road game against the Knicks, or that he was the breakout star of the NBA playoffs, including one 44-point game against the San Antonio Spurs that nearly caused Oakland to leap into the bay.

For each 3-pointer he hit, he donated three bed nets ($10 each), and now he was actually putting them up.

"I'm putting faces to nets right now," he said during a lunch break. "Like, one whole neighborhood is covered now here just thanks to Madison Square Garden. The Knicks covered Block 9, Street 11. I hope they know that."

I'm sure they're touched.

Curry is used to being guarded tightly, but not usually by AK-47s. There are three Tanzanian police carrying them in the bed of the Toyota pickup truck ahead of us as we knuckleball down the red dirt road to the refugee camp. Curry is sandwiched between two bodyguards, the one the Tanzanian government sent and the one his agent sent.

"I feel like I'm in a Bourne movie," he says.

But the refugees aren't dangerous, they're just desperately poor. They beg him for his empty water bottles. They make dishes out of them. Their huts, which they must build themselves, have dirt floors. There's no electricity, and they can't afford candles to light them at night. One boy we met had only one shirt to wear, period, and that one only thanks to the Indianapolis Colts' loss to New Orleans in Super Bowl XLIV.

"And to think that the day before I left I was complaining about our condo," Curry thought aloud.

And yet it's better than where these refugees came from in the Democratic Republic of the Congo, where civil war forced them out of their homes in 1996. Many of them have never been outside the camp fences.

So it didn't matter what Curry did for a living. He was helping and he was strong and he was from somewhere else, so they mobbed him. A touch of Curry went a long, long way. He carried one little boy, named Obama, around for an hour. He was continually being handed taped-up balls of yarn—refugees' version of basketballs—to shoot at them. Once he was asked to shoot it into the giant metal pan a woman was balancing on her head twenty feet away. It rimmed out.

He tried to teach their two basketball teams to play. He'd holler "Give and go!" and "Backdoor!" and other instructions they'd never heard of. It wasn't exactly the D League. One kid kissed the ball just before he shot it. The big, 6-foot-5 guy only cherry-picked. The camp's best shooter, Gerrard Mubake, lost to Curry in a 3-point-shooting contest, and then left me this note to give to Curry: *don't let me in this camp. will die. here peaple killed peaple. back in 1996 my father and my mum died in the war, so i'm left alone. i want to be in your two hands.*

"I don't know what to say to him," Curry says.

Stephen Curry's life has hit the turbo button since he torched the playoffs. He will be on the cover of Capri Sun juice squeezers this season. And *GQ*. He's going to have his own reality show on Comcast.

His All-Star snub last season looks even more ridiculous now: The man shot 45 percent from the 3-point line! He is a cinch to make the 2016 USA Olympic team. His life has changed a thousand ways. But none more than from coming to Africa.

"This has been totally eye-opening," he said at the end, covered in red dirt and sweat and joy. "I picked nets because it's a way people can make a huge difference right away. We can really save kids' lives. I've seen it now. I'll never forget it."

When I founded Nothing But Nets in 2006, I begged for help from anybody, anywhere. But I never dreamed we'd get so much from a rising NBA star. I never thought we'd find one who would look up long enough from his Twitter feed and his Piguet watch to notice suffering, much less suffering 8,000 miles from the United States. I couldn't have imagined we'd find a young man who would not only donate us nets, but actually come to Africa and hang them with us.

Should have known it would be Curry. He's always had a beautiful follow-through.

Postscript: *Want some good news? The World Health Organization reports that malaria deaths in sub-Saharan Africa have been cut in half over the last ten years, thanks to people like Curry.*

Woody and Guthrie Play Catch

April 24, 2012

Sure, you hate Twitter. You say it's the biggest waste of time since the Kansas City Royals. And I used to agree with you. Until I saw this happen:

It's April 10. A Tuesday. Off day for the Colorado Rockies baseball team. Except their new pitcher, nine-year vet Jeremy Guthrie, needs his daily "throw," and he's got nobody to give him a catch. So he tweets this to his 34,000-plus followers:

Jeremy Guthrie
@TheRealJGuts
Anybody on a lunch break & up for a catch with me? #offday
#nothrowingpartner

Two minutes before, a 21-year-old stand-up comic named Woody Roseland had just made it home from the greatest doctor's appointment in his life. After spending more than two and a half years of his

life in chemotherapy for five cancer relapses—knee, lungs and calf—
the nurse said, "You're good. We don't need to see you anymore."

Woody practically floated home to his Denver apartment, fixed
himself a sandwich and flipped open his laptop to his Twitter feed,
with Guthrie's offer on top. Which is when this happened:

> Woody Roseland
> @woodyroseland
> @JGuthrie46 My man! I'm downtown and have my glove.
> Let's do this!

> Jeremy Guthrie
> @TheRealJGuts
> Ok, for real. When can you be here? RT @JGuthrie46 My
> man! I'm downtown and have my glove. Let's do this!

> Woody Roseland
> @woodyroseland
> @JGurthrie46 Like 15 minutes!

Next thing you know, Woody and his prosthetic left leg and his
hairless, eyelashless, eyebrowless head and his chemo-sunken eyes
and his soaring heart are jumping in a cab.

"Coors Field, please," Woody says.

"Nope," says the cabbie. "No game today."

"I don't care! Please just get me to Coors!"

Once there, Woody is puzzled as to how to get into the clubhouse
to meet Guthrie. "It's not like they have a sign that reads 'Guys Here
to Play Catch with Players Ring This Bell,'" Woody says.

But security guards tend to trust guys on one leg with a baseball
glove, which is how Guthrie finds himself bumping into Woody in
the clubhouse hallway.

Guthrie is a little speechless. His first guess is: OK, missing leg, doesn't look like much hair under his hat. He's a soldier.

Finally, Guthrie asks, "What happened to your leg?"

"Oh," Woody says, matter-of-factly. "I lost it to cancer. Got it when I was 16."

That's how Woody is, of course. Cancer to him is just another punch line. It's part of his stand-up routine.

"Being a cancer amputee is like being a really hot girl," Woody tells audiences. "Everybody sends you flowers and cards. And they stare all the time. And I'm like, 'Hello? I'm not just a piece of meat. My eyes are up here, thank you.'"

He's even written a comic cancer rap, which includes this: *When will I give up? Never 'Cause I'm literally . . . the illest rapper ever*

No hair on my head No eyebrows neither But my nurse loves me Cuz I know how to treat her

For his part, Guthrie is gobsmacked.

"I'm just like, 'Wow.' Magically, this is how the cards are dealt today. Cool!"

He takes Woody out to right field, puts him against the wall (in case of overthrows), paces off ninety feet and starts throwing.

"He wasn't bad!" Guthrie remembers, which is pretty good, since the last time Woody threw a baseball, he had two legs.

"I couldn't really believe it," Woody says. "Here's me and here's this major league pitcher, trying to teach me how to throw a slider."

From there, Guthrie tosses Woody a little batting practice. ("I pitched bad, he hit bad," Guthrie says.) Then a visit to the mound, then the video room to analyze how Guthrie was going to get San Francisco Giants hitters out the next night (not well—he was knocked out in the fourth inning) and then more laughing and talking in the Rockies' locker room.

In other words, Twitter and Jeremy Guthrie and a chemotherapy nurse gave Woody Roseland the greatest single day in a life that's been a little light on them.

And that was just the start of things for Woody. Since then, he's gone to a Rockies game with Guthrie's wife. Tim Tebow's foundation, W15H, flew him to Florida for a charity golf tournament, where Bubba Watson let him swing his pink driver and Lindsey Vonn hugged him and *American Idol* star Jordin Sparks heard the cancer rap and liked it so much she's working on helping him turn it into a video. Woody's also writing a book for cancer patients, and he's got a video on YouTube: "S#!% Cancer Patients Say" (i.e., "Lance Armstrong NEVER took performance-enhancing drugs!").

Of course, Twitter giveth and Twitter taketh away. When Denver TV station KCNC first broke this story, a lot of tweople thought it was fake.

> FanPOV
>
> @FanPOV
>
> I smell a set-up in the @jguthrie46 and @woodyroseland story—just too perfect a story, too coincidental, and guy has too slick a website

It's all real, pal, and it's all amazing. When you have a way to talk with thousands of strangers instantly and they can talk with you, you find out 140 characters can change lives.

"I went out to make a fan's day," Guthrie says, "and instead he made mine. I not only met a fan, I made a friend for life."

And that's a pretty good catch.

Postscript: *Twitter may be as shallow as a baby pool, but sometimes it redeems itself. Woody (@WoodyRoseland) has become a motivational speaker. Guthrie (@TheRealJGuts) now hurls for the Kansas City Royals and had 15 wins in 2013, a career best. Twitter made them permanent friends. Signed, @ReillyRick*

What a Difference a Year Makes

December 22, 2011

This is the show-stoppingest year for QBs in NFL history, which is how San Francisco 49ers kicker David Akers's story ended up in 4-point font.

Too bad. It would look nice on Paramount Pictures' summer schedule.

Yes, Akers, 37, had the finest kicking season in NFL history this year, but that's just the riding-off-into-the-sunset part.

The crying-in-the-shower part was exactly a year ago last week—wild-card weekend—when his Philadelphia Eagles were about to host the Green Bay Packers. The day before the game, doctors found a tumor on the ovary of Akers's 6-year-old daughter, Halley.

They were still trying to figure out what to do with it Sunday morning when a distraught Akers had to drive to the game to kick inflated pigskins through bars of steel.

Just to add a pint or two of sweat to the gallons Akers was already spilling, there was this: The year before, Akers found out he'd been swindled out of most of his life savings in a Ponzi scheme by Texas investor Kurt Barton, who ended up getting seventeen years in prison for it. Akers had to testify against him.

His $3.7 million was gone, though, which meant this playoff game was crucial to the Akers family's future.

No wonder his brain was a bowl of Jell-O that day.

Akers immediately went out and blew a 41-yard field goal attempt in the first quarter. That was rare. He'd missed only four tries all season. Then he missed a bunny 34-yarder in the fourth. He can usually make those wearing fuzzy slippers. The Eagles lost, 21–16.

The fans booed him. Talk radio slaughtered him. And even Eagles coach Andy Reid singled him out, saying, "We can all count. Those points would've helped."

And so all those demons lay down in bed with Akers on that sleepless Sunday night, knowing Halley would go in for surgery in a morning that would reveal the heaviest—or lightest—kind of news.

"He was just so down and worried that night," remembers Akers's agent, Jerrold Colton. "He was so, so emotional. But he knew he had to present a strong front for his daughter and his family."

"My life was kind of a car wreck right then," Akers says.

The next morning, at Children's Hospital of Philadelphia, he asked the surgeon to go out in the hall and pray with him. Akers, devout, had preached for years. They knelt.

The tumor turned out malignant but small enough that the doctors felt like they removed all of it. Trouble was, it would be months before they'd know.

The NFL, though, decides things much faster. The Eagles went out and drafted Nebraska kicker Alex Henery in the fourth round. Akers didn't even know it until a friend texted him.

So there it was, the trifecta—nearly broke, a sick kid at home and silently dumped by the team he'd given twelve terrific years.

Akers is a guy who's insecure about his footing in the NFL anyway. He'd been a waiter at a LongHorn Steakhouse in Atlanta, a substitute teacher and a kicker for NFL Europe in Berlin, where he nearly died during a one-month hospital stay for salmonella.

The man who saved him from that life was then Philadelphia special teams coach John Harbaugh, who called him up for a tryout in 1998. Akers stuck. And he's been terribly fond of Harbaughs ever since.

No wonder that when John's brother Jim called in that dark, darker, darkest offseason, offering a 49ers contract, Akers couldn't pack fast enough. He may have been leaving the Eagles' ballyhooed Dream Team for the 49ers' Creamed Team (6-10 the year before), but he didn't care.

"God made it abundantly clear where I was supposed to be," Akers says. "I love the Harbaugh family."

Dad Jack Harbaugh recruited him twenty years ago at Western Kentucky.

"Out on the field they might be just killing you, calling you names, yelling at you," Akers says. "But then you go into lunch and they become completely different people. 'How's the family, David?' And you want to go, 'Wait a minute! You just torched me out there!' But that's how it is. Their teams are families."

That's almost literally true. Jim has turned the 49ers into a sort of odd family reunion. Kids and families are welcome at Saturday practices. They serve a special meal for the kids. Players wear jeans and sweats on the plane and the team's signature gas-station-attendant-blue work shirts during the week, an idea Jim stole from John, the coach of the Baltimore Ravens.

"They're always doing that with each other," Akers said. "I've heard Jim say to John, 'That's my story! You stole my story!' And then John will go, 'That was NOT your story! I stole it from Dad!'"

Akers signed a three-year, $9 million deal with San Francisco, which was a relief, though not as big of a relief as the doctor telling them in the summer that Halley was 100 percent cancer free.

From there, life just started showing up on the end of Akers's fork.

The 49ers' offense ignited, giving Akers a hotfoot. He set NFL records for FGs in a season (44) and points (166). He was the Associated Press' first-team All-Pro kicker. He threw his first TD pass. The 49ers went 13-3. The Eagles: 8-8.

And when Akers's new team played Akers's old team? Philly's rookie kicker missed field goals of 39 and 33 yards and the 49ers won, 24–23, with Akers kicking the winning PAT.

You think Andy Reid counted on that?

Postscript: *Akers kicked in a Detroit Lions uniform in 2013 at 39 years of age. But he'd have to make it another ten years to pass the oldest man to ever boot, George Blanda, who retired at 48.*

The Caddie and His Boss

April 9, 2011

If you believe all Augusta National members are walking lumps of dandruff who eat boiled puppies for lunch, you're not going to like this story.

It happened a couple years ago.

Brad Boss, the multimillionaire chairman emeritus of the pen company A. T. Cross, is a member at the National and a decent player, possibly because he never went out on the course without his favorite caddie, Joe Collins.

Joe had the kind of eyes that could see clean into tomorrow. A caddie at Augusta from the time he was 16, he was known as the best reader of greens in the entire caddyshack.

He took a practically unknown player named Jim Jamieson to a tie for fifth place at the Masters in 1972. Even when Augusta National lifted its local-caddies-only rule in 1983, Joe still got bags. Colin Montgomerie used him in 1998 and finished tied for eighth. In 2000,

Tommy Aaron, then 63, rode Joe to a record as the oldest player ever to make the cut. Still stands, too.

No wonder so many guys asked for Joe—Michael Jordan took him three times—but Brad always got him. They were buddies. Sounds crazy, but over the top of a golf bag, nobody cares about your stock portfolio. Princes lean on peasants and peasants kid princes. Boss and Joe were together for more than ten years. If you spend that much time, you're more than player and caddie. You're a kind of grass-stained team.

It didn't matter that Joe dropped out of school in the tenth grade and Brad was educated at the best schools in the East. Didn't matter that Joe's mom gave him up to her sister when he was only three months old and that Brad inherited Cross from his grandfather. Didn't matter that Joe walked to the course (he didn't own a car) and Brad flew there sometimes in a private jet.

They were friends.

Joe sent Brad a card every birthday, every Christmas and Father's Day, without fail. "They'd call each other plenty," says Faye Latson, the aunt who raised him. "Seemed like Joe was always calling Mr. Boss up."

Then Joe got lung cancer. You smoke for forty years, that might happen. Joe moved back in with his aunt. "I had to take him in," she says. "He didn't have nobody else."

He had to quit going to the National. If the cancer wasn't going to kill Joe, that might. "He was so sad," Faye says. "That man loved that golf course and all those people."

When he died at 56 on June 27, 2009, Faye arranged for a simple funeral. She couldn't afford much of a plot, but she and her daughter, Shirley Quarles, came up with enough for one in a shaggy downtown cemetery.

"But then Mr. Boss called," said Faye. "And he was asking me, could he put Joe up on the hill above the golf course? He said he wanted Joe to have a nice view of it. Lord, I thought! Joe won't be able to see nothin', but OK."

It's a golf thing.

"We were just all overwhelmed," says James Quarles, Shirley's husband. "We couldn't really believe it. We told him no, he didn't have to, but Mr. Boss wouldn't have it any other way."

Boss flew down from New England for the visitation and spoke at the funeral. In fact, he was the first to get up. He told the crowd how much he admired Joe, how he wasn't just his caddie, he was like family. Maybe that explains the Father's Day cards.

Afterward, he asked Faye if he could put something in Joe's pocket. Faye said sure. It was a gold Cross pen with Joe's name on it and a Masters logo. Gift No. 2.

In New England, all this made friends of Boss shake their heads. "It just made me smile when I heard," says Brad Faxon. "I thought, 'Man, why aren't there more people who do this stuff?'"

Saturday of Masters week, I went with Shirley and Faye on one of their visits to Joe's grave. It's a sweet little spot Brad gave Joe. The cemetery is nearly as full of flowers as the National. It's on a steep hill with a view of the tenth green at Augusta Country Club, which is the course that abuts Augusta National.

From Joe's grave, a well-hit driver could land a ball on the National. Plus, it's literally only four blocks from Faye's little house on Mount Auburn Road.

As Faye stood there saying a little silent prayer, a huge roar went up from Amen Corner. Faye loosed a big smile. "My Joe loved that golf," she said. "It's nice he's here."

Brad Boss didn't have to do any of this. He paid Joe plenty in caddie's fees. And ever since he did it, he hasn't returned my calls to talk about it.

I know people don't want to believe this, but there are all kinds of guys walking around in green jackets at the Masters every year just like Boss. I know guys who've paid their caddie's insurance bills, picked up entire surgeries and handled the rent. They do it quietly and with a smile.

After all, caddies aren't the only ones who can see.

Postscript: *Yes, this is the same Boss who donated the Bradford R. Boss Ice Arena at the University of Rhode Island, where he was a hockey star back in the 1950s.*

Wooden Set the Bar High

June 7, 2010

The awful thing about knowing John Wooden was that when you left him, you realized how weak you were as a man.

Every time I left his little 700-square-foot condo in Encino, California, full of books and learning and morals, it would hit me how far short of him I fell.

He made me want to be more principled. This is a man who once turned down the Purdue head-coaching job because he felt the university was treating the fired coach "terribly. I wouldn't stand for it."

He once turned down the Minnesota job he and his wife, Nell, wanted—and accepted the UCLA one instead—because Minnesota hadn't called with its offer by the 6 p.m. deadline he'd set. Turns out a storm had knocked down the phone lines. Didn't matter. He went to UCLA and won the Bruins ten NCAA titles. No other coach has won more than four.

He abhorred stardom and showmanship. He was against jerseys being retired at UCLA, even the one worn by Lewis Alcindor (later:

Kareem Abdul-Jabbar). "What about the youngster who wore that number before Lewis? Didn't he contribute to the team?"

One time I asked him, "How many championships do you think Kobe can win?"

"None," he said, flatly.

"None?"

"Kobe doesn't win championships. The Lakers win championships."

He made me want to be more humble. In the most self-obsessed city in the world—Hollywood—he was selfless. It only made him stand out even more, like a priest at a Chippendale's convention. He would hardly even get out of his chair during games. He and his blue eyes and his farm-boy haircut would just sit there and watch his toy spin. I asked him once what he thought about coaches in their Armani suits strutting up and down the entire game, coaching every dribble. "I don't understand it," he said. "What do they do in practice?"

He made me want to be more courageous. For instance, I'm terrified of dying. He used to laugh about it.

One of his favorite stories was about the time he took his great-granddaughter to get her ears pierced. She was 11. They drove home from the mall in his old 1989 Taurus—"greatest car I ever had," he always said—and she was practically unraveling with joy.

"Oh, Papa," she said. "I hope you live five more years so you can take me to get my license!"

He liked to kid about my occasional visits. "Last time I saw you [at 98], I was walking. This year, I'm in a wheelchair. At 100, I'll probably be on a stretcher." If only.

He made me wish I read more, thought more, listened more.

I started noticing something on my visits. The TV was never on. He was always reading. Poetry, history, the Bible. Never sports. Never novels. He knew hundreds of classic poems by heart. Yet when he found himself coaching a bookish 7-footer named Alcindor in 1966, he memorized the poems of Langston Hughes, the black modern poet. It didn't go unnoticed.

He was a nut for Lincoln, yet not for a second did he realize he, himself, was sports' Lincoln, a boy who'd learned to read by the light of a coal lamp, a man of simple wisdom whose pithy nuggets of good advice—"Do not let what you cannot do interfere with what you can"—will be quoted for the next 100 years.

Me? Great books stack up at my bedside while I watch *The Bachelorette*.

Look, John Wooden wasn't perfect. He may have stopped swearing for good at 14, but he said plenty to refs. He'd put his head down and yell things at them into his program as they'd run by. "Their big fella is fouling Nater every time down! Why can't you see that?"

And it's not true he never drank. He did, at 22, with his Purdue teammates. He had a half a bottle of beer "and threw up six," he remembered. That was the last time.

He made plenty of mistakes. He let Alcindor score 60 points in his first collegiate game just to put fear in the rest of the Pac-10. "I'm ashamed of that," he once said.

His and Nell's relationship wasn't perfect. Once, when he was just out of college, they had a huge fight and he left. Started hitchhiking west. Didn't care where he went. Got as far as Lawrence, Kansas, where he got a job helping to build the football stadium. Then he went back home. "I just got a little confused," he said.

At UCLA, he didn't pay enough attention to realize a booster named Sam Gilbert was lavishing his players with gifts and cars. But I will punch any man in the mouth who says Wooden knew. He couldn't have known it or he'd have stopped it. He'd have sooner cut off his own hand than cheat.

He made me want to love more deeply.

He took me into his bedroom once, in 2000. The clocks were all wrong. He stopped them at the time of Nellie's death, fifteen years before. Only one side of the bed was slept in, and above the sheet, not under them, and hadn't been since the day she died. On her pillow were hundreds of little letters in envelopes tied up in bundles by yellow ribbons. He wrote her every month telling her how much he loved her and what all the kids were doing. Did it right up until the last few months of his life, when his eyes stopped working.

"Coach, were you never tempted in all those years to go on a date?" I asked him once. "Didn't other women come flirting around after you?"

"Oh, yes," he said. "But there's no one else for me."

She'd been dead twenty-four years by then.

Once, when he was missing Nell terribly, one of his great-granddaughters—she was 5 at the time—saw how sad he was, tugged on his pants leg and said, "Papa, I know you miss Mama. So I'm going to rent you an airplane so you can fly up in the clouds and see her."

Here's to Coach for finally getting back with his girl—no airplane necessary.

And here's to all of us striving to be half the person he was.

Postscript: *One of the coolest museums you can visit is the John Wooden Den at UCLA. It's an exact replica of that den I visited so many times in his Encino condo, right down to the scribbled plates of his grandchildren. It's eerie, breathtaking and a pile of goose bumps. Go.*

A Day on the Links with the Round Mound Whose Swing Will Astound

July 15, 2008

Have you ever secretly longed to comb through airplane wreckage? Had a morbid curiosity about autopsies? Wanted to tour a torture camp?

I have. That's why I purposely set out to play golf with Charles Barkley. Wait, don't get mad! I've never met anybody in sports I admire more than Sir Charles. He is more fun than a Dubai expense account. He is unfailingly hilarious, generous and honest.

But his golf swing? Technically, it's not even a swing. It's a lunge. Scientists study it. He gets to the top, starts down and then—two feet from impact—just stops! Totally freezes! He looks like a man waiting for a rattlesnake to pop up so he can kill it. It's the only swing in the world with an intermission. Me, I'd quit and take up the tuba. But not Barkley. He plays golf all the time.

Which is where I came in. Through a clerical error, I was invited to play in this country's best celebrity golf tournament, the American Century Championship on the shore of Lake Tahoe. It was bizarre and cool at the same time. There were rooms in which every face you saw was famous. When was the last time the four people ahead of you in the taco-bar line were Lance Armstrong, Kate Hudson, Al Michaels and Lou Holtz?

(Random celebrity observations from the week: Michael Jordan's girlfriend is scorching. Aaron Rodgers nearly gets a facial tic when asked about Brett Favre. Ray Allen can actually rap. After a bad shot, Ray Romano will yell, "I could rip off my own ear!" Jessica Simpson, in town with boyfriend Tony Romo, is not a stickler for detail. When I asked her, "Jessica, is today your birthday?" she replied: "Yes! No! Wait! Yesterday! No, wait, is today the twelfth? Then, day before yesterday? I don't know!")

Anyway, after much begging I was paired with Barkley for the first round. The night before, as I walked through the casino to go to bed, I saw him. He was standing on a stage, pouring mobs of people shots of Patrón, on his tab, which would top $10,000. So you knew he was taking me seriously.

We had the day's largest gallery for two reasons: (1) The mayor of South Lake Tahoe declared it Charles Barkley Day to honor the $100,000 he donated to locals who'd lost their homes in fires, and (2) people wanted to see the Incredible Hiccuping Swing.

I have bad news. I saw it up close—and it's getting worse. In one fairway bunker Barkley took it back, froze as usual, then suddenly flinched and aborted the swing altogether. Balk. He gathered himself and made another run but, again, could not bring himself to finish the last two feet. It was like a man trying to shoot a favorite old cow. The third time, he finally swung but whiffed. On the fourth, he hit it. And this was only the first hole.

When Barkley freeze-flails, people laugh, shriek and gasp, but it's not funny. It is a pox on his life. "I've tried everything," Barkley says. "Tiger can't help me 'cause the hitch is there no matter what. I even tried getting hypnotized for forty-five minutes and still woke up with the same crappy swing." And so it went the rest of the day: Barkley making people laugh and hug him, interrupted by these sporadic fits that made them look away in sympathy. "Hey, I know I suck," he yelled on the eighth hole, "but I got nice equipment."

Thing is, he never stops having fun. I missed a putt badly on twelve and told the crowd, "I forgot—every green breaks toward Charles." He counterpunched with "Uh-oh, God don't like you bein' mean to fat people." Toward the end, I asked him why he puts himself through it. "Beats working," he said, and shrugged.

Overall, in this fifty-four-hole Stableford tourney, in which double bogey is the most you can take, Barkley took the max on forty-one holes and finished last by a large county. No wonder that, in Barkley's group, the sign boy was given no numbers.

The best player of the week was ex–MLB pitcher Rick Rhoden. The wettest was Romo, who fell in a pond at No. 1 on Saturday. And perhaps the happiest was Rodgers, who was introduced at the first tee on Sunday as a "Green Bay Packers quarterback." Rodgers corrected the announcer, "Starting quarterback."

As for the nobody among the eighty-two celebs, I finished with a plus-two, good for fifty-third place. But on the plus side, I was low sportswriter and beat Michael Jordan. One other crucial thing: I can remember when my birthday is.

Postscript: *Charles Barkley's golf swing is proof that you can't have it all. Even after a month with teaching great Hank Haney, Barkley made no improvements and, at last report, was trying it left-handed.*

Acknowledgments

Big thanks to John Hassan, my ESPN editor, confessor, therapist, suicide prevention hotline and better angel. Bottomless gratitude to John Skipper, who's a friend first and a fabulous boss second and who was willing to let an old dog learn new tricks. Large IOUs to Patrick Stiegman, the Red Adair to all the fires I started. Double knuckles to Blue Rider's David Rosenthal, who seemed to like the idea for this book against all good sense. Warm hugs to my agent, Janet Pawson, who, like a good hotel, never seems to say no. E-thanks to Rex W. Post, who feeds me ideas the way Dunkin' Donuts feeds cops. A-frame guy-hug to my best buddy, Gene Wojciechowski, who always picks up the phone even though he knows I'm usually at the other end. Kisses on the forehead to my kids, who are way cooler than me. And undying love to TLC, the warmest and safest arms to fall into in the known universe. The circle is forever unbroken.